First Steps
in Old English

Stephen Pollington

Anglo-Saxon Books

BY THE SAME AUTHOR

Wordcraft
An Introduction to the Old English Language & its Literature
Rudiments of Runelore
The English Warrior
Leechcraft: Early English Charms, Plantlore and Healing
The Warrior's Way

First Published 1997
Revised and Expanded 1999
Reprinted 2001

Published by
Anglo-Saxon Books
Frithgarth
Thetford Forest Park
Hockwold-cum-Wilton
Norfolk
England

Printed by
Antony Rowe Ltd
Bumper's Farm
Chippenham
Wiltshire
England

The cover illustration is by Brian Partridge

British Library Cataloguing-in-Publication Data. A catalogue record for this book is available from the British Library.

ISBN 1–898281–19–X

ACKNOWLEDGEMENTS

I would very much like to record here my thanks to both Kathleen Herbert and L. A. Hood for reading this course in draft and offering many valuable suggestions for the improvements to the general style as well as to the detailed arrangement of the material. This second edition benefits from the comments and criticisms of many others, friends and strangers alike, but most notably Mr. Hugh Roth of Woodmere, NY who kindly gave me a critique of each section on reading it. I need hardly say that any faults and inconsistencies still in the text after all the intensive effort of the last two years remain my own.

Thanks are also, as ever, due to Tony and Pearl Linsell of Anglo-Saxon Books whose efforts to bring the earliest English material alive have resulted in the publication of so many worthwhile and interesting volumes.

I must record here my acknowledgement of a continuing debt of gratitude to Dr. O. D. Macrae Gibson of the University of Aberdeen, in the handling of whose "Learning Old English" course I began to see the immense difficulty many people have with formal grammar, mainly due to the forbidding terminology in which it is expressed. It was this revelation more than anything that persuaded me that a beginner's course in a specific language such as Old English should teach only as much formal grammar as is absolutely necessary, and if possible using the minimum of technical terms. This guiding principle in the writing of the course should make it a good deal less forbidding – and so more enjoyable – for this reason. I still maintain this belief, even though some dislike pre-digested information and others continue to be baffled and deterred by the remaining technical terms. You can't please all the people, all the time…

Steve Pollington
Essex 1999

CONTENTS

Contents (continued)

INTRODUCTION

This book, and the course of which it forms a part, is designed particularly for three types of user:

- the interested general reader who wishes to learn the basics of Old English (abbreviated to OE throughout this book) at his own pace and who has to work without a tutor;

- the more serious student of the language who has tried the commonly available grammars and guides, but who would feel more comfortable starting with a book which gives a general background in the subject, without too much jargon;

- the student of English language and literature who would like to get a feel for the earliest stages of the language without getting involved in a lot of technical detail.

For these users, the course is designed not to overburden the memory and patience, particularly at the beginning when a handful of possibly unfamiliar ideas have to be understood before proceeding to looking at the language in detail.

With all these types of user in mind, the course assumes no previous knowledge of the language nor familiarity with the terminology of linguistics generally. In other words, **you need not have any background knowledge before you begin this course**, other than a good grasp of Modern English (NE, or New English, throughout this book). The bad news is that Old English is more complicated in its formal grammar than the modern language so you will have to be willing to learn a certain amount of grammatical detail, and you must have an interest in the language and the culture it represents to sustain you through the learning by rote which forms part of the work necessary to complete the course – this is true of learning any language, of course, or indeed any other subject with a fairly high degree of detail.

One drawback with Old English is that there are no 'native' speakers of this ancient language to practice on; on the other hand, since there is no real necessity to speak the language out loud, no one need feel apprehensive about being required to produce those bizarre and unfamiliar sounds which other languages always insist on using! The sounds of Old English have been studied for over a century and I have dealt with them in a later section.

It is important to remember that the speakers of that language knew that they spoke *Englisc* "English" just as we do, and the deepest core of the language remains much the same more than a thousand years later. They had, by and large, far less formal education than we have today - probably the comparative lack of written records meant much greater reliance on memory and consequently a greater feeling for spoken language as something to be preserved, and in which to preserve knowledge and tradition, as well as to create entertainment and enlightenment. There is virtually nothing in OE grammar which is not present (though sometimes vestigially, I admit) in NE grammar. The three genders of noun are echoed in our words *he, she* and *it*. The two tenses of the verb are still with us, as well as the use of auxiliaries like *shall, must, will* to express the future. Perhaps the adjective has come the furthest from OE and is now almost an absolute, unalterable form - though even here a word such as *fast* has forms *faster, fastest* formed in the OE manner.

I think most students will agree that the study of Old English is interesting in itself, as well as in the relationship it has to NE, and there is more than enough absorbing and worthwhile literature in the language to make it worth learning for its own sake. Since the early history of the English language is a minor part of general education even in English-speaking countries, the availability of an accessible introduction to its study is perhaps more important now than ever before: a vast amount of information is available on the subject (whole volumes devoted to word-order and the details of verbal inflection), yet without a ground-level introduction to the basics the non-specialist finds himself totally unable to make use of any of the more specialised works.

This book is not intended to avoid the hours of study needed to master the language, but if it serves to take some of the pain and dreariness out of that study it will have served its purpose.

The Course

My aim has been to produce a clear and useful guide such as I would have wished for when I was teaching myself OE from textbooks, and which would be 'complete in itself', by which I mean that it should not be necessary to refer to other books in order to understand the information being presented.

I have tried to stick to the outlines of the language in use and have generally avoided discussing theoretical or structural matters; but where this is necessary for a reasonable understanding of the language's mechanisms (e.g. the heavy-stemmed monosyllables dealt with in section 9.4) I have presented the data in as straightforward a manner as I could, with the minimum of jargon and technical detail.

With a view to keeping things manageable, I have generally confined my approach to knowledge which is directly relevant to the language in its basic West Saxon guise, because most documents survive in that dialect, and most standard students' editions of the texts work from that norm. (There are at least four regional variants of OE identifiable from the various surviving texts, but the West Saxon dialect of King Alfred is the normal starting point for mastering the grammar. The others are all interesting in their own right and in the fascinating detail of their survival into modern dialects of English, but it is obviously more beneficial for a beginner to learn the 'standard' language first.) Non-essentials and variants have been relegated to the notes, leaving the student free to get on with the task of mastering the various grammatical forms without getting side-tracked into a mass of detail. Having said that, the *Grammar* section, which is mainly meant for future reference, does use the nomenclature of the traditional grammar books – this is to assist the learner who goes on to read further texts, which still tend to refer in their notes to nouns as *a*-stems, *o*-stems, etc., or verbs as 'reduplicating' and so on; these terms are virtually meaningless within the context of OE itself (hence their exclusion from the course) but do form part of the technical literature which surrounds the study of the language. Those who do not wish to be bothered with them at this stage can simply treat them as arbitrary names.

As users of this course who have been defeated or deterred by the available guides and grammars for Old English will know only too well, it is a particular failing of many of these works that they insist on explaining everything in terms of historical processes, for example tracing the various forms of the strong verb back to their Proto-Indo-European antecedents, or classifying the nouns according to their thematic vowels in Proto-Germanic. The weakness of this approach is that the wealth of detailed, subsidiary data it is necessary to include in order to present such explanations is enormous – and it is not very illuminating unless the student is already familiar with Latin, Greek, Gothic and Sanskrit! Students learning from these books who find themselves faced with the intricacies of determining the stress patterns of words in ancient Asian languages may well question why they need to do this just to read the *Anglo-Saxon Chronicle* or *The Dream of the Rood* ! In short, this traditional approach can be like taking a sledgehammer to crack a nut: I hope that this book proves to be more precise and more efficient, more like a scalpel than a sledgehammer. I also hope that, having completed the course and acquired a familiarity with the language and its literature, the reader who wishes to do so will feel confident enough to tackle the more formal, traditional books on equal terms.

The data are presented in an orderly (even if not strictly logical) sequence so that the student may make real progress on several fronts at once. This has entailed certain compromises, particularly where I have given an initial summary treatment of a topic and then returned to it some while later in more detail. The earlier sections are roughly evenly weighted, but coverage of the noun precedes the necessarily more extensive coverage of the strong verb. Only after most of this 'heavy' material has been dealt with have I touched upon peripherals such as word-formation and personal names.

The various numbered sections of the course help to split the information up into manageable parts, and users may wish to set themselves deadlines for completion if this motivates them more (e.g. finish each section in two weeks). The length of each section is determined more by my feeling that some exercises and reading practice are due, than by adherence to any theory of structured learning. The Exercises are generally complete statements which cover aspects of everything dealt with so far: further into the course I have made some of them into short pieces of OE prose. The later sections are also heavier on new vocabulary, as a more detailed treatment of verbs and nouns brings in examples for completeness. For the very last sections, dealing with general matters, there are no Exercises at all.

It will become clear from quite early on that OE is <u>not</u> the same as NE, dressed up in quaint spelling. The language is a thousand years older, first recorded in the seventh century though it had been developing orally for perhaps three centuries before that; while NE had evolved out of Middle English by the beginning of the sixteenth. Old English has its own ways of doing things that often seem strange to us and so have to be learnt, for example, the fact that there are a good many 'endings' to various types of word – though not so many as for Latin or Russian, still more than we use in present-day English – and until you are reasonably familiar with most of them little real progress can be made. I have tried to take the hard 'slog' out of the process by introducing them one part at a time, and not expecting you to remember seventeen types of noun before you get to look at a single verb! Nonetheless, success in the subject – which is to say, acquisition of the language for reading purposes – depends in large part on how familiar you become with the endings of nouns, verbs and adjectives in particular. For this reason, most sections of the course are linked to a 'Practice' exercise in which your knowledge of the topic just covered is tested.

The course is designed to be worked through at whatever speed is most appropriate to the individual; there is no 'grind' of monotonous weekly tests, nor the frantic last-minute revision of an evening class (if you are fortunate enough to have access to one). However, we all learn by 'reinforcement', by acquiring and using data, so the longer and harder you study, the more thorough your knowledge will be. I would suggest that someone who cannot devote half an hour a day to this or any other subject is not serious about wanting to learn it. How quickly the various sections can be worked through depends on a host of variables such as innate skill with language, previous relevant learning, background reading, demands on time and energies, and a great many others, so take the course at your own pace.

Once you have successfully completed the course, you will be equipped to tackle texts in for example Sweet's *Reader* with the help of the notes and glossary in that book. You may prefer to work through Mitchell and Robinson's *Guide to Old English* first, where a more detailed, diachronic presentation of the patterns of Old English is given.

How to Use this Book

1. Read through the individual subsections, numbered x.x, looking up any unfamiliar terms in the Glossary. Make notes separately for your own use – nothing familiarizes the mind with new information like using it.

In the language course sections I have, as far as possible, explained each new 'concept' as it is introduced, as well as including a Glossary of the principal terms for handy reference in the Grammar section – at the beginning, one always forgets what the new word means and where to read about it! Readers with some previous experience of language-learning may wish to skip this elementary matter, although there are surprisingly large numbers of people who, when put to the test, cannot explain the difference between, say, an adjective and an adverb. Rather than try to guess what background information a potential student might be expected to have, I have opted to play safe and explain as much as is practicable in a book of this size.

The subsections are shown in the Summary of Section Contents with the technical, grammatical name for the subject covered. This is for the guidance of those who already have some experience of language learning, and for users who complete the course and go on to study from more conventional textbooks, for whom a quick cross-reference may be useful. The grammatical names given are nonetheless largely irrelevant in terms of this book.

2. Having read and understood the subsection, cover the answers to the 'practice' drills and work through them. Referring to one's notes is not inexcusable at any stage, and more than one attempt at the drills may be necessary before acceptable results are achieved. In fact I recommend that you do these short exercises at least twice each so that you can both reinforce the recall of the information, and, equally important, identify those areas where there is weakness and more work needs to be done.

The 'practice' sections (keyed to the corresponding coursework) are useful for familiarization with the topics discussed. Many have the answers underneath, not to encourage reliance on them as a 'crib', but so that where mistakes occur they can be rectified immediately; if there is still doubt once the answer has been seen, check the coursebook and read the relevant section again. Learning takes place most naturally when the memory is stretched a little, but there is no obvious way to make this course into a 'conversational' exercise in linguistic acquisition; I have therefore tried to make the subsections and drills brief and varied, building on knowledge already gained.

3. At the end of each numbered section, read through and learn the Vocabulary, then complete the Exercises. The vocabulary tables are designed to introduce further words which you will need for the Exercises. The Exercises themselves are mostly sentences for translation into and out of OE; the earlier ones are a little contrived due to the limitations of vocabulary and expression available at the beginning. I have tried to make them not too absurd! Do not be reluctant to turn back to earlier sections if your work on the Exercises shows that you consistently have difficulties with some aspect of the course: you may have misread or not fully grasped something in the early stages which is causing you problems later on. (The answers to the Exercises are given in Part Four.)

4. The last few sections have no Exercises, but edited Texts from Old English for you to read. Here you should refer to the Texts section at the back of the book, in which there are short excerpts from Old English literature which have been 'deconstructed' and parsed for you, to demonstrate the analytical processes necessary to understand the language in use. This sounds complicated but is in fact the very same train of thought processes we all use to read and understand words in any language. The last few sections deal mostly with less critical aspects of the study, such as personal names and word formation.

Having completed the Course, you will be well equipped to tackle pretty well anything the average Anglo-Saxon Reader can throw at you, as well as to read most edited texts. Some suggestions for what to do next are given in the Afterword. Happy reading!

Explanatory Note

*   before a word denotes a form *not* recorded in the language but presumed to have existed before written forms begin, e.g. ***seohan** is presumed to be the original of the word written as **sēon** in the existing texts. Sometimes I have used it to mark incorrect forms e.g. ***willon** a form which does not occur but might be expected.

🗆   denotes additional notes, to be read in conjunction with the section.

⌘   denotes matter which is historical or is given as background to assist with understanding the history of the word.

❖   denotes matter of a dialectal or variant nature, as for example an alternative spelling.

Conversational Old English

While the course in the following pages of this book presents the grammar necessary to master the written language, I would suggest that those who intend to use the language actively - for example, in 'living history' situations - will also need the pleasantries and other social odds-and-ends which make real communication possible.

The evidence for such usages is scarce but not wholly lacking, and I summarise below some of the commoner phrases which may be helpful in starting to use the language in this way. As you progress through the course, familiarity with grammar and syntax will enable you to expand this short list indefinitely.

Greetings

Good day	**gōdne dæg**
Good evening	**gōd ǣfen**
Good morning	**gōdne mergen**
Hail / Be well	**wes ðū hāl**
Hello	**ēalā** (can also be used to hail somebody)
I greet you / you all	**ic grēte þē / ēow ealle**
Welcome	**welcumen**

Address

Dear	**Lēof** (used in direct address to a superior, as **ēalā lēof** 'well, lord')
Father, my dearest	**Fæder mīn se lēofesta**
Lady	**Hlǣfdige**
Lord	**Drihten, Hlāford**
My darling	**Mīn dēorling**

Remarks

Alas!	**wā lā wā**
Hey!	**hig**
I believe so	**ðæs ic wēne**
Listen!	**hwæt, hīerað**
Lo and behold!	**heonu hwæt**
Look!	**lā**
Never so	**nǣfre swā**

Remarks *(continued)*

No	**nā, nese**
Not at all	**nā, nælles**
Not likely	**ungewēne**
Not true	**unsōð**
Oh!	**ēalā**
Please	**ic bidde þē**
Probably	**gewēne**
Thank you	**ic þoncie þē**
True	**sōð**
Yes	**gēa, gīese**

Trade

A good weight	**gōd wǣge**
A small piece / portion	**lytel dǣl**
Count them	**tellað hīe**
How many for one sceatt?	**hū fela wið ānum sceatte?**
How many pennies, sceattas?	**hū fela pendinga, sceatta?**
I like that colour	**sēo dēag līcaþ mē**
Not enough	**nō genōg**
That isn't good enough	**þæt nis gōd genōg**
Too much	**tō fela**
When will you be back here?	**hwonne cymst ðū hider eft?**
Who made this?	**hwā worhte ðis?**

Part One

OE Course

SUMMARY OF SECTION CONTENTS

OLD ENGLISH COURSE – SECTION 1

1.1 Nouns are words denoting things, for example concrete items such as 'table', 'lamp', or abstract ideas such as 'beauty', 'hardness', 'nationality'. They fall into three groups or *genders*, called masculine *(m)*, feminine *(f)* and neuter *(n)*. We still retain a memory of this three-way system in our words 'he' *(m)*, 'she' *(f)* and 'it' *(n)*. Of course, we generally use 'it' for anything other than a human being, but still conventionally refer to ships as 'she', and household pets as 'he' or 'she'. In OE, any masculine noun can be replaced by the masculine pronoun **hē**, and likewise feminines by **hēo** and neuters by **hit**. Nouns are more or less evenly distributed among the three genders.

Mann (a man) and **stān** (a stone) are both masculine and are used with the word **se** (the). **Se mann** can mean both 'the man' and 'that man', since there was no separate word for 'that'.

Talu (a tale) is feminine; its word for 'the' or 'that' is **sēo**.

Land (a land) is neuter; it takes **ðæt** to mean 'the / that land'.

Even today we can often use 'the' and 'that' interchangeably, as in "Do you know the/that boy who delivers the newspapers?" or "How much is the/that doggy in the window?".

⚯   The letters þ and ð are used pretty well interchangeably in Old English so that ðæt can also be spelt þæt. Anglo-Saxon scribes were apparently content to spell the same word in the same sentence with different characters! Throughout this course I have varied the letters so that you will become familiar with the idea.

⚯   A noun used with 'the', 'that' or 'this' is said to be *definite*. This will have some effect on the words used with it, as we shall see later on (section 12.1).

⌘   **Mann** actually means 'adult human being, person' without reference to sex; the sex words were **wer** for a male and **wīf** for a female.

1.2 **Se mann, sēo talu** and **ðæt land** all refer to one example each (one man, tale or land) and are said to be *singular (sing.)*. When referring to more than one, there are separate forms, called *plural (pl.)*, so that just as 'man' has a plural 'men', 'stone' a plural 'stones', and 'tale' has 'tales', the OE words change their endings to show the number.

Equally, some modern words do not undergo any change (e.g. 'sheep', 'deer') and can be singular or plural, so **land** retains the same form:

mann	(a man)	**menn**	(men)
stān	(a stone)	**stānas**	(stones)
talu	(a tale)	**tala**	(tales)
land	(a land)	**land**	(lands)

Se, sēo and **ðæt** are all singular forms (like *he, she* and *it*) to which there corresponds one plural form for all genders, **ðā** :

singular		*plural*
se stān	*(m)*	**ðā stānas**
se mann	*(m)*	**ðā menn**
sēo talu	*(f)*	**ðā tala**
ðæt land	*(n)*	**ðā land**

Question: If **land** has the same spelling in the singular and the plural, how can anyone tell which it is? Fortunately, there are ways other than looking for **þæt** or **þā**, as we shall see below (1.4).

⊠ There is no word corresponding to the modern 'a, an' so that **stān** is both 'stone' and 'a stone'.

⊠ Apart from a few oddities like **mann** and some others, the masculines mostly add -**as** in the plural.

⊠ While many neuters (like **land**) add no ending in the plural, some (like **scip**, a ship) add -**u** (i.e. **scipu**); rules for determining which pattern a noun belongs to will be given later (section 9.4).

Practice 1.2: give the correct word for 'the' for the following nouns, then check your answers. Bear in mind that for one word there is more than one correct answer!

mann stānas talu land stān scipu tala scip menn

Continue with this until you are confident with these words.

Answers: se mann; þā stānas; sēo talu; þæt / þā land; se stān; þā scipu; þā tala; þæt scip; þā menn.

22

1.3 Parallel to the words for 'the/that' are the words for 'this':

ðes mann	this man	**ðās menn**	these men
ðēos talu	this tale	**ðās tala**	these tales
ðis land	this land	**ðās land**	these lands

You can see that the NE words 'this' and 'that' are from the OE neuters **ðis** and **ðæt.**

Practice 1.3: give the correct words for 'the' and 'this' for the following, then check your answers. Again, beware of one particular example!

stānas   scipu   talu   mann   land   scip   tala   stān

Answers: þā, þās stānas; þā, þās scipu; sēo, þēos talu; se, þes mann; þæt, þis, þā, þās land; þæt, þis scip; þā, þās tala; se, þes stān.

1.4 All these forms given above can act as the *subject* of the sentence, which is to say that they denote the performer of the action, the 'doer'. In the sentence 'the man rides', the man is the subject and 'rides' is what he does, the *action*. Words expressing the action are called *verbs* (for example *ride, like, see, hesitate, shine*). Every sentence must contain a verb, and most contain a subject also – the only exception is the *command* type of sentence (Go! Kneel! Look! Come here!) where only the action (the verb) is expressed.

The subject dictates the ending of the verb, just as in NE we say "the man hesitates" (with *-s* inflexional ending) and "the men hesitate" (with no inflexional ending on the verb). OE has a fuller set of endings but the principle is the same; in this way, it is possible to tell by the verb the singular from plural uses of words like **land**, as in **land is...** "a land is..." versus **land sind...** "lands are...". However, this only works when words like **land** are the subject of their sentences (see further in the Exercises section).

✠   The grammatical name for the set of endings showing the subject is the *nominative* case.

✠   The *nominative* case and *singular* number are important to the student because dictionaries almost always use these forms for their alphabetical listings of head words. It follows that if you want to know what **stānas** means, you have to recognise it as a plural and look up the singular **stān** .

Vocabulary (1)

Nouns

(where needed, plurals are shown in brackets beneath)

masculine		*feminine*		*neuter*	
mann (menn)	a man	**talu** (tala)	a tale	**land** (land)	a land
cyning (cyningas)	a king	**brȳd** (brȳda)	a bride	**scip** (scipu)	a ship
mōna	(a) moon	**sunne**	(a) sun	**hors** (hors)	a horse
stān (stānas)	(a) stone	**niht** (nihta)	a night	**tungol** (tunglu)	a star

Verbs

sing.		*pl.*	
is	is	**sind**	are
rīdeð	rides, is riding	**rīdað**	ride, are riding
wadeð	walks, is walking	**wadað**	walk, are walking
cymþ	comes, is coming	**cumaþ**	come, are coming
scīnð	shines, is shining	**scīnað**	shine, are shining
sweorceþ	darkens, is darkening	**sweorcað**	darken, are darkening
ābīdeþ	awaits, is awaiting	**ābīdaþ**	await, are awaiting
hæfð	has	**habbaþ**	have

There are no separate progressive forms, so that for example **cymþ** can mean 'comes' or 'is coming' according to the context.

Exercises (1)

1. Translate the following into NE.

(a)   **ðes mann rīdeð**
(b)   **sēo sunne scīnð**
(c)   **ðis hors bīteð**
(d)   **sēo niht sweorceð**
(e)   **ðās menn cumað**
(f)   **ðæt scip ābīdeð**

Exercises (1) (continued)

2. Translate the following into OE.

(a)   the men ride
(b)   the king is walking
(c)   the moon is shining
(d)   horses bite
(e)   this bride walks
(f)   stars are shining

OLD ENGLISH COURSE – SECTION 2

2.1 The object   2.3 Negation

2.2 Word order

2.1 In section (1.1) we looked at sentences such as **se mann rīdeð** 'the man rides' where the verb's meaning and action are confined to the subject and there are no other people or things involved. Similarly **sēo sunne scīneð** 'the sun is shining' or **ðā menn cumað** 'the men are coming' – verbs like this are called *intransitive,* meaning that the action is confined to the performer, the subject. What if I want to say 'the man is riding a horse'? Here there is more than one party involved, since the action now affects something else (the horse, the thing which is ridden). This kind of verb is called *transitive*, because the action crosses over from the performer (subject) to another person or thing whom it affects, called the *object*. In OE there are sometimes special ways of marking out the object, particularly with words for 'the' and 'this':

Subject   Object

masculine		*masculine*	
sing.	*pl.*	*sing.*	*pl*
se/ðes mann	ðā/ðās menn	ðone/ðisne mann	ðā/ðās menn
se/ðes stān	ðā/ðās stānas	ðone/ðisne stān	ðā/ðās stānas
feminine		*feminine*	
sēo/ðēos talu	ðā/ðās tala	ðā/ðās tale	ðā/ðās tala
sēo/ðēos brȳd	ðā/ðās brȳda	ðā/ðās brȳde	ðā/ðās brȳda
neuter		*neuter*	
ðæt/ðis land	ðā/ðās land	ðæt/ðis land	ðā/ðās land
ðæt/ðis scip	ðā/ðās scipu	ðæt/ðis scip	ðā/ðās scipu

You can see from the above that it is mainly the words for 'the' and 'this' which change to show subject from object, because **mann, stān, scip** and **land** do not have any (inflexional) ending and the plurals **menn, stānas, scipu, land** don't distinguish between the two uses. The feminines do have separate forms in the singular but not in the plural, which is to say that **talu, brȳd** are marked as subject of the verb and **tale, brȳde** as object, while **tala, brȳda** can be either.

Question: How can I separate the various meanings of **þā/þās**? Briefly, **þā** will be found most often with plurals, where it doesn't help in distinguishing subject from object. However, with a *singular* noun, it can only mark a *feminine object*.

✠   **brȳd** (bride) and others differ from **talu** only in that the latter has a **-u** ending in the nominative singular. This is parallel to the correspondence **land** : **scipu** we noted in the neuter plural nouns (see 9.4).

✠   the ending **-ne** of the masc.acc.sing.(e.g. **ðone**) is unique and specific to that role, and so is very useful in picking out object from subject in OE.

Practice 2.1: give the OE for the following, then check your answers against the table above. Continue until you are confident in the use of these forms.

this land *(subj.)*	these ships *(obj.)*	these tales *(obj.)*
this knowledge *(obj.)*	that man *(obj.)*	this man *(subj.)*
those stones *(subj.)*	those men *(obj.)*	those ships *(subj.)*
this land *(obj.)*	this tale *(subj.)*	that stone *(obj.)*

Answers: þis land; þās scipu; þās tala; þās lāre; þone mann; þes mann; þā stānas; þā menn; þā scipu; þis land; þēos talu; þone stān.

2.2   The reason that object has to be distinguished from subject is that OE word order was less rigid than it is in the modern language. To return to our example 'the man is riding a horse' we can see that the subject (i.e. the rider) here is the man while the object (the thing ridden) is the horse. Knowing that 'the man' as the subject is **se mann**, and 'the horse' as the object is **ðæt hors**, we can construct the sentence

se mann	**rīdeð**	**ðæt hors**
subject	verb	object

However, in OE one might wish to vary this by calling special attention to the horse – as for example, in answer to the question **Hwæt rīdeð se mann?** 'What is that man riding?', by saying

ðæt hors	**rīdeð**	**se mann**
object	verb	subject

Note that you can still see that the man is the subject (i.e. the rider) by the use of **se**, which can only mark the subject of the verb. Or to take another example:

se cyning	**grēteð**	**ðone ðegn**
subject	verb	object
the king	greets	the thane

27

which can equally be expressed as

    ðone ðegn   **grēteð**   **se cyning**

where, because **ðone** and **se** tell you which is object and subject, you can tell who is greeting whom. A further example with feminine nouns

    sēo brȳd   **hīerþ**   **ðā tale**
    the bride *(subject)*   hears   the story *(object)*

where **sēo** marks out the subject and **ðā** the object, which is also indicated by the inflexional ending -**e**.

It is important to be familiar with the concepts of subject and object since OE can be deceptive in suddenly reversing the expected order without warning.

⊞   Subject forms are referred to as being in the *nominative* case, and object forms in the *accusative* case. This is a shorthand method of referring to the form as well as function, since the accusative has other functions than the simple object.

Practice 2.2: identify subject and object in the following phrases:

se cyning grēteð ðone biscop; ðās word hīerð se biscop; lāre hīerð ðes mann; ðisne mann grēteð sēo brȳd.

Answers:

se cyning	**grēteð**	**ðone biscop**
subject-nominative		*object-accusative*
ðās word	**hīerð**	**se biscop**
object-accusative		*subject-nominative*
lāre	**hīerð**	**ðes mann**
object-accusative		*subject-nominative*
ðisne mann	**grēteð**	**sēo brȳd**
object-accusative		*subject-nominative*

Question: How can one tell subject from object in the last example – neither noun has any inflexional ending to show which case it is in? True, the nouns don't provide enough information by themselves to tell which case they are in, but we know from the grammar of the sentence that one must be the subject (nominative) and the other must be the object (accusative). But the words for 'this' and 'the' come to our rescue, as **þisne** can only be accusative singular masculine (characteristic -**ne** ending) and **sēo** can only be nominative singular feminine. If the nouns had been plural, would the corresponding words for 'the/this' have helped?

2.3 Negation is the grammatical term for saying that something is *not* so. In NE we normally make use of a clumsy construction with 'do(es) not' (e.g. I do not know, that does not matter, etc.). The OE system is simpler: the word **ne** (not) is inserted before the verb:

> **se mann rīdeþ hors** versus **se mann ne rīdeþ hors**
> the man rides a horse the man does not ride a horse (rideth not)

It is possible to use **ne** more than once in a sentence, since it can also mean 'neither' and 'nor': **se cyning ne lufað ne bātas ne scipu** 'the king loves neither boats nor ships'. In such cases **ne** still usually precedes the verb as well, i.e. '...does not love neither... nor...'. While this is bad (modern) English, it was perfectly normal in OE.

✠ There are other, stronger negative words, such as **nā** (not at all) **nǣfre** (never) or **nælles** (by no means).

✠ Some verbs have special negative forms such as **nis** from **ne + is** (not + is). These will be dealt with as the verbs occur (in 5.2,6; 9.3;10.6;15.2, 5,6).

Vocabulary (2)

Conjunctions

and	and	**oþþe**	or	**ac**	but
oþþe ... oþþe	either ... or	**ne ... ne**	neither ... nor	**ēac**	also

❖ the word 'and' can be spelt **and** or **ond**; generally, variant spellings with -on- for -an- are West Saxon e.g. **lond** for **land**.

Nouns (plurals are shown in brackets beneath)

masculine		feminine		neuter	
ðegn (ðegnas)	a thane	**lār** (lāra)	learning, knowledge	**hūs** (hūs)	a house
biscop (biscopas)	a bishop	**giefu** (giefa)	a gift	**word** (word)	a word
stān (stānas)	a stone, rock	**glōf** (glōfa)	a glove	**rīce** (rīciu)	a kingdom
āð (āðas)	an oath, promise	**cearu** (ceara)	care, grief, worry	**brim** (brimu)	a sea
bāt (bātas)	a boat			**bān** (bān)	a bone

masculine		feminine		neuter	
æðeling	a prince,	**sacu**	strife,	**folc**	a folk,
(**æðelingas**)	nobleman	(**saca**)	contention	(**folc**)	nation
līðmann	a sailor			**sweord**	a sword
(**līðmenn**)				(**sweord**)	
				lof	praise

Verbs

ādrecceð	afflicts	**ādreccað**	afflict
sēcð	seeks, is looking for	**sēcað**	seek, are looking for
hīerð	hears, is hearing	**hīerað**	hear, are hearing
lufað	loves	**lufiað**	love
oneardað	inhabits, lives in	**oneardiað**	inhabit, live in
giefð	gives, is giving	**giefað**	give, are giving

A Note on Verbs

In some West Saxon texts, verbs dropped the the -**e**- of the singular ending. This causes unpronounceable sequences of sounds which are simplified – the vowels also change according to definite sequences which will be dealt with later (7.5). For now, you should just be aware of the following correspondences:

rīdeð becomes **rītt**	**wadeð** becomes **watt**
bīteð becomes **bītt**	**befæsteþ** becomes **befæst**
sweorceð becomes **swiercð**	**ābīdeð** becomes **ābītt**.
cumeð becomes **cymþ**	**scīneð** becomes **scīnð**

Exercises (2)

1. Translate the following into NE:

(a)   ðes mann rīdeð ðæt hors

(b)   ðes mann rīdeð ðā hors

(c)   menn bīteð ðis hors

(d)   se cyning hīerð tale ac tala ne lufað se cyning

(e)   oððe se æðeling oþþe se cyning oneardaþ ðis hūs

(f)   ðā biscopas ābīdað ðone cyning

(g)   ðā ðegnas giefað āðas

(h)   ðās bātas ābīdeð se cyning

(i)   ðēos brȳd lufað giefa ond lof

(j)   cearu and sacu ādreccað ðæt folc.

2. Translate the following into OE:

(a)   the king loves learning

(b)   the thane loves this horse

(c)   the sailors are awaiting the ship

(d)   the bride loves this house

(e)   men inhabit this land

(f)   the bishop lives in that kingdom

(g)   the bride loves gifts

(h)   the nobleman is looking for a glove

(i)   bishops love neither grief nor strife

(j)   a sailor neither walks nor rides a horse

Question: In 1(c), how can one tell subject from object? The nouns don't help very much as both can be both subject and object, and **ðis** likewise. The clue is in the verb, which is singular ('bites') – its subject must likewise be singular, and this excludes **menn** (which is plural) and effectively permits only **hors** which, with **ðis**, can only be singular.

OLD ENGLISH COURSE – SECTION 3

3.1 Personal pronouns (nominative)	3.3 Infinitive verbs
3.2 Present tense, weak verbs (*hīeran*)	3.4 Personal Pronouns (accusative)

3.1 The words 'I', 'you', 'they', etc. are called *personal pronouns* – 'pronouns' because they can stand on behalf of (pro) nouns in the sentence, and 'personal' because they indicate the 'person' of the verb. I will explain what this means below.

The personal pronouns are conventionally set out according to a system whereby the person speaking (writing, etc.) is the most 'important' and is called the 'first person' (which is logical, because without a 'first person', a speaker, there would be no speech). A speaker needs an audience, and the person addressed is thus referred to as the 'second person'; the subject about which they speak, if it is something else, is the 'third person'. The speaker may refer to himself alone (*I*) or as part of a group (*we*) and may address one person (*thou* in early NE) or several (*you, ye* in early NE) about a single subject (*he, she* or *it*) or many (*they*).

The table looks like this:

		sing.	pl.
1st		ic	wē
2nd		ðū	gē
	(m)	hē	
3rd	(f)	hēo	hīe
	(n)	hit	

Compare these with the modern forms; only **hīe** and **hēo** have been completely replaced, although *thou* and *ye* are now seldom encountered except in very florid speech and poetry.

Practice 3.1: give the OE for the following:

he, we, I, she, they, thou, you.
Repeat until you have learnt these by heart.

Answers: hē, wē, ic, hēo, hīe, þū, gē

3.2 In the phrases **se mann hīerð** (the man hears) and **ðā menn hīerað** (the men hear) the verb 'hear(s)' changes its ending according to the number of men, which is to say according to whether its subject is singular or plural. The modern English verb does just the same, although the actual endings are different. And **hierð**, like 'hears', can be used with any singular noun, as well as the pronouns such as **hē, hēo, hit** (he, she, it). Similarly, **hīeraþ**, like 'hear' can be used with any plural noun and the word for 'they'. We can set this out in a table (bearing in mind that **hē, hēo, hit** can all be translated as 'it' according to the gender of the noun):

[**hē**]		[he]	
[**hēo**]	**hīerð**	[she]	hears
[**hit**]		[it]	
[**hīe**]	**hīeraþ**	[they]	hear

But it may also be necessary to say 'you hear' or 'we hear', and in such cases **hīeraþ** is used just as in the modern language:

[**wē**]		[we]	
[**gē**]	**hīeraþ**	[you]	hear
[**hīe**]		[they]	

These forms with **hīeraþ** are all plural. What about the singular 'I' and 'you' (referring to one person only)? Here OE does use different endings:

[**ic**]	**hīere**	[I]	hear
[**ðū**]	**hīerst**	[you]	hear

✠   **ðū hīerst** is the archaic 'thou hearest', while **gē** is 'ye'; the ending -(e)ð is the -(e)th of doth, hath, liveth, heareth, etc. All these features will be familiar to readers of the Authorized Version of the Bible, Shakespeare, etc.

✠   There is one modern verb which has the same pattern as the OE examples: 'to be' has the forms:–   *(I) am, (thou) art, (he, she, it) is, (we, you, they) are.*

Compare this with the pattern of separate endings for 'hear' above

Practice 3.2: memorize these four forms (**hīere, hīerst, hīerð, hīeraþ**) particularly the endings (**-e, -st, -ð, -aþ**) since, while there will be variations in detail later, the pattern is fairly constant.

3.3   The forms in 3.2 are all part of the verb 'to hear', which in OE is **hīeran**. Because 'to hear' does not display any information about tense or person or number, it is essentially an 'incomplete' or 'unfinished' form, which is called '*infinitive*' for that reason. In NE, we often mark out the infinitive by adding the word 'to' in front; although we can sometimes drop this e.g. "I want *to go*" but "I will *go*", or "he is obliged *to pay*" and "he must *pay*". The ending **-an** appears on the end of OE verbs in these circumstances: **ic wile fēran, hē sceal gieldan.**

In order to complete the sense of the verb, then, it is necessary to remove the ending – **an** and add the relevant personal ending. NE does exactly this when adding *-s* in the form '(he) hears', of course.

Many verbs follow the pattern of endings set out above; these are random examples, and there are others in the Vocabulary to this section:

lǣran	to teach	**fēran**	to travel
rȳman	to make room	**cwīðan**	to mourn
dēman	to judge	**fēdan**	to feed

You will see that they all have a long vowel in the stem (the part to which **-an** has been added). There are a few that have short vowel followed by two consonants, e.g. **bærnan**, to burn.

※ It is important to be able to recognise the infinitive, because most dictionaries give only this form for the verb – you need to know that **fēde** has **fēdan** for its infinitive in order to be able to look up its meaning.

※ There are a very few OE verbs where the infinitive ends in **-on** rather than **-an**; this is due to changes in pronunciation, so that **sēon** 'to see' replaces an earlier form ***seohan** with the normal **-an** ending (see 10.6 below)

※ Where the stem ends in **-d** or **-t** (e.g. **fēd-**), if the endings **-st** or **-ð** follow, there may be simplification of the clusters of consonants (e.g. ***fēdst** becomes **fētst**, ***fēdð** becomes **fētt**). This is mainly confined to early West Saxon, though, and in later texts forms such as **fēdest**, **fēdeð** are common.

Practice 3.3: put the correct endings onto the verbal stems to make the following OE expressions, using the pronouns also :

I teach; he judges; I feed; she makes room; we mourn; they travel; you (sing.) teach; you (pl.) travel; we teach; it burns; I mourn; you (sing) travel; they make room.

Answers: ic lǣre; hē dēmð; ic fēde; hēo rȳmð; wē cwīðað; hīe fērað; ðū lǣrst; gē fērað; wē lǣrað; hit bærnð; ic cwīðe; ðū fērst; hīe rȳmað.

3.4 The pronouns shown above (3.1) are all used as the subject of the verb, but naturally we sometimes need to use a pronoun as the object (e.g. N.E. me, him, them, us, etc.). Such forms exists in OE also:

person		sing.	pl
1st		**mec**	**ūs**
2nd		**ðec**	**ēow**
3rd	*(m)*	**hine**	
	(f)	**hīe**	**hīe**
	(n)	**hit**	

✠   **ūsic** and **ēowic** sometimes appear instead of **ūs** and **ēow**; remember that **hīe** can mean both 'her' and 'them' (as well as 'they'); NE 'you' is both subject and object, but OE has different forms, **gē** and **ēow**; conversely, **hit**, like 'it', can be subject or object.

Vocabulary (3)

Nouns

masculine		*feminine*		*neuter*	
bæcere (**bæceras**)	a baker	**bōt** (**bōta**)	a remedy	**trēow** (**trēow**)	a tree
hierde (**hierdas, hierde**)	a herdsman	**ecg** (**ecga**)	a sword, blade	**bearn** (**bearn**)	a child
hlāf (**hlāfas**)	a loaf	**benn** (**benna**)	a wound	**scēap** (**scēap**)	a sheep
lǣce (**lǣcas**)	a healer, doctor				
here (**herigas**)	a raiding party, enemy army				

Verbs

Note: only the infinitive of each verb is given below, since the various forms for I, they, he, etc. can be inferred from it. These verbs all behave like **hīeran**, to hear.

ālīesan	set free, release	**dǣlan**	split, divide, share
cȳðan	declare, make known	**bærnan**	burn up
gīeman	heed, obey	**lǣran**	teach
fēran	travel, journey	**dēman**	judge
cwīðan	mourn	**drǣfan**	drive out, expel
fēdan	feed	**flīeman**	drive off, rout
hǣlan	heal, make whole	**lǣfan**	leave behind
nīedan	compel, force	**rǣran**	raise, rear
rȳman	make room	**wēnan**	expect, hope, suppose

Exercises (3)

1. Translate the following into NE :

(a)   ðās menn cȳðað ðā lāre

(b)   se æðeling fērð

(c)   ðā biscopas dēmað

(d)   ðegnas gīemað ðone cyning

(e)   wē bærnað ðæt trēow

(f)   ic hīere word ond gīeme hīe

(g)   ðā hierdas fēdað scēap

(h)   se cyning dræfð ðone biscop

(i)   læce hæfð bōta

(j)   ðū rȳmest bāt

(k)   læcas hælað

2. Translate the following into OE :

(a)   I am teaching this child

(b)   the princes divide the kingdom

(c)   we obey these words

(d)   you (pl.) hear a story

(e)   the bishops are hoping

(f)   you (sing.) obey the bishop

(g)   they divide the loaf and feed him

(h)   I am setting her free

(i)   they are routing the enemy army

(j)   you (sing.) are forcing me

(k)   a nation mourns

OLD ENGLISH COURSE – SECTION 4

4.1 Another important group of words are the adjectives, words which describe nouns or supply additional information. Adjectives don't occur by themselves, but usually with nouns: tall ships, cold weather, hot water, pretty dresses, sad stories; *tall, cold, hot, pretty* and *sad* are all adjectives which help to define and describe the nouns they are with. OE adjectives differ from modern ones in that they change their endings according to the nouns they are linked to and describe, for example: -

gram 'fierce, angry'

	Subject		Object
masculine	**gram cyning**	a fierce king	**gramne cyning**
	grame cyningas	fierce kings	**grame cyningas**
neuter	**gram bearn**	an angry child	**gram bearn**
	gramu bearn	angry children	**gramu bearn**
feminine	**gramu brȳd**	an angry bride	**grame brȳde**
	grama brȳda	angry brides	**grama brȳda**

Other adjectives which take these endings are:

trum	firm, stout	**til**	good, gainful
longsum	enduring	**wilsum**	enjoyable
lufsum	lovable	**lāðlic**	hateful
twēolic	doubtful	**eorðlic**	worldly

(Here and elsewhere, lists of words are given as illustration; it is not necessary to memorize all of them at once as they will recur throughout the course and exercises.) There are large numbers of adjectives formed with **-sum** and **-lic**, all of which follow this pattern. Certain other adjectives do not add the **-u** ending (nom.sing.fem. and nom./acc.pl.neut.), for example:

37

lēof 'dear, precious'

Subject		Object
lēof cyning	a dear king	**lēofne cyning**
lēofe cyningas	dear kings	**lēofe cyningas**
lēof brȳd	a dear bride	**lēofe brȳde**
lēofa brȳda	dear brides	**lēofa brȳda**
lēof bearn	a dear child	**lēof bearn**
lēof bearn	dear children	**lēof bearn**

The great majority of adjectives follow this pattern, for example:

gōd	good	**earm**	poor
blind	blind	**heard**	hard
yfel	evil	**eald**	old

One important point with nouns and adjectives is that those with **-æ-** in the stem (e.g. **glæd** 'happy') change this vowel to **-a-** when the ending begins with a vowel (e.g. **glæd, gladu, glade, glada,** but **glædne**). **Hwæt** 'bold, daring' behaves likewise.

Practice 4.1: there is a lot to remember here. Using the tables if necessary, give the OE for the following (I have deliberately used adjective + noun combinations not given in the coursebook so that you can get used to working out the endings; the answers are given below):

a good king (obj.); a blind horse (subj.); an old herdsman (subj.); poor children (obj.); hard edges (subj.); a lovable child (subj.); a hateful enemy army (subj.); happy princes (subj.); a bold king (obj.); a good (use **til**) remedy (subj.).

Answers: gōdne cyning; blind hors; eald hierde; earm bearn; hearda ecga; lufsum bearn; lāðlic here; glæde æðelingas; hwatne cyning; tilu bōt.

4.2 Some other adjectives already have an **-e** or **-u** ending where those given above have none (e.g. **gram cyning** but **æðele cyning**). Examples of those in **-e** are:

rīce	powerful	**dēore**	dear, precious
æðele	noble	**mǣre**	famous, renowned
grēne	green	**swēte**	sweet

✠ These adjectives follow **lēof** in dropping the **-u** ending of the nom.sing.fem and nom./acc.pl. neut.

Those ending in **-u** have the peculiarity of inserting **-w-** before a vowel ending, and **-o-** before a consonant, for example **fealu** 'dark':

masculine

fealu stede	a dark place	**fealone stede**
fealwe stede	dark places	**fealwe stede**

feminine

fealu stōw	a dark site	**fealwe stōwe**
fealwa stōwa	dark sites	**fealwa stōwa**

neuter

fealu land	a dark land	**fealu land**
fealu land	dark lands	**fealu land**

Like **fealu** are **gearu** 'ready, prepared' and **nearu** 'narrow, close'.

Furthermore, the handful of adjectives which end in **-h** drop this when adding the ending; any tricky vowel clusters are then simplified as for example with **hēah** 'high':

masculine

hēah stede	a high place	**hēane stede**
hēa stede	high places	**hēa stede**

feminine

hēa stōw	a high site	**hēa stōwe**
hēa stōwa	high sites	**hēa stōwa**

neuter

hēah land	a high land	**hēah land**
hēa land	high lands	**hēa land**

Like **hēah** are

ðweorh	awkward, perverse		**fāh**	hostile
flāh	treacherous		**nēah**	near
frēoh	free			

Practice 4.2: as for 4.1 above, but I have substituted different adjectives taken from this section:

a noble king (obj.); a ready horse (subj.); a free herdsman (subj.); precious children (obj.); narrow edges (subj.); an awkward child (subj.); a hostile enemy army (subj.); treacherous princes (subj.); a renowned king (obj.); a sweet remedy (subj.).

Answers: æðelne cyning; gearu hors; frēoh hierde; dēore bearn; nearwa ecga; ðweorh bearn; fāh here; flā æðelingas; mǣrne cyning; swēte bōt.

4.3   Numerals (numbers) in OE are generally very similar to our own. They are divided into two main types: cardinal (one, two, three,…) and ordinal (first, second, third,…). We will look first at the cardinal numbers; the basic series is:-

1	**ān**	30	**ðrītig**
2	**twēgen**	40	**fēowertig**
3	**ðrīe**	50	**fīftig**
4	**fēower**	60	**siextig**
5	**fīf**	70	**hundseofontig**
6	**siex**	80	**hundeahtatig**
7	**seofon**	90	**hundnigontig**
8	**eahta**	100	**hund, hundred, hundtigontig**
9	**nigon**	110	**hundendleofontig**
10	**tīen**	120	**hundtwelftig**
11	**endleofon**	200	**tū hund**
12	**twelf**	231	**tū hund ān ond ðrītig**
13	**ðrēotīene**	300	**ðrīe hund**
14	**fēowertīene**		etc.
	etc.		
20	**twentig**	1000	**ðūsund**
21	**ān and twentig**	2000	**tū ðūsund**
22	**twēgen ond twentig**		etc.
	etc.		

   – **ān** can take normal adjectival endings (**ic sēo ānne mann** 'I can see one man')

– **twēgen** has a feminine form **twā**, and a neuter **tū**

– **ðrīe** has a separate feminine form **ðrēo**

(See also 12.4 for ordinal numerals and 14.3 for more on the cardinals.)

✠   Anglo-Saxon number notation was based on the Roman practice:

1	**i**	20	**xx**
2	**ij**	50	**l**
3	**iij**	60	**lx**
4	**iiij**	100	**c**
5	**u**	120	**cxx**
6	**uj**	500	**d**
7	**uij**	1000	**m**
8	**uiij**	2000	**mm**
9	**uiiij**		
10	**x**		

Note that the practice of subtracting a number to the left of a higher one (e.g. iv = v minus i = 5 minus 1 = 4) was not used in Anglo-Saxon times. The last stroke of a set often had a definite descender, like modern 'j', to assist in counting the number of minims (i).

Practice 4.3: give the OE for the following: 7, 17, 77; 1, 10, 100, 110, 1000, 1001; 4, 44, 444; 666; 999; 365.

Answers: seofon, seofontīene, seofon ond hundseofontig; ān, tīen, hund, hund ond tīen, þūsund, ān ond þūsund; fēower, fēower ond fēowertig, fēower hund fēower ond fēowertig; siex hund siex ond siextig; nigon hund nigon ond nigontig; ðrīe hund fīf ond siextig.

4.4   Prepositions are words which indicate position or direction or some other relationship between nouns: in the phrases 'up the road', 'over the hill', 'along the river', 'for king and country' *up, over, along, for* are all prepositions. Here are a few OE examples:-

fore	before, in front of
geond	across, throughout
ofer	over, beyond, on the other side of
on	onto, into, against
ongēan	towards, against
oð	as far as, until, up to
ðurh	through, by means of
wið	against, towards, along
ymb(e)	around, about

The nouns with which they are used are in the accusative case :

fore ðæt hūs	in front of the house
geond ðis land	across this country
ofer ðā stānas	beyond the stones
on ðæt stēorbord	on the starboard (side)
ongēan ðā scipu	towards the ships
ðurh his lāre	through his learning
wið ðæt rīce	against that kingdom
ymbe ðā trēow	around the trees
oð ðone dæg	until that day

Practice 4.4: Cover the answers below and give the OE for the following:-

across the sea; through that stone; as far as that tree; beyond the ships; into this kingdom.

Answers: geond ðæt brim; ðurh ðone stān; oð ðæt trēow; ofer ðā scipu; on ðis rīce.

4.5 There are other prepositions which require a different set of endings, those of the *dative* case. This case has a great many uses in OE, although it has largely dropped out of our modern language. Its form are as follows:-

Nouns

	sing.	pl.
masc	**ðǣm stāne** **ðissum**	**ðǣm stānum** **ðissum**
neut.	**ðǣm lande** **ðissum**	**ðǣm landum** **ðissum**
fem.	**ðǣre lāre** **ðisre**	**ðǣm lārum** **ðissum**

Personal Pronouns

masc	*neut.*	*fem.*	*pl.(all)*
him	**him**	**hire**	**him**

Adjectives

	sing.	pl.
masc.	**gōdum stāne**	**gōdum stānum**
neut.	**gōdum lande**	**gōdum landum**
fem.	**gōdre lāre**	**gōdum lārum**

The type of adjective ending in -**h** (e.g. **hēah**) has forms ending -**m** and -**re** (e.g. **hēare** in the fem. sing., **hēam** elsewhere.)

Beware – there are a very few nouns which have the ending **-um** in the nominative singular; the commonest ones are **fultum** (m) 'help, assistance', **maððum** (m) 'treasure, valuable possession' (e.g. dative singular **fultume**, plural **fultumum**).

✠ The endings for the noun are **-e** (sing.) and **-um** (pl.) and for the adjective **-re** and **-um**.

❖ **ðæm** is sometimes written as **ðām** and **ðisre** as **ðisse**.

4.6 Prepositions which use the dative case include the following:

æfter	after	**for**	for, on behalf of
ǣr	before	**fram**	from, by
æt	at	**mid**	with
be (bī)	by, beside	**of**	off, from, away from
betwēonan	between	**on**	on, in
betwux	betwixt	**tō**	to, as
būtan	without, except for		

Examples are:

æfter þissum gelimpum	after these events
ǣr ðǣm dagum	before those days
æt ðǣm stāne	at the rock
be gōdum cyningum	by good kings
betwēonan stānum	between stones
betwux ðǣm muntum	betwixt the hills
būtan þissum ānum	except for this one
for ðǣm æðelinge	for the prince
mid his sweorde	with his sword
of Englalande	from England
tō frōfre	as a comfort
on ofoste	in haste

❖ **betwux** has alternative spellings **betwuh, betwih**.

Practice 4.6: Again, there is a lot to remember here, but the endings are not difficult and are easily identified in reading – any word ending in **-um** will automatically call to mind the dative. Give the OE for the following:-

after this day; at the tree; between the houses; to England; without a remedy.

Answers: æfter ðissum dæge; æt ðǣm trēowe; betwēonan ðǣm hūsum; tō Englalande; būton bōte.

Vocabulary (4)

Adjectives

trum	firm, stout	**til**	good, gainful
longsum	enduring	**wilsum**	enjoyable
lufsum	lovable	**lāðlic**	hateful
twēolic	doubtful	**eorðlic**	worldly
gōd	good	**earm**	poor
blind	blind	**heard**	hard
yfel	evil	**eald**	old
hwæt	bold, daring	**gram**	fierce, angry
glæd	happy	**dēad**	dead
hēah	high	**gearu**	ready
lȳtel	small	**smæl**	slender

Nouns

(plurals are given in brackets beneath)

masculine		*feminine*		*neuter*	
munt	a mount, hill	**hyll**	a hill	**stēorbord**	starboard side
(muntas)		**(hylla)**		**(stēorbord)**	
stede	a place	**lāf**	inheritance	**mynster**	a minster-
(stede)				**(mynster)**	church
æcer	a field				
(æceras)					

⌘ The type of ship used in Anglo-Saxon times was conventionally steered by a large rudder-like oar mounted at the rear on the right-hand side (looking forward) and called the steer(ing)-board, **stēorbord**; a memory of this has survived as our word 'starboard' for the right side of a ship.

Exercises (4)

1. Translate the following into NE:

(a)   sacu ādrecceð cyningas on Englalande

(b)   twegen rīce cyningas and twelf ðegnas cumað

(c)   ðæt mynster is mære geond Englaland

(d)   se biscop fēdeð earme menn

(e)   līðmenn fērað be scipum

(f)   grēne trēow ne bærnað nā

(g)   cwīðað hīe and hǣlað mec mid gōdum bōtum

2. Translate the following into OE :

(a)   a famous man has enduring praise

(b)   poor men leave a small inheritance

(c)   the thanes drive off the raiders with their swords – they travel towards the ships

(d)   the site is between those hills in front of the trees

(e)   green fields and good are in this land

(f)   the herdsman is by the stones on the other side of the field

(g)   neither kings nor bishops will travel through that land

OLD ENGLISH COURSE – SECTION 5

5.1   Another use of the dative is to mark out the indirect object of the verb. To explain what this means: in an expression such as "the nobleman gives a gift to the bride" the subject (i.e. the giver) is the nobleman and the object (i.e. the thing given) is the gift; there is a third party involved, however, the recipient to whom the object is given: this is the indirect object.

In OE this sentence would appear as **se æþeling giefð giefe þǣre brȳde**, where **þǣre brȳde** is the dative singular of **sēo brȳd**. Another example: 'the king entrusts his sword to the thane'; here the subject (entruster) is the king and the thing entrusted is the sword, while the indirect object is the thane: **se cyning befæsteð his sweord ðǣm þegne**.

The indirect object is usually marked in modern English with 'to' (…to the bride, …to the thane) although there are other instances of the dative in use where 'to' does not figure in the modern translation ("gives the bride a gift").

Practice 5.1: translate the following:-

the sailor entrusts his ship to the bishop; the bishop gives an oath to the prince; the king gives his horse to the bride.

Answers: se līþmann befæsteð his scip ðǣm biscope; se biscop giefð āþ ðǣm æðelinge; se cyning giefþ his hors ðǣre brȳde.

5.2   There are two sets of forms of the verb 'to be' in the present tense. While this may seem unnecessary to us, there are important differences in use which will be discussed below. There are special negated forms of the verb **wesan**:

	wesan	*negated*	bēon
1st sing	eom	neom	bēo
2nd	eart	neart	bist
3rd	is	nis	biþ
all pl.	sind		bēoþ

❖ These are the standard West Saxon forms. Variant spellings occur, including **sindon**, **sint**, **synt** for **sind**. There is also an Anglian (Mercian and Northumbrian) alternative to **sind**: **earon**.

There are different uses for these verbs, which have separate meanings, in effect. Generally, the forms found under **wesan** are commonest and correspond closely to the modern usage of 'be'. **Bēon**, however, refers to more indefinite matters, general statements, the 'usual' rather than the 'actual' e.g. **cyning biδ gram ond fram** 'a king is fierce and bold' – a statement which does not rule out the possibility of mild and indecisive kings; it could perhaps be better translated as 'a king should be fierce and bold' or 'it is fitting that a king be fierce and bold'. Because of this association with generalities rather than specifics, **biδ is often used in proverbs and laws, e.g. fyr biþ þēof** 'fire is a thief' (because it deprives people of their property).

Bēon has another important use – it expresses (in a limited way) the future, e.g. **ic bēo gearu** 'I shall be ready' as opposed to **ic eom gearu** 'I am ready'. This is the closest OE gets to statements about the future – normally the 'present' tense of the verb is used to mean both 'now' and 'in the future', so that **ic rīde** is 'I ride, am riding' and 'I will ride, will be riding'.

5.3 The words for 'my', 'our', etc. in OE could be divided into two sets: those for the 1st and 2nd persons, and those for the 3rd. This latter group are :

masc.	*neut.*	*fem.*	*all pl.*
his	**his**	**hire**	**hiera**

These words, like the NE equivalents, do not vary according to the gender of the noun they occur with, e.g. **his stān, his brȳd, his scip, his bātas, his giefa, his word**.

The 1st and 2nd persons' corresponding forms take the endings of the normal adjective, as set out in 4.1, i.e.

1st. sing	**mīn**	*pl.*	**ūre**
2nd	**þīn**		**ēower**

They behave like **gōd** in that they do not add **-u** before the nom.sing.fem or nom./acc.pl. neut. Here are the forms for **mīn** 'my':-

	masculine	*neuter*	*feminine*
nom. sing.	**mīn stān**	**mīn scip**	**mīn brȳd**
pl.	**mīne stānas**	**mīn scipu**	**mīna brȳda**
acc. sing	**mīnne stān**	**mīn scip**	**mīne brȳde**
pl.	**mīne stānas**	**mīn scipu**	**mīna brȳda**
dat. sing.	**mīnum stāne**	**mīnum scipe**	**mīnre brȳde**
pl.	**mīnum stānum**	**mīnum scipum**	**mīnum brȳdum**

Þīn follows this pattern; **ūre** retains its final -e when no other ending is necessary (**ūre lār**); **ēower** drops the short -e- when an ending is added (**ēowrum bātum**).

❖   **hiera** can also be spelt **hira, heora**; there is another form **ūser** for **ūre.**

✠   There is an old form **sīn** for the 3rd person sing. and pl., which behaves like **mīn, ðīn**. It is found only in poetry.

Practice 5.3: give the appropriate forms for the following :

my words (nom.)	thy gift (acc.)	our lands (acc.)	his sword (acc.)
my ships (nom.)	their houses (dat.)	thy oath (acc.)	your king (dat.)
their nobleman (nom.)	her horses (nom.)	our sheep (acc.)	

Answers: mīn word; þīne giefe; ūre land; his sweord; mīn scipu; hiera hūsum; þīnne āð; þīnum cyninge; hiera æðeling; hire hors; ūre scēap.

5.4   Similar to **mīn**, etc. above is the word **nān** 'no, none', e.g.**nis nān cyning hēr** 'no king is here' or 'there is no king here'. The verb is usually preceded by **ne** 'not':

nāne līþmenn ne rīdað   – no sailors ride
ic ne lufie nānne mann būton him ānum   – I love no man but him alone

✠   **Nān** is a compound of **ne** (not) and **ān** (one), just like NE 'none'

Practice 5.4: repeat the exercise in 5.3, substituting **nān** for **mīn, his**, etc.

Answers: nān word; nāne giefe; nān land; nān sweord; nān scipu; nānum hūsum; nānne āð; nānum cyninge; nān æðeling; nān hors; nān scēap.

5.5   An important and very common verb in OE (as in NE) is **habban** 'to have', of which the present tense forms and their special negated variants are as follows:

	habban	nabban
ic	hæbbe	næbbe
þū	hæfst	næfst
hē		
hēo	hæfð	næfð
hit		
wē		
gē	habbaþ	nabbaþ
hīe		

✠   There are variant singular forms: **ic hafu, þū hafast, hē hafaþ**.

Vocabulary (5)

Adjectives

sār	painful, sore	**rūm**	spacious, roomy
brād	broad, wide	**sēoc**	sick

Nouns

masculine	**wīcing**	(**wīcingas**)	a viking
neuter	**wīf**	(**wīf**)	a woman

Adverbs   Conjunctions

sōna	soon	**ac**	but

Exercises (5)

1. Translate the following into NE:

(a)   se līðmann befæsteð his scip þǣm ðegne.

(b)   nis se bæcere eald ne earm.

(c)   lāþlice menn ne bēoþ nǣfre glade.

(d)   mīn hūs is betwēonan þǣm hyllum.

(e)   nis þīn hūs hēah, ac hit is brād ond rūm.

(f)   þis word is twēolic – ic ne cȳðe hit

(g)   būton nānre bōte ðās menn bēoþ sōna dēade

2. Translate the following into OE:

(a)   the wound is painful and he is sick.

(b)   the raiding party shall not drive off a brave man

(c)   she comes to him as a bride and loves him

(d)   that woman is neither hostile nor treacherous

(e)   a happy man has a ship, a sword and a woman

(f)   neither the king nor his thane will release the vikings

(g)   in England, the fields are broad and the sea is narrow

OLD ENGLISH COURSE – SECTION 6

6.1 The genitive
6.2 Nouns ending in -e (*stede*)
6.3 Present tense, weak verbs (*fremman, nerian*)

6.4 Imperative mood (second person)
6.5 Imperative mood (first person plural)

6.1 Possession. We have seen above (5.3) how certain adjectives show possession. What happens when we need to show possession by someone or something else? That is, how do we say 'the king's thane' or 'the sword's edges' or 'my mother's brother' and so on? In NE, as I have just shown, we use a special ending (- *'s*), so it comes as no surprise to discover that OE does likewise. However, the ending varies according to the gender and the number.

Nouns

	sing.	*pl.*
masc.	ðæs stānes	ðāra stāna
	ðisses	ðissa
neut.	ðæs scipes	ðāra scipa
	ðisses	ðissa
fem.	ðǣre lāre	ðāra lāra
	ðisre	ðissa

  The name of this case is the *genitive*.

Evidently, in the singular the feminines have the same form here as for the dative, while the masculines and neuters take the **-es** which has given rise to our modern -'s (for all genders in NE). Again, in the plural, there is one set of endings for all genders, the same pattern as is found in the dative.

Possessive Pronouns

masc.	*neut.*	*fem.*	*pl. (all)*
his	**his**	**hire**	**hiera**

These forms have already been met with as the possessive adjectives (his, its, etc.)

Adjectives

	sing.	*pl.*
masc.	**gōdes stānes**	**gōdra stāna**
neut.	**gōdes scipes**	**gōdra scipa**
fem.	**gōdre lāre**	**gōdra lāra**

The type of adjective ending in **-h** (e.g. **hēah**) has forms ending **-s**, **-re** and **-ra** (masc./neut.sing. **hēas**, fem.sing. **hēare**, pl. **hēara**).
The endings of the adjectives follow the pattern of the words 'the' and 'this', and of the personal pronouns.

Examples of the genitive case in use are common:

ðæs cyninges ðegn	the king's thane	or	the thane of the king
ðæs līþmannes scip	the sailor's ship	or	the ship of the sailor
þære brȳde hors	the bride's horse	or	the horse of the bride
ðāra bæcera hlāfas	the bakers' loaves	or	the loaves of the bakers
ðāra ecga benna	the swords' wounds	or	the wounds of the swords
ðāra scēapa hierde	the sheeps' herdsman	or	the herdsman of the sheep

Use of **of** with the modern meaning in OE is *very* late; normally this word means 'off, away from' and will not translate NE 'of': **of Englalande** is 'from England' not 'of England'. The genitive case is the normal way of expressing both 'the ship's side' and 'the side of the ship' (**scipes sīde**).

> ✠ **Englaland** is transparently **Engla** (gen.pl) and **land** – it is the 'land of the Angles' (i.e. the English).

6.2 There is a group of masculine nouns whose plurals are not formed with **-as** (i.e. like **stānas**). Some of the nouns in this group have **-e** in the singular (e.g. **stede** 'a place') but most have no singular at all, being the names of nations or peoples. Here is the set of forms:

	sing.	*pl.*
nom.	**stede**	**stede**
acc.	**stede**	**stede**
gen.	**stedes**	**steda**
dat.	**stede**	**stedum**

Like **stede** are the common nouns **wine** 'friend', **here** 'army' with occasional genitive plural form **winigea, herigea**.

The group of words for which there are no singular forms include:

ylde	men, human beings	**Seaxe**	Saxons
ylfe	elves	**Mierce**	Mercians
lēode	people	**Norþanhymbre**	Northumbrians
Engle	Angles, Englishmen	**Dene**	Danes, vikings

❖ Sometimes **Mierce** and **Seaxe** have genitive plural **Miercena, Seaxna;** the 'weak' form **Seaxan** (nom.acc.pl) also occurs (see 11.3 for 'weak' nouns). **Engle** may also be a variant of **Angle** dat.sing. of **Angul** 'Angeln, the (continental) home of the Angles'.

6.3   Having looked at verbs like **hīeran** 'to hear' in 3.2, there are other verbs of a similar kind with the same endings but slightly different treatment of the stem (the part of the verb to which the endings are added). As an example, here are the forms of **fremman** 'to carry out, perform'

1st.	*sing.*	**fremme**
2nd.		**fremest**
3rd		**fremeþ**
	pl.	**fremmað**

As you can see, the 2nd and 3rd person singular have altered the stem which would be expected (**fremm-*) by deleting the final '-**m**-'. There are a good many verbs of this type, easily detected by the fact that they have a double consonant before the infinitive ending -**an**. Here are some further examples:-

trymman	strengthen	**settan**	set
dynnan	make a loud noise	**lettan**	hinder
cnyssan	strike	**cnyttan**	tie a knot

A parallel pattern operates with a small group of verbs whose infinitives end in -**erian**, e.g. **nerian** 'save':

1st.	*sing.*	**nerie**
2nd		**nerest**
3rd		**nereþ**
	pl.	**neriaþ**

Here, the -**i**- is removed from the stem in the 2nd and 3rd. sing., just where the verbs like **fremman** reduce the doubled consonants.

Like **nerian** are:-

erian	plough	**ferian**	carry, ferry
derian	harm, hurt	**werian**	defend, protect
herian	praise	**spyrian**	ask, inquire

Practice 6.3: cover the answers and give the OE for the following:-

I plough; you praise; he protects; we strengthen it; it makes a noise; thou strikest; that hinders me; they are tying a knot; you (sing.) are hurting me (use the dative 'me'); she is enquiring.

Answers: ic erie; gē heriaþ; hē wereð; wē trymmaþ hit; hit dyneþ; þū cnysest; þæt leteð mec; hīe cnyttaþ; þū derest mē; hēo spyreð.

6.4 The imperative is the name for the 'command' form of the verb. In NE, we use the infinitive without 'to' (come! look! be quiet!), but OE has two forms, according to whether one person (ðū) or more (gē) is addressed:-

hīeran	*sing.*	**hīer**	*pl.*	**hīerað**
fremman	*sing.*	**freme**	*pl.*	**fremmaþ**
nerian	*sing.*	**nere**	*pl.*	**neriað**

In the plural, the imperative is the same as the normal 'statement' form, but in the singular of the latter two types there are special forms ending in -**e**.
'Be!' in OE may be formed on both **wesan** and **bēon**:

    sing.   **wes, bēo**   *pl.*   **wesað, bēoð.**

✠   A common greeting was **wes ðū hāl** 'be hale', 'be whole' from which the modern word *wassail* is derived.

Practice 6.4: cover the answers below and give the OE for the following:-

    singular – hear! defend! strengthen! strike! judge! release them!
      plural – perform! plough that field! obey! teach me!

Answers: hīer, were, tryme, cnyse, dēm, ālīes hīe; fremmaþ, eriaþ ðone æcer, gīemað, lǣrað mec.

6.5 There is another kind of imperative for the 1st person plural, which in NE is formed with the phrase 'Let's...' before the infinitive (minus 'to') e.g. 'let's go!'. In OE, such expressions are usually formed with the similar phrase **uton** (sometimes **wuton**) e.g. **uton ālīesan hine** 'let's set him free!'.

Vocabulary (6)

Nouns

henceforth are given in the nom. sing. only, and are followed by the abbreviation of their gender.

eorðling *(m)*	a farmer, ploughman
æcs *(f)*	an axe
wull *(f)*	wool
galdor *(n)*	a charm, spell, incantation
eard *(m)*	an estate (for more on this word, see 9.5), farm

Adverbs

oftost	most often	**swīþe**	very, very much, greatly
hwȳ	why?	**forðǣm ðe**	because
seldan	seldom		

Adjectives

fremful	effective, potent	**forhtful**	afraid, fearful

Exercises (6)

1. Translate the following into NE:

Dudda is eorþling on Miercena lande; his sunu hāteþ Dunnere. Oððe se eorðling oþþe his sunu ereþ ðā æceras on hiera earde. Þæs eorþlinges sunu is swīþe strang – hē cnyseþ trēow mid his æcse. Ac Dudda nis nō strang – hē is eald ond sēoc ond ereð seldan. His wīf is dēad, ac Dunnere lufaþ hine ond ereþ oftost. Hiera eard is lȳtel ac hīe habbað scēap for wulle and tō mete.

Hwȳ ne ereþ Dudda? Forðǣm þe hē is eald ond sēoc.

Hwȳ ereþ Dunnere? Forþǣm þe hē is geong ond strang.

2. Translate the following into OE:

The farm of Berhtwulf is in East Anglia. Elves afflict it, he says (**cweðan**, to say), but Swæppa his friend protects him against them with charms. His words are effective and the elves are fearful. A charm is hateful to the elves.

OLD ENGLISH COURSE – SECTION 7

7.1   There are a number of ways of expressing 'who' or 'whom' or 'which' or 'that' in OE. These words are called 'relative pronouns' because they relate one statement to another, forming a link between the two statements. The commonest are:-

(i) using the word for 'the', with the gender and number appropriate for the word in the main statement (principal clause) being linked, but with the case required by the grammar of the secondary statement (subordinate clause). This sounds more complicated than it actually is, so let's take an example: **se mann se oneardaþ þis hūs is sēoc** 'the man who lives in this house is sick'

The main statement here is 'the man is sick', and the word **mann** is linked to 'who lives in this house'; in this latter phrase we need a word for 'who' which is masculine singular (like **mann**) and as it is the subject of the phrase it should be in the nominative case. Therefore the correct form here is **se**.

Another example: "the bride who loves treasures will not love a proud man" with the principal statement "the bride (subject = nominative) will not love a proud man (object = accusative)" and the secondary "the bride (subject = nominative) loves treasures (object = accusative)" **sēo brȳd sēo lufað maðmas ne lufað wlancne wer**

Yet another example: **ðes stede ðone menn oneardiað is hēah** 'this place which men inhabit is high'. The main statement is 'this place is high', and the secondary statement is 'men inhabit it', so that the place is the *object* of this secondary statement (of which **menn** is the subject), and thus in the accusative case (**ðone**); again **mīn brȳd þā ic lufie is gladu** 'my bride, whom I love, is happy' – the main statement is 'my bride is happy' so the word for 'whom' must be feminine singular (like **brȳd**) and as it is the object of 'I love' it must be accusative (and singular), **þā**.

(ii) using the word **þe**, which does not change for gender, number or case: **hierdas þe fēdað scēap** 'herdsmen who feed sheep'; **bōta þe hǣlað menn** 'remedies which heal people'; **þæt scip ðe ic befæste** 'the ship which I entrust'.

(iii) using both (i) and (ii) together: **eorþling se ðe ereð æceras** 'a farmer who ploughs fields'; **ceara þā ðe ūs ādreccaþ** 'worries which afflict us'.

'Whose' and 'to whom' can be expressed using the genitive and dative respectively: **se cyning ðæs rīce is brād fērþ oft** 'the king, whose realm is wide, often travels'; **hierdas þāra scēap sind sēoc sēcað bōte** 'herdsmen whose sheep are sick will seek a remedy'; **sēoce menn þǣm giefað lǣcas tila bōta ne sweltaþ** 'sick men to whom healers give good remedies will not die'.

Here is a schematic of some of the possibilities outlined above:

masc.

nom.	Se wer	se gǣþ tō ðǣm mōre	The man	who travels to the moor
acc.		þone ic sēah on þǣm mōre		whom I saw on the moor
gen.		þæs fōr wæs on ðǣm mōre		whose journey was on the moor
dat.		ðǣm wæs lang fōr on ðǣm mōre		for whom (it) was a long journey on the moor

neut.

nom.	Þæt bearn	þæt andswaraþ	The child	who answers
acc.		þæt ic andswarie		whom I answer
gen.		þæs andswaru is forhtful		whose answer is fearful
dat.		þǣm wæs gōd andswaru		for whom (it) was a good answer

fem.

nom.	Sēo brȳd	sēo lufaþ giefa	The bride	who loves gifts
acc.		ðā lufað se wer		whom the man loves
gen.		ðǣre lufu is hold		whose love is true
dat.		ðǣre is þæs weres lufu hold		for whom the man's love is true

Þæt can also introduce following clauses, like NE 'that', e.g. **ic wāt þæt hē is eald** 'I know that he is old'. (See (15.2) for the form **wāt**.)

Practice 7.1: cover the answers and give the OE for the following:

> a farmer whose sheep are sick; the nobleman who protects the king; the house which is on the hill; these fields which I plough; a sword of which the edges will harm these vikings (use the dative).

Answers: eorþling ðæs scēap sind sēoc; se æðeling se þe wereð þone cyning; þæt hūs þæt is on ðǣre hylle; ðās æceras þā þe ic erie; swēord þæs deriaþ ðā ecga ðissum wīcingum.

7.2 An extended use of **se ðe** is as 'he who' in expressions such as 'he who hesitates is lost' and the like. Naturally, **se ðe** refers to masculines, **sēo ðe** to feminines and **þæt þe** (often written **þætte**) to neuters, the latter often translatable as 'that which': **se þe fērð biþ wērig** 'he who travels will be weary', **sēo ðe oneardað þis hūs** 'she who lives in this house', **þætte menn lufiað** 'that which men love'.

7.3 We have looked at verbs ending in **-rian** in 6.3; there is another, larger group of verbs which end in **-ian** in the infinitive. We have already used **lufaþ** 'loves', **oneardaþ** 'inhabits' and **lufiaþ** 'love', **oneardiaþ** 'inhabit' in previous exercises. The set of present tense forms runs:-

1st.	*sing*	**lufie**
2nd.		**lufast**
3rd		**lufaþ**
	pl.	**lufiaþ**

The imperative forms are:

sing.	**lufa**	*pl.*	**lufiaþ**

All infinitives ending in **-ian** (except those endings in **-rian** above (6.3)) follow this pattern. It is important to note that with these verbs **-að** is the 3rd. sing. ending, not the plural as it usually is elsewhere.

❖   An alternative spelling is **lufige,** etc. for **lufie**, where **-g-** represents a '-y-' sound, a slur between the two vowels.

Verbs of this type are numerous: examples can be found in the Vocabulary to this section.

Practice 7.3: cover the answers and give the OE for the following:

you are learning; do not grieve (sing.)!; the tree is trembling; I shall remain; obey!; he is looking; the sea is ebbing; the wound is painful.

Answers: gē leorniaþ; ne sorga; þæt trēow bifað; ic wunie; hīersumiaþ; hē lōcaþ; ðæt brim ebbað; sēo benn sāraþ.

7.4   There are a few nouns in NE which form their plurals in an unusual way: instead of adding an ending, they change the vowel – *man:men; woman:women; foot:feet; tooth:teeth; goose:geese; louse:lice; mouse:mice.* The OE equivalents of these words behave similarly, although there are a few more of them. The vowel change is found in the nom.acc.pl. and also in parts of the sing.:-

(i) *masculine*
     fōt 'a foot'

	sing.	*pl.*
nom	**fōt**	**fēt**
acc.	**fōt**	**fēt**
gen.	**fōtes**	**fōta**
dat.	**fēt**	**fōtum**

so also **tōð** 'a tooth'

mann 'a person'	*nom*	**mann**	**menn**
	acc.	**mann**	**menn**
	gen.	**mannes**	**manna**
	dat.	**menn**	**mannum**
frēond 'a friend'	*nom.*	**frēond**	**frīend**
	acc.	**frēond**	**frīend**
	gen	**frēondes**	**frēonda**
	dat.	**frīend**	**frēondum**

so also **fēond** 'an enemy'

(ii) *feminine*

bōc 'a book'	*nom.*	**bōc**	**bēc**
	acc.	**bōc**	**bēc**
	gen.	**bēc**	**bōca**
	dat.	**bēc**	**bōcum**

so also **gōs** 'a goose'

burg 'a stronghold'	*nom.*	**burg**	**byrig**
	acc	**burg**	**byrig**
	gen.	**byrig**	**burga**
	dat.	**byrig**	**burgum**
āc 'an oak'	*nom*	**āc**	**ǣc**
	acc.	**āc**	**ǣc**
	gen	**ǣc**	**āca**
	dat.	**ǣc**	**ācum**
mūs 'a mouse'	*nom.*	**mūs**	**mȳs**
	acc.	**mūs**	**mȳs**
	gen.	**mȳs**	**mūsa**
	dat.	**mȳs**	**mūsum**

so also **lūs** 'a louse'

There are other nouns which also have occasional forms of this type, e.g.: **cū** 'a cow' has nom.acc.pl **cȳ**; **hnutu** 'a nut' has dat.sing., nom.acc.pl. **hnyte**.

Practice 7.4: cover the answers and give the following OE forms:

man (nom.pl); foot (gen.sing.); tooth (acc.pl.); tooth (gen.sing.); friend (dat.sing.);tooth (dat.sing.); man (gen.sing.); man (dat.pl.); mouse (acc.pl.); louse (nom.pl); book (gen.sing.); enemy (gen.pl.); goose (dat.sing.); tooth (gen.pl); mouse (gen.sing.); friend (dat.pl.); enemy (acc.sing.); stronghold (nom.sing.); book (acc.pl.); oak (gen.pl.); oak (gen.sing.); stronghold (dat.sing.).

Answers: menn; fōtes; tēþ; tōþes; frīend; tēð; mannes; mannum; mȳ; lȳ; bēc; fēonda; gēs; tōþa; mȳ; frēondum; fēond; burg; bēc; āca; ǣc; byrig.

7.5 The correspondences in vowels shown above are part of an entire system which has an effect on the ways words behave. In brief, the changes are as follows:-

Vowels

a + m, n, ng	*becomes:*	e	**standan** 'to stand'	**stent** 'stands'
a	*becomes:*	æ	**faran** 'to travel'	**færþ** 'travels'
æ	*becomes:*	e	**sæt** 'he sat'	**settan** 'make sit, set'
e	*becomes:*	i	**helpan** 'to help'	**hilpþ** 'helps'
u	*becomes:*	y	**cuman** 'to come'	**cymþ** 'comes'
ā	*becomes:*	ǣ	**gān** 'to go'	**gǣþ** 'goes'
ō	*becomes:*	ē	**flōwan** 'to flow'	**flēwþ** 'flows'
ū	*becomes:*	ȳ	**brūcan** 'to enjoy'	**brȳcþ** 'enjoys'

The **diphthongs** all become -ie- (short) and -īe- (long):

eo	*becomes:*	ie	**ceorfan** 'to cut'	**cierfð** 'cuts'
ea	*becomes:*	ie	**weaxan** 'to grow'	**wiext** 'grows'
ēo	*becomes:*	īe	**hrēowan** 'to rue'	**hrīewþ** 'rues'
ēa	*becomes:*	īe	**hēawan** 'to hew'	**hīewþ** 'hews'

These alternations have a profound effect on many groups of OE words, and a knowledge of them will be helpful when we come to look at the 'strong' verb (in 8.1). For the meantime, you can see from this tabulation that the change **mann>menn** is an example of **a+n>e+n** (line 1) while the changes **cū>cȳ āc>ǣc, frēond>frīend**, etc. are all deducible from the table, as is the interchange of vowel in **hæfð** 'has' and **habbað** 'have'. Furthermore, you are already familiar with the adjectives **trum** 'firm', **fram** 'effective' – the table shows their connection to the words **trymman** 'make firm, strengthen', **fremman** 'be effective, perform'. OE has an entire section of its vocabulary linked together in this way, with verbs, adjectives and nouns forming part of a 'network' of words which are related to each other (see 18.4).

We will return to these correspondences from time to time. In the meantime, it is enough to be aware of them in preparation for the 'strong' verb data in the next section.

�֍ This change of vowel is sometimes called *i-mutation* or *i-umlaut*.

Vocabulary (7)

Verbs

endian	end, finish	**andswarian**	answer
āscian	ask, enquire	**bēotian**	boast, promise
bismrian	besmirch, insult	**blissian**	be happy, rejoice
bodian	preach	**clipian**	call, call out to
eardian	dwell	**ebbian**	ebb away
fandian	try, test	**folgian**	follow
gaderian	gather	**geæmetigan**	empty
hergian	ravage, harry	**hīersumian**	obey
leornian	learn	**lōcian**	look
losian	be lost	**macian**	make
scēawian	look at, inspect	**trūwian**	trust, believe
weorðian	honour	**wunian**	remain, dwell
wundian	wound	**ārian**	honour, endow
forhtian	be afraid, fear	**maþelian**	make a speech
sārian	be painful	**sorgian**	sorrow, grieve
gehālsian	take an oath	**bifian**	tremble

Nouns

gesīþ *(m)*	a companion, fellow traveller
gefeoht *(n)*	a battle, fight
rāp *(m)*	a rope

Exercises (7)

1. Translate the following into NE:

(a)   ic ne trūwie ðone þe bēotaþ

(b)   se here hergaþ on þissum lande

(c)   hīe weorþiaþ heora frīend ond deriaþ heora fēondum

(d)   se cyning fērþ mid ānum menn tō gesīþe

(e)   þā wīcingas þe bēotiað swīþe forhtiaþ on gefeohte

(f)   ðā Mierce trymmaþ ðā burg wiþ ðā Dene

2. Translate the following into OE:

(a)   the bishop is lost and is very afraid

(b)   follow me and look at that oak which is in my field *(use sing. forms)*

(c)   do not be afraid, the wound is painful but will not harm you *(use sing. forms)*

(d)   I will take an oath with my friend whom the king trusts

(e)   set a rope about the tree and tie a knot *(use pl. forms)*

(f)   these people are Mercians, they do not live in the land of the Saxons

OLD ENGLISH COURSE – SECTION 8

8.1   OE verbs are conventionally divided into three types: *weak*, *strong* and *preterite-present*. The *weak* verb is the type we have already met in detail (e.g. **hīeran** (in 3.3), **fremman, nerian** (in 6.3), **lufian** (in 7.3). The *strong* verb is not very different in the present tense from the weak type, although it does incorporate the vowel correspondences which we noted above (in 7.5) in some forms. The great difference between weak and strong verbs is in the way they form their past tense (called the *preterite* in most grammars): where a typical weak verb adds *-ed* to its stem to make the past tense in NE, a strong verb will change its vowel instead.

Examples are:

Weak	Strong
I like : I liked	I strike : I struck
I arrive : I arrived	I drive : I drove
I mind : I minded	I find : I found

Another test is with the past tense using 'have' (the perfect tense) where weak verbs continue to use *-ed* forms, but many strong verbs have *-en* forms, usually with a different vowel from that of the present tense:

arrive : arrived	drive : driven
deride : derided	hide : hidden
fake : faked	take : taken

(There is an apparent flaw in the argument here, in that we don't say 'I have founden' or 'he has stricken again', but this is due to later changes in the language and the word 'stricken' does still occur as an adjective with the meaning 'afflicted, blighted'.)

Preterite-present verbs are few in number but very important; they are the class of words like 'can', 'will', 'must', 'should', etc. which are used to show shades of meaning with other verbs: 'I may go' for example. The name 'preterite-present' is due to the fact that they behave as if they are past tense (preterite) forms, but their meaning is that of a present tense. If this seems odd, remember that their modern equivalents generally behave likewise: we say 'he may go', 'that must be true' not 'he mays go', 'that musts be true'; also, these verbs don't usually have a real infinitive form, so we don't say 'you must can ride a bicycle' but 'you must be able to…'. The preterite-present verbs are an interesting and useful group, but we shall not look at them until later (in 15.1-6).

8.2   There are different groups of strong verbs (called 'classes') depending on the vowels they use to show the tense. Conventionally, there are seven such classes; in practice, there are rather more patterns due to some verbs having suffered a change in the vowel of the stem. For the purposes of the present tense, however, only those correspondences set out under 7.5 are of importance.

Taking a sample verb (in this case, one which has no vowel change in the present tense) to begin with, the endings are as follows:-

		scīnan 'to shine'
1st.	*sing.*	**scīne**
2nd		**scīnst**
3rd		**scīnþ**
	pl.	**scīnað**

Alternatively, one of the numerous strong verbs with simplification of final consonant clusters:

		glīdan 'to glide'
1st	*sing.*	**glīde**
2nd		**glītst**
3rd		**glītt**
	pl.	**glīdaþ**

Evidently, the endings are substantially the same as for the weak verbs like **hīeran**. But there is no vowel before the -**st**, -**þ** of the 2nd and 3rd sing., and it is in these forms that the alterations to the stem vowel occur. The pattern is reflected in the following example:-

		beran 'to bear, carry'
1st.	*sing*	**bere**
2nd		**birst**
3rd		**birþ**
	pl.	**berað**

Here, the -**i**- of the 2nd, 3rd sing. is the altered ('mutated' is the usual grammatical term) form corresponding to -**e**- in the infinitive and stem. Obviously, each stem vowel has a different corresponding mutated vowel; here are some further examples:-

		standan 'to stand, be situated'	**faran** 'to fare, travel'	**cuman** 'to come'
1st	*sing.*	stande	fare	cume
2nd		stentst	færst	cymst
3rd		stent	færð	cymþ
	pl.	standaþ	faraþ	cumaþ

		gān 'to go'	**dōn** 'to do, put'	**lūcan** 'to lock'
1st	*sing.*	gā	dō	lūce
2nd		gǣst	dēst	lȳcst
3rd		gǣþ	dēþ	lȳcð
pl.	*pl.*	gāð	dōð	lūcað

		feohtan 'to fight'	**weaxan** 'to grow'	**cēosan** 'to choose'
1st	*sing.*	feohte	weaxe	cēose
2nd		fiehtst	wiext	cīest
3rd		fieht	wiext	cīest
pl.	*pl.*	feohtaþ	weaxaþ	cēosaþ

		hēawan 'to hew, carve'
1st	*sing.*	hēawe
2nd		hīewst
3rd		hīewþ
pl.	*pl.*	hēawaþ

It is worth noting that verbs which have -i-,-ie-,-ī-,-ǣ- in the stem already do not alter the vowel, but can still undergo the changes to the endings when consonants fall together – hence the form '**glītt**' under **glīdan**. Since the endings affect all verbs with final **-d-** and **-t-**, it is not possible to tell whether the word **bītt** (in isolation) means 'waits' (**bīdan**, to wait) or 'bites' (**bītan**, to bite). But there can seldom be any doubt, due to the very different meanings, as to which one is being used!

Practice 8.2: give the OE for the following:-

I hew; thou comest; she glides; the house stands on the estate; the farmers are going; children grow.

Answers: ic hēawe; þū cymst; hēo glītt; þæt hūs stent on ðǣm earde; ðā eorþlingas gāþ; bearn weaxaþ.

8.3 'When' and 'then' can both be expressed in OE with the word **þā**; but first we need to distinguish between two meanings each of the NE words 'when' and 'then'.
    – *when* can introduce a question about time (when?), and in such expressions its OE equivalent is **hwonne** – **hwonne gǣst þū?** "When are you going?"

– it can also begin a statement which is linked to (and dependent upon) another statement which may or may not begin with *then*. This use is detailed below.

– *then* can introduce a 'linked' statement, to which the corresponding linked statement begins with 'when'.

– it can also indicate the next in a series of ideas or statements, such as "he comes to the house, then enters and greets his wife" (where 'then' means 'thereafter, next'). Here, OE uses the word **þonne**: **hē cymþ tō ðǣm hūse, þonne gǣð in ond grētt his wīf.**

Where 'when' and 'then' co-ordinate two statements, making one relative to the other, OE uses the word **ðā** to begin both the statements "When you go (then) I shall go too." But note the word order in OE: **þā ðū gǣst, þā gā ic ēac.** The word order in the second (dependent) statement is different – the verb (**gā**) comes before the pronoun (**ic**). And note that the order of the statements could be reversed without affecting the meaning: **ðā gā ic, ðā þū gǣst.**

To summarize, (i) statements may be linked by both beginning with **þā**, in which case (ii) where the verb comes before the (pro)noun **þā** means 'then' and (iii) where the (pro)noun comes before the verb **þā** means 'when'. This inversion of (pro)noun and verb is common also when any adverb begins its phrase or sentence.

Practice 8.3: decide the meanings of **þā** in the following sentences (be careful – there is one example which is not what it seems – it is underscored in the answers):

þā ic rīde, þā bið mīn hors werig; ðā lǣre ic þec, þā ðū spyrest; þa þa Seaxe cumaþ, þa gretað we hie; þā leornast þū, þā ic lǣre þec.

Answers: when I ride,(then) my horse will be tired; (then) I will teach you, when you ask; when the Saxons come, (then) we shall greet them; (then) you will learn, when I teach you.

8.4 'Interrogatives' are words used to form questions; you have already met **hwonne** 'when?' in the previous section and **hwæt** 'what?' earlier. There are a few others, most of which resemble their modern equivalents:

where?	**hwǣr**
when?	**hwonne**
why?	**hwȳ**
how?	**hū**
whither?	**hwider**
whence?	**hwanon**
which (of two)?	**hwæðer**
which (of many)?	**hwilc**, which takes normal adjectival endings:
	hwilcne mann lufast ðū? Which person do you love?

Who?, whose? what? etc., are dealt with by means of a set of forms which behave like a pronoun:

	masc./fem.	*neut.*
nom.	**hwā**	**hwæt**
	masc./fem.	neut.
acc.	**hwone**	**hwæt**
gen.	**hwæs**	**hwæs**
dat.	**hwǣm**	**hwǣm**

Usually, the masc./fem. forms mean 'who?' and the neuter means 'what?', **hwæs** means 'whose?' and 'of what?' and **hwǣm** 'to whom?' and 'to what?'. There are further forms **hwȳ** and **hwon** meaning 'by whom?' and 'by what?', representing the *instrumental* case which had all but disappeared from OE (see section 17.3 for more on the instrumental).

⊠ The difference between *where, whence* and *whither* (words which are easily confused since the latter two are seldom used these days) can be set out like this (see also section 17.5):

where?	= at which place? answer:	here / there	**hēr**	**þǣr**
whither?	= to which place?	hither / thither	**hider**	**þider**
whence?	= from which place?	hence / thence	**heonan**	**þonan**

❖ **hwilc** may also be spelt **hwelc, hwylc**.

Practice 8.4: cover the answers and give the OE for the following (using the 2nd person singular throughout):

Where are you going? what are you doing? whom do you trust? where do you live? when will you preach? how do you make swords? why are you sad?

Answers: Hwider gǣst þū? hwæt dēst þū? hwone trūwast þū? hwǣr eardast ðū? hwonne bodast þū? hū macast ðū sweord? hwȳ sorgast þū?

8.5 Apart from the personal pronouns which were dealt with in sections 3.1, 3.4, 4.5, 6.1, there are also 'indefinite' pronouns, words such as 'everyone', 'something', etc. which do not refer to any specific example (hence the name 'indefinite'). Many are based on the pronoun **hwā**, and change ending according to the grammar of the sentence; others are based on **hwilc**, which takes normal adjectival endings. Here are some examples:

anyone	**hwā, āhwā, ǣghwā, āhwelc, ǣghwelc**
each one	**gehwā, ǣghwā, gehwelc, ǣghwelc**
something	**hwæthwugu**
someone	**hwelchwugu, nāthwā, nāthwelc**
none, no-one	**nǣnig**

e.g. **āhwā mōt spyrian** 'anyone may ask'; **ǣghwæs sweord cierfþ** 'anyone's sword will cut'.

A common construction in poetry and the more 'florid' prose is to use the genitive plural of a noun with **gehwā** , e.g. **cyninga gehwā mōt dēman** 'any king may judge' or more literally 'of kings, any may judge'. Sometimes **hwā** alone is used: **gif hwā biþ ðēof** 'if anyone shall be a thief'.

The generalising prefix **ge-** can be added to other interrogatives, **for example gehwǣr** 'everywhere', **gehwā** 'everyone', **gehwilc** 'whoever, whatever, whichever'.

For NE phrases like 'whoever, no matter who' OE uses **swā** both before and after the pronoun:

whoever	**swā hwā swā**
whatever	**swā hwæt swā**
wherever	**swā hwǣr swā**
whenever	**swā hwonne swā**
whosoever	**swā hwæs swā**

for example, **swā hwæt swā ic hæbbe fēst ðū** 'whatever I have you will receive', **swā hwider swā þū gǣst þider gā ic** 'wherever you go I will go'.

However, the commonest use of an indefinite pronoun in OE is the word **man** or **mon** 'a person, anyone, someone'. This can be used whenever it is not necessary to name or specify the subject of a verb, when we would use 'one' in formal NE: **man mōt dēman** 'one may judge'. It is used much more than 'one', however: **mon sēcþ ðone cyning** 'one seeks the king' or 'the king is sought'; **man flīemð ðā Dene** 'one routs the Danes' or 'the Danes are routed'; **mon letteþ þæt scip** 'one hinders the ship' or 'the ship is hindered'. Also note expressions such as: **se tūn þe mon nemnaþ Oxenaford** 'the estate which is called (which one calls) Oxford'.

Vocabulary (8)

Adverbs

sōna	immediately, soon	**āwā**	always
hwīlum	sometimes	**nōðȳlǣs**	nonetheless

Verbs

biddan	to bid, command	**gremian**	to anger, irritate

Adjectives

wīs	wise	**welgelǣred**	well-taught

66

Exercises (8)

1. Translate the following into NE:

(a) Þā ic clipie, þā cymð mīn hors sōna tō mē. Þæt is gōd hors ond strang, ac hit ne hīersumaþ āwā. Hwīlum bið hit fāh ond ne dēþ ðæt ic bidde. Þonne gremaþ hit mē swīþe.

(b) Swā hwider swā ic gā, þider gǣst þū mid mē tō gesīðe; þū mē eart gōd frēond ond wilsum, ond ic trūwie þæt þū cwiðst.

(c) Leorna hwæthwugu fram ðisse bēc – þonne bist þū wīs ond welgelǣred.

2. Translate the following into OE:

(a) I am hindered whatever I do. People do not love me and I am afraid but my charms protect me.

(b) The king's son rides to the estate of his friend Burgred in Mercia.ō

(c) He has not any gold in his land but he is powerful nonetheless.

OLD ENGLISH COURSE – SECTION 9

9.1   We saw in 8.1 that the great difference between 'weak' and 'strong' verbs lies in the ways these groups form their past tenses. Let's now look at this tense in practice, starting with the weak verb, which uses a set of endings containing -**d**- for this purpose. We have seen already that there are four principal types of weak verb (**nerian, fremman, hīeran, lufian**); their past tense forms look like this:

	nerian	fremman	hīeran	lufian
	'save'	'carry out'	'hear'	'love'
ic	nerede	fremede	hīerde	lufode
þū	neredest	fremedest	hīerdest	lufodest
hē				
hēo	nerede	fremede	hīerde	lufode
hit				
wē				
gē	neredon	fremedon	hīerdon	lufodon
hīe				

It is obvious that the verbs which follow **nerian** and **fremman** have the same endings (-**ede**, etc.) and those which follow **hīeran** differ only in not putting an -**e**- before the -**de** (but see 9.4 below); those which follow **lufian** have the same pattern of endings, but insert -**o**- instead of -**e**- before the -**de**.

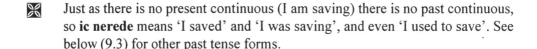 Just as there is no present continuous (I am saving) there is no past continuous, so **ic nerede** means 'I saved' and 'I was saving', and even 'I used to save'. See below (9.3) for other past tense forms.

Practice 9.1: give the OE for the following (the infinitive of the relevant verb is given in brackets to help you): I loved (lufian); it made a noise (dynnan); they were ploughing (erian); we strengthened (trymman); we used to protect the king (werian); you (sing.) answered (answarian); you (pl.) rejoiced (blissian); he taught (lǣran); I declared (cȳþan); we were travelling (fēran); they judged (dēman).

Answers: ic lufode; hit dynede; hīe eredon; wē trymedon; wē weredon þone cyning; ðū andswarodest; gē blissodon; hē lǣrde; ic cȳðde; wē fērdon; hīe dēmdon.

9.2   As well as the past tense forms of the verb, there is also an adjectival form which can be used separately.

Consider 'I love her' – 'she is loved' or 'they judge me' – 'I am judged', where 'loved' and 'judged' are acting purely as adjectives, not showing tense at all (that is, they are not just reflecting something that *was*, but something that *is, was* or *will be*). Another example: in the phrase 'we have pleased' there is reference to past action (i.e. the act of pleasing is over) while in 'we are pleased' the reference is to a present condition, and 'pleased' is an adjective – we could as easily say 'we are happy' or 'we are glad' (but we could not say 'we have happy', etc.). The use of 'have' shows that we are dealing with a past tense, while the use of 'be' is naturally associated with an adjective.

OE forms this class of words on similar lines to the past tense, just as NE does:

nerian	-nered
fremman	-fremed
hīeran	-hīered
lufian	-lufod

These endings are much like the past tense forms, but without the final syllables showing person and number (**-e**, **-est**, **-on**). Most often these words have an element **ge-** attached at the beginning: **genered** (saved), **gefremed** (carried out), **gehīered** (heard), **gelufod** (loved); however, **ge-** is not added when the verb already has a prefix (an element added before the stem) such as **ā-**, **be-**, **for-**, etc. We will look at prefixes in a later section (18.3)

Usually when these words are used as adjectives they need to take the appropriate endings: **gelufode menn** 'beloved people', **on geeredum æcerum** 'in ploughed fields'.

There are times when these so-called participles are indistinguishable from verbs, e.g. **gelufode** could be the 1st or 3rd sing. preterite of **gelufian** 'love' (**ic / hē gelufode** 'I/he loved') or the inflected form of the past partciciple (**hīe sind gelufode** 'they are loved').

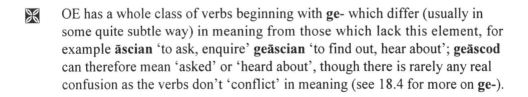

OE has a whole class of verbs beginning with **ge-** which differ (usually in some quite subtle way) in meaning from those which lack this element, for example **āscian** 'to ask, enquire' **geāscian** 'to find out, hear about'; **geāscod** can therefore mean 'asked' or 'heard about', though there is rarely any real confusion as the verbs don't 'conflict' in meaning (see 18.4 for more on **ge-**).

Practice 9.2: give the OE for the following: taught, made room, travelled, mourned, judged, set free, split, declared, burnt, obeyed, expelled, routed, healed, left behind, compelled, raised, expected, strengthened, praised, harmed, protected, boasted, insultted, preached, called, dwelt, ebbed, tried, followed, gathered, ravaged, learnt, looked, made, inspected, trusted, honoured, endowed, trembled.

Answers: gelǣred, gerȳmed, gefēred, gecwīþed, gedēmed, ālīesed, gedǣled, gecȳþed, gebærned, gegīemed, gedrǣfed, geflīemed, gehǣled, gelǣfed, genīeded, gerǣred, gewēned, getrymed, gehered, gedered, gewered, gebēotod, gebismrod, gebodod, geclipod, geeardod, geebbod, gefandod, gefolgod, gegaderod, gehergod, geleornod, gelocod, gemacod, gescēawod, getrūwod, geweorþod, geārod, gebifod.

9.3 The forms given above (9.2) are called 'past participles' (or 'passive participles' in some grammars) and can be used to make the 'perfect' tense, a special form of the past relating to actions which are regarded as totally completed (hence the name 'perfect').

ic nerede	I saved	**ic hæbbe genered**	I have saved
ic fremede	I performed	**ic hæbbe gefremed**	I have performed
ic hīerde	I heard	**ic hæbbe gehīered**	I have heard
ic lufode	I loved	**ic hæbbe gelufod**	I have loved

However, such 'perfect' constructions are much less common in OE than in NE and the preterite often expresses the 'perfect' meaning: **ic hīerde þæt þū cwiðst** 'I (have) heard what you are saying'. Similarly the 'pluperfect' (past-in-the-past) tense ('I had saved', etc.) using the preterite of **habban** (or its negated forms):

		negated	
ic	**hæfde**	**næfde**	**genered**
ðú	**hæfdest**	**næfdest**	**genered**
hē			
hēo	**hæfde**	**næfde**	**genered**
hit			
wē			
gē	**hæfdon**	**næfdon**	**genered**
híe			

although again the preterite is more usual: **ic hīerde þæt þū gewendest** 'I (had) heard what you (had) translated' and only the sense of the phrase is the guide to the most appropriate NE expression. The adverb **ǣr** 'formerly, before, previously' assists: **þonne lufode hē ðæt hē ǣr hatode** 'then he loved what he (had) previously hated'.

9.4 Before going on to look at another small but common type of noun, it is worth taking a moment away from the formal 'grammar' to review something in the structure of OE which has had an effect on some of the nouns, verbs and adjectives we have met so far. This is the concept of '*syllable weight*' which can alter a word's endings.

A syllable is a speech unit containing a peak of loudness (the vowel) often bounded by one or more consonants. The word 'syllable' has three syllables (*syll-ab-le*) while many other common words may have one (*word*), two (*vow-el*), four (*com-po-si-tion*) or more. Some syllables consist of a consonant and a vowel (*see*) or a vowel and a consonant (*at*) or even have no consonants at all (*eye, a, owe*).

Syllables may be *light* or *heavy* according to their rhyme (everything including and after the vowel). Generally a light syllable consists of a short vowel followed by one consonant (e.g. **til**, **gram**, **scip**) while a heavy one may contain a long vowel (e.g. **bān**) or have more than one consonant in the rhyme (e.g. **land**). Two short syllables in a word (e.g. **feðer** 'a feather') have the weight of one long one.

What has all this got to do with OE? Briefly, OE does not allow a heavy syllable to be followed by **-u** (unless it is part of a longer ending like **-um**) and where the grammar calls for such an ending the **-u** is simply deleted. We can check this in practice as for example with neuter nouns which form their nominative and accusative plural by adding **-u**:

light	**scip** *(sing)*	**scipu** *(pl.)*	
heavy	**land** *(sing.)*	**land** *(pl.)*	(not ***landu**)

or with the nominative singular feminine which is also marked by **-u**:

light	**giefu**	(**-ie**- is a diphthong, not two separate vowels)
heavy	**lār**	(not ***lāru**)

while with the adjective **-u** occurs in the same instances (nom.acc.pl.neut./ nom.sing.fem.):

light	**tilu**	
heavy	**gōd**	(not ***gōdu**)

Where a word has two syllables, these may both be light (**feþer**) or both heavy (**hengest**, a stallion) or a mixture: light/heavy (**ofost** 'haste') or heavy/light (**hēafod** 'head'). There is a strong tendency to reduce the second syllable of such words if it is light, when grammatical endings are added; this is achieved by removing the vowel:

feþer	*dat.pl.*	**feþrum**
hēafod	*nom.pl.*	**hēafdu**
winter	*gen.sing.*	**wintres**

This is commonest when the first syllable is heavy (**hēaf-**, **wint-**); this explains the 'missing' **-e** of **hīerde**, compared to **nerede**, **fremede** where it is retained because the preceding syllable is light.

✠ Light syllables are called *short*, and heavy syllables *long* in some grammars.

9.5 There is a small but important group of nouns with endings like **sunu** 'a son':

	sing.	*pl.*
nom	**sunu**	**suna**
acc	**sunu**	**suna**
gen	**suna**	**suna**
dat	**suna**	**sunum**

Masculine nouns of this type include **meodu** 'mead' and **sidu** 'a custom'; feminines include **duru** 'a door'. The initial syllable of **sunu** is light (see 9.4), but there are a good many nouns in this class with a heavy first syllable, like the feminine **hand** 'a hand':

	sing.	*pl.*
nom	**hand**	**handa**
acc	**hand**	**handa**
gen	**handa**	**handa**
dat	**handa**	**handum**

Masculines of this type include **eard** 'homeland', **feld** 'open country', **ford** 'a ford', **sumor** 'summer', **weald** 'forest, woodland', **winter** 'winter', **wudu** 'a wood'; feminines include **flōr** 'a floor', **cweorn** 'a quern, handmill'.

❖ Sometimes **flōr** behaves like **stān** (i.e. a masculine noun) and **winter** may often behave like a neuter (e.g. nom.acc.pl **wintru**).

Practice 9.5: give the OE for the following: hand (nom.sing.); homeland (gen.sing.); homeland (gen.pl.); floor (acc.pl.); open country (dat.sing.); winter (gen. pl.); wood (dat. sing.); forest (dat.pl.); son (acc.sing.); door (nom.pl.); mead (gen.sing.).

Answers: hand; earda; earda; flōra; felda; wintra; wuda; wealdum; sunu; dura; meoda.

9.6 A group of feminine nouns denoting mainly abstract qualities have the endings **-u**, sometimes spelt **-o**, and **-þo** e.g. **strengo, strengþo** 'strength', **lengu, lengþu** 'length', **yrhþo** 'cowardice, worthlessness, slackness', **yrmðo** 'poverty'. They are unusual in that they do not have plural forms (which is not *so* unusual for abstract qualities) and their endings do not change in the singular i.e. **yrmðo** is nom./acc./gen./dat. sing.

❖ There is an anomalous noun **sǣ** 'sea' which can be either masculine or feminine as follows:

	masc.	*fem.*
nom.	**sǣ**	**sǣ**
acc.	**sǣ**	**sǣwe**
gen.	**sǣs**	**sǣwe**
dat.	**sǣ**	**sǣwe**

Vocabulary (9)

Nouns

hǣs (*f*)	command, behest	**hergung** (*f*)	raiding, harrying
hlāford (*m*)	lord, master	**risc** (*f*)	rush
sige (*m*)	victory	**storm** (*m*)	storm
tīd (*f*)	time, occasion	**unweder** (*n*)	bad weather

Adverbs

būton ende	without end, ceaselessly	**miclum**	greatly, mightily
hām	(to) home, at home	**wel**	well, greatly

Verbs

forhtian	to be afraid, fear	**rēafian**	rob, plunder
wæs	was	**wǣron**	were

Conjunctions

swā	so (that)

Adjectives

ādreht	oppressed	**ceald**	cold
Denisc	Danish	**Englisc**	English
gewrigen	covered	**micel**	great, large
sum	a certain (one)		

Exercises (9)

1. Translate the following into NE:

(a) Mīn handa sind cealda þā ic fēre ðurh feld on wintertīda be mīnes hlāfordes hǣse.

(b) On mīnum earda is micel wudu, on þǣm eardiað ylfe.

(c) Ðæs hūses flōr is gewrigen mid riscum.

(d) Þīnes suna brȳd lufode hine wel and hē werede hīe wið ðǣm wīcingum.

(e) Þā eorþlingas eredon on ðǣm æcerum, þonne fērdon hīe hām on ǣrlicum ǣfne.

(f) Denisce wīcingas hergodon geond Englalond on þǣm dagum, ond menn forhtodon swīþe oþþæt sum Englisc cyning nerede hīe.

2. Translate the following into OE:

In those days a great Danish army was in this land, which harried and robbed ceaselessly. Wherever it went it had victory, and the English were mightily oppressed; also there was bad weather and storms throughout the land, so that men did not plough, and hunger followed (the) raiding.

OLD ENGLISH COURSE – SECTION 10

10.1 Nouns expressing close family relationships (other than **sunu** 'son') form a group by themselves, with characteristic endings – or rather lack of them:

masculine	*sing.*	*pl.*		*sing.*	*pl.*
	fæder 'father'			**brōðor** 'brother'	
nom.	fæder	fæder		brōðor	brōðor
acc.	fæder	fæder		brōðor	brōðor
gen	fæder	fæder		brōðor	brōðra
dat.	fæder	fædrum		brēþer	brōðrum

feminine					
	mōdor 'mother'			**dohtor** 'daughter'	
nom.	mōdor	mōdor		dohtor	dohtor
acc.	mōdor	mōdor		dohtor	dohtor
gen	mōdor	mōdra		dohtor	dohtra
dat.	mēder	mōdrum		dehter	dohtrum

	sweostor 'sister'	
nom.	sweostor	sweostor
acc.	sweostor	sweostor
gen	sweostor	sweostra
dat.	sweostor	sweostrum

There are variants to many of the above, for example gen.sing **fædres**, (to bring it into line with **stān**) and **dehter**, **mēder** (with vowel interchange like **bōc:bēc**). There are also special 'collective' forms such as **gebrōðru** nom.acc.pl. meaning a 'group' of brothers; the prefix **ge-** is very productive in making names for groups of things (see 18.4).

10.2 In 9.1 we looked at the preterite (past tense) of the weak verb, which may end in **-de**, **-ede**, or **-ode**. The latter two are straightforward enough, but where the ending **-de** (after a heavy syllable -see 9.4) occurs there are simplifications similar in kind to those which apply to -þ (e.g. **sendþ** becomes **sent**). Briefly, where the root ends with a voiceless sound (e.g. **p, s, t, x**) the **-d-** becomes **-t-**, as with the following:

infinitive		*past singular*	*past participle*
scierpan	'sharpen'	**scierpte**, etc	**gescierped**
cȳssan	'kiss'	**cȳsste**, etc	**gecȳssed**
mētan	'meet'	**mētte**, etc	**gemētt**
līxan	'gleam'	**līxte**, etc	**gelīxed**

and where its ends with just **-c** this becomes **-h-**:

tǣcan	'teach'	**tǣhte**, etc	**getǣht**

while **-h-** also occurs in certain verbs without **-c**:

bycgan	'buy'	**bohte**, etc	**geboht**
brengan	'bring'	**brōhte**, etc	**gebrōht**

and others change the vowel:

þencan	'think'	**þōhte**, etc	**geþōht**
þyncan	'seem'	**þūhte**, etc.	**geðūht**
sēcan	'seek'	**sōhte**, etc	**gesōht**
reccan	'care for'	**rōhte**, etc	**gerōht**
wyrcan	'make, work'	**worhte**, etc	**geworht**
lǣccan	'catch, grab'	**lǣhte**, etc	**gelǣht**
reccan	'tell, reckon'	**reahte**, etc	**gereaht**

There are a few other verbs like **reccan** 'tell, reckon, narrate', for example:

dreccan	'afflict'	**dreahte**, etc	**gedreaht**
streccan	'stretch'	**streahte**, etc	**gestreaht**
weccan	'wake up'	**weahte**, etc	**geweaht**
cweccan	'quake, shake'	**cweahte**, etc	**gecweaht**
leccan	'moisten'	**leahte**, etc	**geleaht**
ðeccan	'cover over'	**þeahte**, etc	**geþeaht**

However, those ending in **-nc** mix the types:

swencan	'distress'	**swencte**, etc	**geswenced**

This softening to **-t** still occurs in NE where e.g. *helped, asked, missed, mixed* are pronounced *helpt, askt, mist, mixt*, although the spelling does not reflect this change; comparison of NE *teach:taught, buy:bought, bring:brought* will show that these changes are not as unfamiliar as they appear at first.

A further group of weak verbs alters its vowel while retaining -**de**:

sellan	'hand over'	**sealde**, etc	**geseald**
stellan	'set down'	**stealde**, etc	**gesteald**
tellan	'count'	**tealde**, etc	**geteald**
cwellan	'kill'	**cwealde**, etc	**gecweald**
dwellan	'be mistaken'	**dwealde**, etc	**gedweald**
secgan	'say'	**sægde**, etc	**gesægd**

while those with -**d** ending the stem simplify the -**dd**-:

sendan	'send'	**sende**, etc	**gesend** (or **gesended**)

Practice 10.2: give the OE for the following (1st person singular throughout):

caught, moistened, thought, seemed, distressed, kissed, woke up, counted, told, gleamed, worked, sent.

Answers: lǣhte, leahte, þōhte, þūhte, swencte, cȳsste, weahte, tealde, reahte, līxte, worhte, sende.

10.3 Adverbs are words which describe the manner in which an action is performed, e.g. *he drives fast but she drives carefully; I understand fully; they sing sweetly,* where *fast, carefully, fully, sweetly* are all adverbs. OE has more than one way of making such words, like NE mostly from adjectives (*fast, careful, full, sweet*).

Many OE adverbs can be formed from the appropriate adjective by adding -**e**:

blind	blind	**blinde**	blindly
dēop	deep	**dēope**	deeply
gram	fierce	**grame**	fiercely
wrāþ	angry	**wrāðe**	angrily
swift	swift	**swifte**	swiftly

There is a group of OE adjectives ending in -**lic** which form their adverbs in -**līce**:

sārlic	painful	**sārlīce**	painfully

It is this -**līce** ending which has given rise to the commonest NE adverbial ending -*ly*, although we still have a few adjectives from those with the ending -**lic**, e.g. 'lovely' (**luflic**). There are numerous adverbs formed with different endings, though, such as -**inga**/-**unga**:

eall	all	**eallunga**	entirely
nīw	new	**nīwinga**	recently, newly
ierre	angry	**ierringa**	angrily

the genitive case ending -**es**:

eall	all	**ealles**	completely
el-(prefix)	other	**elles**	else, otherwise
ungemete	large	**ungemetes**	excessively

the dative case ending -**um**:

hwīl *(f)*	period of time	**hwīlum**	at times, sometimes
wearn *(f)*	refusal	**unwearnum**	irresistably, suddenly

or the ending -**a**:

til	good	**tela**	well
-		**sōna**	soon

Other than these common patterns, there are certain exceptional adverbial formations which we will come to later (16.3).

It is perhaps worth repeating that where an adverb begins a sentence or phrase, the (pro)noun usually comes after its verb: **nīwinga sægde hē þæt...** "he recently said that...".

Practice 10.3: give the OE for the following:

blindly, deeply, painfully, well, wisely, dearly, hardly.

Answers: blinde, dēope, sārlīce, tela, wīse, dēore, hearde.

10.4 There are a few groups of 'exceptional' nouns, most of which have very few members; they are given here together for convenience.

The first ends in -**end** and is a common form of 'agent noun', which is to say that its ending is equivalent to *-er* in NE words like *baker, rider, fighter, flyer* which are formed from the verbs *bake, ride, fight, fly.* OE verbs make such forms with the ending -**end**, for example **wīgan** 'to fight' gives **wīgend** 'fighter, warrior' as follows:

	sing.	*pl.*
nom.	**wīgend**	**wīgende**
acc.	**wīgend**	**wīgende**
gen.	**wīgendes**	**wīgendra**
dat.	**wīgende**	**wīgendum**

All the -**end** nouns are masculine, and the endings reveal that they began as adjectives (e.g. -**ra** in the gen.pl.); in later texts they are remodelled as ordinary masculines (like **stān**) with nom.acc.pl. **wīgendas**.

Note: **wīgend** is by origin a present participle – see 13.5

The second group is characterized by the ending -**ð**, and is not confined to one gender:

masculine		*feminine*		*neuter*		
hæleð 'a hero'		**mægð** 'a maid, girl'		**ealu** 'ale'		
sing.	*pl.*	*sing.*	*pl.*	*sing.*	*pl.*	
nom.	hæleð	hæleð	mægð	mægð	ealu	ealoðu
acc	hæleð	hæleð	mægðe	mægð	ealu	ealoðu
gen.	hæleðes	hæleða	mægð	mægða	ealoð	ealoða
dat.	hæleðe	hæleðum	mægð	mægðum	ealoð	ealoðum

Again with the masculines, an alternative nom.acc.pl **hæleðas** can be found, (with the -**as** ending, like **stān**), and the neuters may have nom.acc.sing. **ealoð**.

The third group has barely survived into NE; it consists of a few neuters which insert -**r**- before the plural endings. The three commonest words are:

cild 'a child'		**lamb** 'a lamb'		**æg** 'an egg'		
sing.	*pl.*	*sing.*	*pl.*	*sing.*	*pl.*	
nom.	cild	cildru	lamb	lambru	æg	ægru
acc	cild	cildru	lamb	lambru	æg	ægru
gen.	cildes	cildra	lambes	lambra	æges	ægra
dat.	cilde	cildrum	lambe	lambrum	æge	ægrum

Forms are found with -**ri**- (e.g. **cildriu**) as well as nom.acc.pl **cild** treating the word as if it were a normal heavy-stemmed neuter noun like **land** (see 9.4).

Practice 10.4: give the OE for the following:

hero (gen.sing), ale (nom.pl), girl (gen.sing.), hero (dat.pl), girl (acc.sing.), warrior (acc.pl.), child (gen.pl.), lamb (nom.pl.), egg (gen. sing.).

Answers: hæleðes, ealoðu, mægð, hæleðum, mægðe, wīgend, cildra, lambru, æges.

10.5 The strong verb's main characteristic is the way it uses vowel changes to show the present and past tenses, just as in NE we say I ride : I rode : I have ridden or I bite : I bit: I have bitten. Why are there two past tense vowels here (r<u>o</u>de, b<u>i</u>t)? OE actually uses two vowels, one for the 1st and 3rd person singular, the other for the 2nd person singular and the plural:

	rīdan 'to ride'	**bītan** 'to bite'
ic	rād	bāt
ðū	ride	bite
hē		
hēo	rād	bāt
hit		
wē		
gē	ridon	biton
hīe		

As you can see, both verbs have the same vowel correspondences in OE, and 'bite' has generalized the -i- of the plural ('bit') while 'ride' has done likewise with the -ā- of part of the singular (**rād** > 'rode').

This set of correspondences is only one of many such patterns in OE, although it is one of the more easily recognized. A good many common verbs follow **rīdan** and **bītan**, e.g.

slītan tear	**gewītan** go along	**stīgan** climb, go up	**blīcan** shine, glitter
flītan contend	**bīdan** wait	**drīfan** drive	**swīcan** fail
(æt)wītan blame	**slīdan** slide	**hrīnan** touch	**wrītan** write

Practice 10.5: give the following forms:

I tore; you (sing.) slid; I rode; we waited; it shone; they drove; you (pl.) failed; he wrote; she touched; we went along.

Answers: ic slāt; ðū slide; ic rād; wē bidon; hit scān; hīe drifon; gē swicon; hē wrāt; hēo hrān; wē gewiton.

10.6 Having seen the principle behind the past tense of the strong verb with respect to **rīdan**, it is as well to introduce two further matters in which such verbs may deviate from the pattern set out. First, so-called 'contracted verbs', which have a variant form of infinitive and present tense. We have already seen the type in **sēon** 'to see' which replaced an earlier form reconstructed as ***seohan**; we will here consider **lēon** 'to lend' which has the following forms:

		present	*past*
1st.	*sing.*	**lēo**	**lāh**
2nd.		**līehst**	**lige**
3rd.		**līehð**	**lāh**
all	*pl.*	**lēoð**	**ligon**

The regular form of infinitive here would be ***līhan**, but OE abhors an -h- between vowels and has dropped it, and simplified the resulting vowel cluster. There are three more such verbs which follow **lēon**, namely **tēon** (to accuse), **þēon** (to thrive, prosper), **wrēon** (to cover). The second point of deviation is in the final consonant of the past tense forms, which you can see alternates between -h and -g with the vowel. This pattern is usual in strong verbs of all classes and can be summarized thus:

root ending	*1st,3rd sing.* *past ending*	*2nd sing.,* *pl.past ending*
h	*h*	*g*
ð	*ð*	*d*
s	*s*	*r*

An example of the correspondence is found in **līðan** 'to travel by sea' with past tense forms **ic, hē lāþ, þū lide, wē lidon**. Only one OE verb in this group ends in -s and it has generalized this sound to the plural (**rīsan** 'to rise'; **ic, hē rās, ðū rise, wē rison**) which **mīþan** 'to hide' has also done (**māð, miðe, miðon**). Like **līþan** are **scrīþan** (move) and **snīðan** (cut).

One NE verb still uses the *s/r* correspondence in its past tense: *was/were*. The forms for this verb (and its special negated forms) are:

ic	**wæs**	**næs**
þū	**wǣre**	**nǣre**
hē		
hēo	**wæs**	**næs**
hit		
wē		
gē	**wǣron**	**nǣron**
hīe		

Practice 10.6: give the OE for the following:

I accuse; he accused; they throve; I hid; you (sing.) travelled by sea; we rose; I moved; you (pl.) cut (both tenses); we covered; they lend:

Answers: ic tēo; hē tāh; hīe þigon; ic māð; ðū lide; wē rison; ic scrāð; gē snīþað, snidon; wē wrigon; hīe lēoþ.

Vocabulary (10)

Verbs

scierpan	'sharpen'	**reccan**	'care for'
cȳssan	'kiss'	**wyrcan**	'make, work'
mētan	'meet'	**læccan**	'catch, grab'
līxan	'gleam'	**reccan**	'tell, reckon'
tǣcan	'teach'	**dreccan**	'afflict'
bycgan	'buy'	**streccan**	'stretch'
brengan	'bring'	**weccan**	'wake up'
þencan	'think'	**cweccan**	'quake, shake'
þyncan	'seem'	**leccan**	'moisten'
sēcan	'seek'	**ðeccan**	'cover over'
		swencan	'distress'

Nouns

drȳ *(m)*	magician, wizard
cræft *(m)*	skill, power
ǣnne	once, at one time

81

Exercises (10)

1. Translate the following into NE:

I heard a blind man; he blamed his children who had hidden the warriors' ale. They called fiercely and insulted him, and he shook but they did not harm him (dative). The children had covered the ale with geese's feathers; they were very afraid. Their father accused them and they trembled; then they were sorry.

2. Translate the following into OE:

Ǣnne on ðissum lande wæs micel drȳ ond rīce, ðæs fæder wæs ēac drȳ ond hæfde micelne cræft. His galdras wæron fremfule ond menn cweahton fore his hūs.

OLD ENGLISH COURSE – SECTION 11

11.1   Nouns ending -*h*
11.2   Dative: further uses
11.3   Weak nouns
11.4   Past tense, strong verbs
         (*hrēowan*); aorist-presents

11.5   Past participle, strong verbs
         (*rīdan*, *hrēowan*)
11.6   Accusative: further uses

11.1   In the previous section I mentioned that OE does not tolerate -**h**- between vowels, hence the alteration to verbal infinitives which originally had this feature (***seohan** becomes **sēon**). This principle also applies to adjectives (see 4.2) so it would be surprising if it did not equally apply to nouns. Actually, not many OE nouns end in -**h** but two typical examples are **eoh** 'a horse' with a short vowel, and **scōh** 'a shoe' with a long vowel. They are both masculine.

	eoh	'a horse'	**scōh**	'a shoe'
	sing.	*pl.*	*sing.*	*pl.*
nom	eoh	ēos	scōh	scōs
acc.	eoh	ēos	scōh	scōs
gen.	ēos	ēona	scōs	scōna
dat.	ēo	ēom	scō	scōm

Where the short-vowelled (i.e. light-stemmed – see 9.4) type adds its endings the -**h**- is dropped, then the vowel cluster simplifies and lengthens (because the original two light syllables are equivalent to the one heavy one which replaces them). This doesn't just apply where -**h** is preceded by a consonant: **wealh** 'a foreigner' and **mearh** 'a horse', both masculine, behave similarly:

	wealh	'a foreigner'	**mearh**	'a horse'
	sing.	*pl.*	*sing.*	*pl.*
nom	wealh	wealas	mearh	mearas
acc.	wealh	wealas	mearh	mearas
gen.	weales	weala	meares	meara
dat.	weale	wealum	meare	mearum

These words, ending -**rh**, -**lh**, don't have vowel lengthening.

⌘ The word **wealh** means both 'foreigner' and 'servant'; it is used exclusively of Celtic-speaking peoples, and is the English name for the native British population. The plural **Wealas** is our name 'Wales', while the adjectival form **wealisc** gives our word 'Welsh'.

11.2 Some further uses for the dative case should be mentioned, as we have already seen it with certain prepositions (4.6) and for the indirect object (5.1). An important use is as the direct object of certain verbs, mostly connected with 'separation' of some kind. Here are a few of the commoner ones:

ætwindan escape from	**ætwītan** blame, reproach
andswarian answer, reply	**ārian** honour, endow
bedrēosan deprive of	**bēodan** offer
beorgan protect, save	**betǣcan** entrust
bodian announce, preach	**bregdan** pull, draw, wave
gedafenian suit, be fitting	**dēman** judge
derian harm, hurt	**gefēon** rejoice, exult
gefremman benefit, serve	**fulgān** accomplish
fylgan follow	**fylstan** help, assist
helpan help	**hīersumian** obey
līcian please	**gelīefan** believe
linnan desist	**miltsian** take pity on
mislimpan go wrong	**genēalǣcan** approach, near
ōleccan flatter	**onfōn** receive, acquire
sǣlan happen, come about	**sceþþan** injure, scathe
þegnian serve	**þēowian** serve
ðingian talk, reconcile	**wealdan** rule, wield
wīsian guide	**gewītan** go along

e.g. **ic þegnie him** (dat.) "I serve him"; **se cyning ārieð ðǣm hæleðe** (dat.) "the king honours the hero"; **þæt cild hīersumað ðǣm menn** (dat.) "the child obeys the man".

⌘ **Þegnian** and **ðēowian** can both be translated as 'to serve' but there is an important difference in meaning. A **ðegn** was a royal official, somewhat like a mediaeval knight, with military and manorial duties; a **þēow**, in contrast, was a hireling or thrall. Therefore **þegnian** is to serve as a **þegn**, and **þēowian** is to serve as a **þēow**; in other words, the first is the service of an officer and the second that of a menial.

✠ The verb **helpan** can also have a direct object in the genitive case.

84

Another important use for the dative is to show possession or association; normally this is handled by the genitive, of course (see 6.1), but there is an extension of the idea of expressing 'with' by means of the dative; bearing in mind that the phrase 'my son' involves the unexpressed (but logically inescapable) necessary further idea 'I have a son'. Aside from using **habban** (**ic hæbbe sunu**) OE can say **mē is sunu** (to-me is (a) son). This kind of expression is commonest in poetry: **mē wæs noma Dēor** 'my name was Dēor' (to-me was (the) name Dēor), **næs him hrēoh sefa** ' he did not have a cruel heart' (not-was to-him (a) cruel heart).

A few adjectives also require a dative, such as **gelīc** 'alike, similar', e.g. **gelīc mīnum suna** 'similar to my son'.

Rarely, situation or location can be shown with the dative ending e.g. **wīcum wunian** 'to live in dwellings' where one would expect **on wīcum**. Far commoner is a dative ending showing the means by which something has been done: **mundum bregdan** 'to brandish in the hands' (**sēo mund** = the hand) **eallum mægne geworht** 'made with all (his) strength' (**ðæt mægen** = strength).

Lastly, adverbial phrases can be made with the dative case forms, similar to the way they can show 'means', but usually indicating something happening at the same time as the 'action' e.g. **āstrehtum earmum clipode hē** 'he called out with outstretched arms'.

11.3 There is one further large class of nouns, of all three genders, which are of very common occurrence in OE. The whole group is characterized by the ending -**an** in many of the various forms. The masculines, of which there are very many, have -**a** in the nom.sing., while the feminines have -**e**; there are only two neuters, which have -**e** in the nom. and acc.sing: **ēage** (an) eye and **ēare** (an) ear.

masculine			*sing.*	*pl.*
boda	(a) messenger	*nom.*	**boda**	**bodan**
		acc.	**bodan**	**bodan**
		gen.	**bodan**	**bodena**
		dat.	**bodan**	**bodum**
feminine				
heorte	(a) heart	*nom.*	**heorte**	**heortan**
		acc.	**heortan**	**heortan**
		gen.	**heortan**	**heortena**
		dat.	**heortan**	**heortum**
neuter				
ēage	(an) eye	*nom.*	**ēage**	**ēagan**
		acc.	**ēage**	**ēagan**
		gen.	**ēagan**	**ēagena**
		dat.	**ēagan**	**ēagum**

The masculine type in particular is very productive in making nouns from verbs, for example from **bodian** 'announce, declare, preach' comes **boda** 'one who declares, a messenger, a herald'; here are some more such forms:

huntian	to hunt	**hunta**	hunter
cuman	to come	**cuma**	one who comes, guest
flīeman	to rout	**flīema**	exile, outlaw, man on the run
fēran	to travel	**gefēra**	companion, traveller
andsacan	to contend, compete	**andsaca**	opponent
witan	to know	**wita**	wise man, sage, adviser
willan	to want, wish	**willa**	wish, desire, intention
giefan	to give	**giefa**	donor

There are a good many masculines not made from verbs, however, e.g. **mōna** (moon), **steorra** (star), **guma** (man, warrior), **nama** (name). The feminines are also very common words, such as **nunne** (nun), **hlǣfdige** (lady), **sunne** (sun), **byrne** (mailcoat), **tunge** (tongue), **cirice** (church), **eorðe** (earth).

✠ This class of words is known as the 'weak' nouns.

Practice 11.3: give the OE for the following: messenger (nom.pl); name (acc.sing); name (dat.sing.); name (nom.pl.); hunter (gen.pl.); adviser (nom.sing.); star (dat.sing.); church (gen.sing.); sun (dat.sing.) mailcoat (nom.pl.); earth (acc.sing.); eye (acc.sing.); ear (nom.pl.).

Answers: bodan; naman; naman; naman; huntena; wita; steorran; cirican; sunnan; byrnan; eorþan; ēage; ēaran.

11.4 A second set of strong verbs are recognized by having the vowel -**ēo**- in the infinitive, just as those we looked at before (10.5) have -**ī**-. The forms are:

> **hrēowan** 'to rue, mourn, be sorry'

ic	**hrēaw**
þū	**hruwe**
hē	
hēo	**hrēaw**
hit	
wē	
gē	**hruwon**
hīe	

There are some common verbs in this class including:

bēodan command	**brēotan** break	**flēotan** float
gēotan pour out	**scēotan** shoot	**crēopan** creep
drēogan endure	**flēogan** fly	**lēogan** lie (tell lies)

and some others with the consonantal correspondences e.g. **cēosan** 'choose' **ic, hē cēas, þū cure, hīe curon,** including:

lēosan lose	**hrēosan** fall	**frēosan** freeze
drēosan fall	**sēoðan** boil	

while two have contracted infinitives:

flēon flee, run away   **tēon** draw, pull

A further detail with this class are a few verbs which don't have -ēo- in the present tense but -ū-, e.g.

brūcan 'to enjoy, use'

	present	*past*
ic	**brūce**	**brēac**
þū	**brȳcst**	**bruce**
hē		
hēo	**brȳcþ**	**brēac**
hit		
wē		
gē	**brūcað**	**brucon**
hīe		

Such verbs include:

lūcan lock	**būgan** bend, bow, turn
dūfan dive	**scūfan** shove

✤   Verbs in this group and similar ones with the same vowel in the plural past tense as in the present (even though the present tense has a long vowel and the past a short one) are known as *aorist-presents*.

11.5 Just as the weak verbs have passive participles, there are corresponding forms for strong verbs. They also mostly add **ge-** at the beginning, and in common with their means of forming the past tense they have a different vowel from the present:

bītan	bite	**gebiten**	bitten
slītan	tear	**gesliten**	torn
wlītan	behold	**gewliten**	beheld, observed
rīdan	ride	**geriden**	ridden
mīþan	hide	**gemiþen**	hidden
stīgan	climb	**gestigen**	climbed
bēodan	command	**geboden**	commanded
crēopan	creep	**gecropen**	crept
gēotan	pour out	**gegoten**	poured out

flēogan	fly	**geflogen**	flown
cēosan	choose	**gecoren**	chosen
frēosan	freeze	**gefroren**	frozen
sēoþan	boil	**gesoden**	boilt
dūfan	dive	**gedofen**	dived

Evidently, the vowel in the **rīdan** type (called Class I) is the same as for the past plural, while in the **hrēowan** type (Class II) it is a different one. These forms also share in the consonant correspondences like the past plural e.g. **curon** and **gecoren**, both with **-r-**.

11.6 The accusative has other functions than simply showing the direct object, perhaps the most important of which is to show extent in space or time, e.g. **hē rīcsode fēower gēar** *(acc.pl.)* 'he ruled for four years'; **ealne weg rād hēo swifte** 'she rode swiftly all the way'. Many prepositions can be used with both the accusative and the dative; as a general rule, with the accusative they will denote *motion* and with the dative *location*, e.g. **hē rād on ðone feld** 'he rode *into* the open country' (motion), **sēo cirice stent on felda** 'the church stands *in* open country' (location).

Vocabulary (11)

Verbs

cēosan	choose	**hrēosan**	fall	**drēosan**	drip, fall
lēosan	lose	**frēosan**	freeze	**hrēowan**	mourn
bēodan	command	**brēotan**	break	**flēotan**	float
gēotan	pour out	**scēotan**	shoot	**crēopan**	creep
drēogan	endure	**flēogan**	fly	**lēogan**	lie
dūfan	dive	**sēoðan**	boil	**lūcan**	lock
flēon	flee	**tēon**	draw, pull	**scūfan**	shove, thrust
būgan	bend, turn				
rīcsian	rule, reign				

Nouns

unfrið (*m*)	breach of peace	**heretoga** (*m*)	war-leader
gimm (*m*)	gemstone	**smiþþe** (*f*)	smithy
bune (*f*)	cup	**īren** (*n*)	iron
flān (*m*)	arrow	**ealu** (*n*)	ale, beer
boga (*m*)	bow	**wīga** (*m*)	warrior
smiþ (*m*)	smith	**sweord** (*n*)	sword

Adjectives

frēosende	freezing	**gylden**	golden

Exercises (11)

Translate the following into NE:

1. Þā wīgan curon Berhtwulf tō cyninge and hē rīcsode twelf gēar on ðǣm lande būton unfriðe. Hē wæs swīðe rīce heretoga and his fīend flugon oft fram his here; hiera wīf hruwon.

2. Þā līðmenn scufon heora scip on ðǣre sǣwe, ac ān ðēow dēaf fram him and flēat on ðǣm wætre, frēosende, ond ðā wīgan scuton mid bogum. Flānas flugon ac him ne deredon.

Translate the following into OE:

3. The servant poured the ale as the messengers lied about the name of their war-leader. Gems shone and gleamed on the golden cups.

4. Two smiths worked in a smithy; they sharpened swords, bent iron and thrust it in water (so) that it boiled.

OLD ENGLISH COURSE – SECTION 12

12.1 The endings of the adjective given in 4.1 are for so-called 'indefinite' uses: **swift scip** '(a) swift ship' **swift scipu** 'swift ships'. But what about when we need to refer to a particular one: 'the swift ship (which brought me here)', etc.; in other words, a 'definite' rather than indefinite usage? In these circumstances there are different endings to the adjective, which correspond to the endings of the weak noun (11.3) e.g. **ðæt swifte scip** 'the swift ship', **ðā swiftan scipu** 'the swift ships'. Here is a tabulation of the endings:-

masculine   *sing.*   *pl.*

'the swift man'   *nom.*   **se swifta mann**   **ðā swiftan menn**
                     acc.   **ðone swiftan mann**   **ðā swiftan menn**
                     gen.   **ðæs swiftan mannes**   **ðāra swiftena manna**
                     dat.   **ðǣm swiftan menn**   **ðǣm swiftum mannum**

feminine

'the swift mouse'   *nom.*   **sēo swifte mūs**   **ðā swiftan mȳs**
                     acc.   **ðā swiftan mūs**   **ðā swiftan mȳs**
                     gen.   **ðǣre swiftan mȳs**   **ðāra swiftena mūsa**
                     dat.   **ðǣre swiftan mȳs**   **ðǣm swiftum mūsum**

neuter

'the swift horse'   *nom.*   **ðæt swifte hors**   **ðā swiftan hors**
                     acc.   **ðæt swifte hors**   **ðā swiftan hors**
                     gen.   **ðæs swiftan horses**   **ðāra swiftena horsa**
                     dat.   **ðǣm swiftan horse**   **ðǣm swiftum horsum**

   These endings are called the 'weak' declension, and those in 4.1 the 'strong' declension. You can remember that the 'weak' declension needs the support of other words (e.g. 'the', 'our', etc.) and follows the pattern of endings of the 'weak' noun.

❖ The genitive plural ending -**ena** is often replaced by the indefinite ending -**ra**, especially in later texts.

These endings are used whenever the noun being described is *definite*. What does this mean? Generally, a noun when definite will be preceded by the appropriate word for 'the' or 'this', or by a possessive adjective e.g. 'my' (5.3).

Where an adjective ends in -**u**, -**e**, -**h** the same rules as for the strong endings apply (see 4.2) e.g. **se hēa stede, ðæs hēan stedes**, etc.

 There are groups of adjectives which can only take weak endings, such as the comparative forms (see13.1) and the ordinals (see 12.4); two have only strong endings, **ōþer** 'other, second' (see 12.4) **āgen** 'own'.

Practice 12.1: give the OE for the following: our swift messenger (nom.sing.); this old house (nom.sing.); for my little son (dat.sing.); the high land (dat sing.); the noble queen (gen.sing.); the blind man (gen.sing.); the blind men (gen.pl.); the hostile foreigners (dat.pl.); your poor ploughman (acc.sing.).

Answers: ūre swifta boda; ðis ealde hūs; for mīnum lȳtlan suna; ðǣm hēan lande; ðǣre æðelan cwēne; ðæs blindan mannes; ðāra blindena manna; ðǣm fām wēalum; ðīnne earman eorðling.

12.2 Another important use for the adjective with its 'weak' endings is to act as a noun. For example, we might say 'the sick and the poor deserve our support' where 'the sick' means 'sick people', and 'the poor', 'poor people'. Or another example might be 'victory goes to the brave', or 'the future belongs to the young'. The word 'people' is not expressed in any of these phrases, and the simple adjectives nonetheless act as nouns.

To do likewise, the OE adjective will have its weak endings which is not unnatural since it is referring to something definite, and it will often be preceded by 'the'. Examples are:

þā earman ðurfaþ	the poor are in need	(adj. **earm**, poor)
þā hwætan feohtaþ	the brave will fight	(adj. **hwæt**, brave)
se blinda ne sīehþ	the blind (man) does not see	(adj. **blind**, blind)
þæt hwīte līxte	the white (thing) gleamed	(adj. **hwīt**, white)

An expression such as **mīn lēofa frēond** 'my dear friend', **mīn lȳtle dohtor** 'my little daughter' can be reduced to **mīn lēofa** 'my dear (one)', **mīn lȳtle** 'my little (one)'.

⌘ Many weak nouns, especially those for particular types of people, began as adjectives with weak endings (like **lēofa, lȳtle** above) although dictionaries may define them as separate words. An example is **freca** 'warrior' which comes from the adjective **frec** 'dangerous, fierce', in such expressions as **se freca cnyste** 'the dangerous (one) struck'.

12.3 To return to the strong verb, there are two more large groups with similar vowel-change patterns, which may be illustrated by the verbs **weorðan** 'become', **helpan** 'help' and **findan** 'find':

ic	wearþ	healp	fand
þū	wurde	hulpe	funde
hē			
hēo	wearþ	healp	fand
hit			
wē			
gē	wurdon	hulpon	fundon
hīe			
past participle	geworden	geholpen	gefunden

Obviously **weorþan** features the alternation of consonants mentioned in 10.5. Verbs similar to **weorþan** (but without this feature) are:

hweorfan turn, go	**ceorfan** carve, cut	**weorpan** throw
beorgan protect	**sweorcan** grow dark	**feohtan** fight

Like **helpan** are:

swelgan swallow	**meltan** melt	**delfan** delve, dig
belgan be angry	**sweltan** die	

The following verbs drop the -**i**- :

gieldan pay, give up	**gielpan** boast	**giellan** shout

(i.e. **geald, gulde, guldon, gegolden**)

Like **findan** are:

bindan bind, tie	**grindan** grind	**windan** wind
drincan drink	**swincan** labour, toil	**winnan** fight
gewinnan win, gain	**onginnan** begin	**singan** sing
springan spring, jump	**stingan** stab	**þringan** throng
swimman swim	**gelimpan** happen	

Practice 12.3: give the OE for the following:

they turned; it grew dark; you (pl.) were fighting; he was angry; we protected him; they were throwing stones; you (sing.) boasted; she swallowed it; we bound them; I drank the ale; they laboured; we fought; I carved; he died (sweltan); he died (steorfan); it happened; it began to grow dark; he jumped; she swam; they crowded; I was grinding; it is ground; I was helped.

Answers: hīe hwurfon; hit swearc; gē fuhton; hē bealg; wē burgon hine; hīe wurpon stānas; þū gulpe; hēo swealg hit; wē bundon hīe; ic dranc þæt ealu; hīe swuncon; wē fuhton; ic cearf; hē swealt; hē stearf; hit gelamp; hit ongann sweorcan; hē sprang; hēo swamm; hīe ðrungon; ic grand; hit is gegrunden; ic wæs geholpen.

12.4 In section 4.3 we looked at the cardinal numerals (one, two, three,...); the ordinal numerals are as follows:

1st	**forma**	8th	**eahtoþa**	20th	**twintogoþa**
2nd	**ōþer**	9th	**nigoða**	30th	**þrītigoþa**
3rd	**ðridda**	10th	**tēoða**	etc.	
4th	**fēorða**	11th	**endleofoða**	100th	**hundtēontigoða**
5th	**fīfta**	12th	**twelfta**		
6th	**siexta**	13th	**ðrēotēoða**		
7th	**seofoða**	etc.			

With one exception, these all behave as adjectives with only weak forms (i.e. the ending **-a** given here is for the nom.sing.masc. and will need to be changed according to the number, gender and case of the noun described), e.g.:

	(masculine)	*(feminine)*	*(neuter)*
	the fourth part	the first story	the tenth ship
nom.	**se fēorða dǣl**	**sēo forme talu**	**þæt tēoþe scip**
acc.	**ðone fēorðan dǣl**	**þā forman tale**	**þæt tēoþe scip**
gen.	**ðæs fēorþan dǣles**	**ðǣre forman tale**	**þæs tēoðan scipes**

and so on.

The exception is **ōðer** 'second, other' which never has weak endings:

	the second part	the second story	the second ship
nom.	**se ōþer dǣl**	**sēo ōþer talu**	**þæt ōþer scip**
acc.	**ðone ōþerne dǣl**	**þā ōþera tale**	**þæt ōþer scip**
gen.	**ðæs ōþres dǣles**	**ðǣre ōþerre tale**	**þæs ōþres scipes**

and so on.

'First', when it is an expression of time (e.g. 'you must first learn to read') meaning 'beforehand, in advance' is **ǣror**; when it means 'foremost' (e.g. 'he is the first of our warriors') it is **fyrmest.**

Practice 12.4: give the OE for the following:

the first king (nom.sing.); the twelfth night (nom.sing.); the third loaf (acc.sing.); the fifth wound (gen.sing.); the ninth battle (acc.sing.); my first companions (nom.pl.); the tenth messenger (gen.sing.); my other eye (dat.sing.); the hundredth sheep (gen.sing.).

Answers: se forma cyning; sēo twelfte niht; þone ðriddan hlāf; þǣre fīftan benne; þæt nigoðe gefeoht; mīne forman gesīþas; þæs tēoþan bodan; mīnum ōþrum ēagan; þæs hundtēontigoþan scēapes.

12.5 Another small but common group of strong verbs follows the examples of **beran** 'bear, carry', **cuman** 'come' and **scieran** 'shear, cut':

ic	bær	cōm	scear
þū	bǣre	cōme	scēare
hē			
hēo	bær	cōm	scear
hit			
wē			
gē	bǣron	cōmon	scēaron
hīe			
past participle	geboren	gecumen	gescoren

There are no other verbs like **scieran** and only **niman** 'take' is like **cuman** (**nōm, nōme,** etc.). Like **beran** are:

stelan steal	**helan** hide	**cwelan** die
teran tear	**brecan** break	

Practice 12.5: give the OE for the following:

I was carrying; it broke; it tore; they died; we hid; you (sing.) stole; you (pl.) stole; she took; we came; I cut; they are stolen; it is torn.

Answers: ic bær; hit bræc; hit tær; hīe cwǣlon; wē hǣlon; þū stǣle; gē stǣlon; hēo nōm; wē cōmon; ic scear; hīe sind gestolene; hit is getoren.

Vocabulary (12)

Verbs

hweorfan	turn, go	**mǣrsian**	glorify	**weorpan**	throw
beorgan	protect	**ceorfan**	carve, cut	**feohtan**	fight
weorðan	become	**sweorcan**	grow dark	**findan**	find
delfan	delve, dig	**steorfan**	die	**sweltan**	die
meltan	melt	**belgan**	be angry	**gielpan**	boast
swelgan	swallow	**gieldan**	pay, give up	**windan**	wind
bindan	bind, tie	**helpan**	help	**winnan**	fight
drincan	drink	**grindan**	grind	**singan**	sing
gewinnan	win, gain	**swincan**	labour, toil	**þringan**	throng
springan	spring, jump	**onginnan**	begin	**gelimpan**	happen
swimman	swim	**stingan**	stab		

Nouns

hilt (*m*)	hilt	**ecg** (*f*)	edge, blade
scēaþ (*f*)	sheath, scabbard	**spearc** (*m*)	spark
sleg (*m*)	blow	**wǣpn** (*n*)	weapon
anfilt (*n*)	anvil		

Adjectives

sweart	dark	**gehroden**	ornamented, decorated

Exercises (12)

1. Translate the following into NE:

Torhta, se swearta smið, ongann swincan, his hlāfordes sweord scierpan; þæs ecg hē grand, þone hilt hē band, his naman cearf on þǣre gehrodenan scēaþe. Þā hwīle þe hē swanc on ðǣre deorcan smiððan, sang hē ond dranc ealu; þā spearcas flugon ymb, hruron ond sturfon. Þā se dæg swearc, þā wearð hē werig æt his anfilte; hæfde gemǣrsod þæt wǣpn mid heardum slegum ond mid wīsum cræfte. Þā his hlāford feaht mid þǣm miclan sweorde, ðā stang hē ðone fēond swifte. Ne swāc hine þæt sweord on gefeohte.

2. Translate the following into OE:

When I grew angry I threw my golden cup onto the floor; my heart grew dark. I broke an axe against a tree as I cut it and pulled. No remedy did I find for this strife.

OLD ENGLISH COURSE – SECTION 13

13.1 The comparative adjective

13.2 Past tense, strong verbs (*specan, etan, giefan*)

13.3 The superlative adjective

13.4 The irregular comparative/superlative adjective

13.5 The present participle

13.1 The ordinal numeral, as we have seen (12.4), has only weak endings which is what one would expect because we would normally refer to '*the* fourth day of the week' not '*a* fourth day...' – items in a numbered series are naturally 'definite'.

There is another set of adjectives which are always weak, the *comparatives*. A comparative adjective is used for comparing one thing with another: 'faster than a speeding bullet', 'my one is bigger than yours', etc. where *faster, bigger* are the comparative forms of *fast, big*. In NE we have two ways of making comparatives: adding -*er* (faster) or putting *more* in front (more interesting). OE only uses the former method:

swift	'fast, swift, speedy'	**lēof**	'dear, precious'
swiftra	'faster, swifter, speedier'	**lēofra**	'dearer, more precious'

Fāh 'hostile' has the form **fāra**, **fealu** 'dark' **fealora**, and others ending in -**u** likewise, while those with -**æ**- in the stem retain it (**glæd, glædra**).

'Than' is usually expressed by **ðonne**: **swiftra þonne ic** 'faster than I', **beorhtra ðonne seo sunne** 'brighter than the sun' although (mainly in poetry) the dative case alone may be used instead: **swiftra mē** (dat.), **beorhtra sunnan** (dat.).

Again, these are the masc.nom.sing.forms ending in -**a** which needs to be altered to agree with the number, gender and case:

fealore hors	*(nom.sing.neut.)*	a darker horse
fægerran brȳde	*(gen.sing.fem.)*	of a fairer bride
Ðā Mierce sind swīþran ðonne þā Norþwealas	*(nom.pl.masc.)*	The Mercians are mightier than the Welsh

Practice 13.1: below are some OE adjectives taken from part 4; put them into their comparative form with the correct endings for the number,case, and gender stated:

'firmer' trum (nom.sing.masc.); 'more enjoyable' wilsum (acc.sing.fem.); 'braver' hwæt (gen.sing.masc.); 'blinder' blind (dat.pl.masc.); 'harder' heard (nom.pl.neut.); 'more doubtful' twēolic (gen.pl.neut.); 'more slender' smæl (dat.sing.fem.).

Answers: trumra; wilsumran; hwætran; blindrum; heardran; twēolicrena; smælran.

13.2 Similar to the verbs given in 12.5 is the group given below, which have a different vowel in the past participle. Typical examples are **specan** 'speak', **etan** 'eat' and **giefan** 'give':

ic	spæc	ǣt	geaf
þū	spǣce	ǣte	gēafe
hē			
hēo	spæc	ǣt	geaf
hit			
wē			
gē	spǣcon	ǣton	gēafon
hīe			
past participle	gespecen	geeten	gegiefen

There is only one verb like **etan** with a long vowel in the singular and plural: **fretan** 'devour', and one like **giefan**: **ongietan** 'perceive, sense, understand'. Like **specan** (which has an alternative form with -**r**-: **sprecan**) are:

wrecan avenge	**tredan** tread	**wefan** weave
metan measure	**biddan** ask	**sittan** sit

The verb **cweþan** 'say' shows the consonant alternation referred to in 10.6 (**cwæð**, **cwǣde**, etc.) while **genesan** 'survive, be saved' does not (**genæs**, **genǣse**, etc.). The pair **licgan** 'lie (down)' and **ðicgan** 'partake, taste' show change to the cluster -**cg**- (the latter verb partly following **giefan** in its vowel):

ic	læg	ðeah
þū	lǣge	ðǣge
hē etc	læg	ðeah
wē etc	lǣgon	ðǣgon
past participle	gelegen	geþegen

A single contracted verb belongs in this group: **sēon** 'see' with the forms:

ic seah, ðū sāwe, hē, etc. **seah, wē,** etc. **sāwon** past participle **gesewen**

Practice 13.2: give the OE for the following: you (sing.) asked; we were eating; they avenged him; I trod; he lay down; I tasted; you (pl.) sat; she was weaving.

Answers: þū bǣde; wē ǣton; hīe wrǣcon hine; ic trǣd; hē læg; ic þeah; gē sǣton; hēo wæf.

13.3 Having seen in 13.1 how the word *faster* can be formed from *fast*, we should now look at the way *fastest* is formed, the so-called *superlative*. This is usually with the ending -ost e.g. **swiftost** 'fastest', **lēofost** 'dearest', **trumost** 'firmest', etc. This form of adjective can take weak or strong endings according to the usage, e.g. **mīn hors is swiftost** 'my horse is fastest' but **þæt swiftoste hors is mīn** 'the swiftest horse is mine' where the weak ending is used because the adjective comes after **ðæt** 'the' (see 12.1).

13.4 In 13.1 and 13.3 we have seen the adjective in its regular comparative and superlative forms; there are however a handful of adjectives which do not follow the basic rule. Some involve alterations to the stem, like NE *elder, eldest* from *old* with an altered vowel; others substitute a completely different stem, like NE *better, best* from *good*.

The commonest are:

(i) with vowel change

old	**eald**	**ieldra**	**ieldest**
young	**geong**	**gingra**	**gingest**
high	**hēah**	**hīerra**	**hīe(h)st**
strong	**strang**	**strengra**	**strengest**
long	**lang**	**lengra**	**lengest**

(ii) with different stem

good	**gōd**	**betera**	**betst**
		sēlra	**sēlest**
bad	**yfel**	**wiersa**	**wierst**
great	**micel**	**māra**	**mǣst**
little	**lȳtel**	**lǣssa**	**lǣst**

For the comparatives, again the nom.sing.masc. only is given and the ending will need to be changed to suit the number, gender and case of the noun it describes.

Practice 13.4: give the OE for the following:

a ship is bigger than a boat (use **bēon**); he was better than I; the house is higher than a tree; they are the worst vikings who now sail (use **līðan**); this is the greatest battle I have seen.

Answers: scip biþ māre þonne bāt; hē wæs betera ðonne ic; þæt hūs is hīerre þonne trēow; hīe sind þā wierstan wīcingas þe nū līðað; þis is þæt mǣste gefeoht þæt ðe ic sēah.

13.5 Although OE has no continuous tenses of the type *I am going, we were playing, you are joking* there is nevertheless an ending which can be added to the present tense stem of the verb to make a so-called 'present participle'. The form this ending takes is **-ende** e.g.

bodian	to preach	**bodiende**	preaching
secgan	to say	**secgende**	saying
wlītan	to look	**wlītende**	looking
hogian	to think	**hogiende**	thinking

although contracted verbs take **-nde** only:

sēon	to see	**sēonde**	seeing

In use, the present participle is an adjective and so it may take the adjectival ending appropriate to the noun it describes: **ic band stelendne ðēow** 'I tied up a thieving slave' although it often remains unchanged: **hīe sǣton specende ond etende** 'they sat talking and eating'. When used with 'to be' the present participle can sometimes indicate the beginning of an action: **ne bēoþ etende ðās wyrte** 'do not (start to) eat this plant!' although the difference from the simple present or past tense is not always clear.

It is necessary to be careful over phrases such as 'I saw him coming' or 'we heard them riding', in which OE does not use the participle at all but the infinitive: **ic seah hine cuman, wē hīerdon hīe rīdan**. This is largely confined to expressions where the idea is perception (seeing, hearing, knowing, etc.) – which rather unusually can be translated with a present participle into NE – **and is parallel to phrases such as ic bēad hine cuman** 'I asked him to come' where we would not think of putting 'I asked him coming'.

Practice 13.5: give the OE for the following:

finishing; learning; testing; teaching; working; shaking; being; killing; breaking; mourning; diving; protecting; finding; weaving.

Answers: endiende; leorniende; fandiende; tǣcende; wyrcende; cweccende; bēonde; cwellende; brecende; hrēowende; dūfende; beorgende; findende; wefende.

Vocabulary (13)

Verbs

wrecan	avenge	**tredan**	tread	**wefan**	weave
metan	measure	**biddan**	ask	**sittan**	sit
sp(r)ecan	speak	**etan**	eat	**fretan**	devour
giefan	give	**ongietan**	perceive	**licgan**	lie down
þicgan	taste	**ðurhdrīfan**	pierce		

Noun

flēot (*m*)	stream	**burg** (*f*)	fortress
hæftling (*m*)	captive	**fyrd** (*f*)	defence force, army
ealdormann (*m*)	commander, leader	**gewuna** (*m*)	custom
bātweard (*m*)	ship's watchman		

Preposition

binnan	inside

Exercises (13)

1. Translate the following into NE:

Þā wīcingas fuhton wið Engle æt flēotes mūðan; hæfdon hīe burg getimbroda þǣr. Binnan sǣton hæftlingas, wefende ond grindende, swincende mid micelre sorge. Hīe forhtodon forþām þe hīe nǣron frēo. Wīcinga gewuna wæs þæt hīe ne burgon hiera hæftlingas, ac sendon hīe forþ on gefeohte, ond þǣr sturfon hīe. Sum hæftling crēap fram þǣre byrig ond dēaf on þæt wæter, swamm oþ Engla fyrde hors ond rǣhte þone ealdormann hwǣr þāra wīcinga scipu wǣron. Þonne sende se Englisca heretoga sume wīgan forð, ond hīe crupon on riscum ond sprungon wiþ Dene, bātweardas flīemende mid miclum bennum. Þā þā Dene ongēaton þæt hiera scipu ðurhdrifenu wǣron, þā ongunnon hīe forhtian swīðe.

OLD ENGLISH COURSE – SECTION 14

14.1 Past tense, strong verbs (*wadan*)
14.2 Genitive: further uses
14.3 Numerals: oblique cases
14.4 Past tense, strong verbs
       (*cnāwan, slǣpan*)
14.5 Pronouns (*se, wit, git*)

14.1 A small set of strong verbs follows the pattern of **wadan** 'walk':

ic	wōd
þū	wōde
hē etc	wōd
wē etc	wōdon
past participle	**gewaden**

Like **wadan** are:

hladan load	**sacan** contend	**scacan** shake
dragan draw, pull	**faran** fare, go	**galan** chant

The verbs **standan** 'stand', **swerian** 'swear' have past participles **gestanden, geswored** (but normal forms **stōd, stōde, stōdon; swōr, swōre, swōron**) while **hebban** 'raise, lift' replaces -**bb**- with -**f**- in the past tense and participle (**hōf, hōfe, hōfon, gehafen**). As elsewhere the -**i**- of **scieppan** 'create, make, shape' is dropped in the past (**scōp, scōpe, scōpon, gescapen**).

There are two contracted verbs: **lēan** 'blame' and **slēan** 'strike', the latter with alternative past participles **slagen, slǣgen**.

Practice 14.1: give the OE for the following:

I loaded; he drew; they contended; we shook; I stood; you (sing.) swore; she walked; they created.

Answers: ic hlōd; hē drōg; hīe sōcon; wē scōcon; ic stōd; þū swōre; hēo wōd; hīe scōpon.

14.2 In NE we can say 'one of my sheep is sick' or 'this is the highest of the hills' where *of* does not show 'possession' (the main use of the genitive – see 6.1) but rather inclusion in the group mentioned. OE does likewise: **ān mīnra scēapa is sēoc, ðēos is sēo hīehste þāra hylla**, where **scēapa, hylla** are both genitive plural. A similar kind of phrase using a superlative adjective is common in poetry, where a royal hall may be

101

referred to as **hūsa sēlest** 'best of houses' and an old king as **manna mildost** 'mildest of men'. This type of phrase is called a *partitive* genitive, because it denotes part of a larger group.

There are a few prepositions which govern the genitive, although none are used only with that case:

andlang	along	**andlang þǣre strǣte**	along the street
tō	until, as far as	**tō ðisses tīman**	up to this time
wið	towards	**wiþ ðæs holtes**	towards the wood

and examples of adverbs with genitive endings:

hāmweardes	homewards
ealles	entirely, all, wholly
wordes oððe dǣde	by word or deed

Some common verbs have a direct object in the genitive, for example:

wēnan hope, expect	**fægnian** rejoice at	**wundrian** wonder at, be amazed
fandian test, try out	**helpan** help	**blissian** rejoice, be happy

so that 'try it!' in OE is **fanda his** and 'I did not expect that' is **ic ðæs ne wēnde**, where **his, ðæs** are in the genitive.

In NE, we use expressions such as 'a lot of people' or 'mindful of words' and so does OE: **fela manna, worda gemyndig;** here the genitive is found not supported by a preposition, and it usually carries the meaning '(in respect) of', e.g. **wiges heard** 'hard (in respect) of warfare'.

 The adjective **monig** 'many' occurs with singular nouns: **monig mann cymð** 'many (a) man shall come'.

Practice 14.2: give the OE for the following:

sickest of men; swiftest of ships; fairest of women; they wondered at that; we tested these swords; a lot of warriors; a lot of nuns; towards those rocks.

Answers: manna sēocost; scipa swiftost; wīfa fægrost; hīe þæs wundrodon; wē fandodon ðissa sweorda; fela wīgendra; fela nunnena; wið ðāra stāna.

14.3 Having looked at the use of the partitive genitive (14.2) it will be well to look at some further aspects of the numerals.

The numbers **twēgen** and **þrēo** have separate genitive and dative forms (plural only, for obvious reasons!), so that the complete set of endings looks like this:

	two	three
nom.	**twēgen** *(m)* **twā** *(f,n)* **tū** *(n)*	**ðrīe** *(m)* **ðrēo** *(f,n)*
acc.	**twēgen** *(m)* **twā** *(f,n)* **tū** *(n)*	**ðrīe** *(m)* **ðrēo** *(f,n)*
gen.	**twēgea** *(m,n)*, **twēgra** *(f)*	**ðrēora**
dat.	**twām, twǣm**	**ðrim**

Parallel to **twēgen** 'two' is **bēgen** 'both' which rhymes with it in all instances but replaces **tw-** with **b-** (e.g. **bēgen** *(m)* **bā** *(f,n)* **bū** *(n)* gen. **bēgra**, etc).

For **ān** 'one' the normal adjectival endings apply (see 4.3) and there is an alternative masc.acc.sing. **ǣnne** which can also mean 'once, at one time'. When **ān** has weak adjectival endings it means 'only, alone' e.g. **ðes wīgend āna cweleð hine** 'this warrior alone shall slay him' **ðās bodan ānan wadaþ hider** 'only these messengers shall walk to this place'.

'Two by two' and similar distributive phrases are rendered with the dative forms, e.g. **twǣm ond twǣm**.

Halves are expressed with the noun **healf** (fem.) 'a half'; they are 'counted' as follows:

half	**healf**	
one and a half	**ōþer healf**	'the second half'
two and a half	**ðridde healf**	'the third half'
three and a half	**fēowerþe healf**	'the fourth half'

even up to much higher numerals: **þridde healf hund scipa** 'two hundred and fifty ships' i.e. the third half hundred.

Another expression using numbers is that of adding the genitive plural ending **-a** to the number with the word **sum** 'a certain one' e.g. **se cyning wæs twelfa sum** 'the king was one of twelve' i.e. one person in a group of twelve people. This is another case of the partitive genitive.

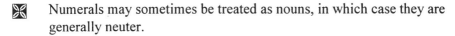 Numerals may sometimes be treated as nouns, in which case they are generally neuter.

Practice 14.3: give the OE for the following: with two swords; towards two rocks; with one companion; my only friend; he is one of five; from two vikings; only the hunter survived; I helped both my friends.

Answers: mid twǣm sweordum; wið twēgra stāna; mid ānum gesīþe; mīn āna frēond; hē is fīfa sum; fram twǣm wīcingum; se hunta āna genæs; ic healp bēgea mīnra frēonda.

14.4 The last two groups of strong verbs are among the commonest in OE and all have -**ē**- or -**ēo**- in their past tense forms. Examples are **cnāwan** 'know' and **slǣpan** 'sleep':

ic	**cnēow**	**slēp**
ðū	**cnēowe**	**slēpe**
hē etc	**cnēow**	**slēp**
wē etc	**cnēowon**	**slēpon**
past participle	**gecnāwen**	**geslǣpen**

Like **cnāwan** are:

blāwan blow	**māwan** mow	**sāwan** sow

Nearly all verbs in this group have the same vowel in the past participle as in the infinitive:

with -**ō**- are:

spōwan succeed	**blōwan** bloom	**grōwan** grow
flōwan flow	**rōwan** row	

(exception **wēpan** weep: **gewōpen**)

with -**ea**- are:

wealdan rule	**weallan** well, surge	**weaxan** grow up
fealdan fold	**feallan** fall	**healdan** hold

with -**ēa**- are:

hlēapan leap, dance	**hēawan** hew, chop	**bēatan** beat

with -**a**- are:

bannan summon	**spanan** seduce, entice	**spannan** span, link

Like **slǣpan** are:

lǣtan let, allow	**rǣdan** advise	**ondrǣdan** dread
hātan call, command (past participle **gehāten**)		

There are two contracted verbs, **fōn** 'sieze, grab, get' and **hōn** 'hang' which behave as follows:

	present	*past*
ic	**fō**	**fēng**
þū	**fēhst**	**fēnge**
hē etc	**fēhð**	**fēng**
wē etc	**fōþ**	**fēngon**
participles	**fōnde**	**gefangen**

While they do not really belong in this class, there are two very common verbs with an irregular preterite: **gān**, to go and **dōn**, to do (see 8.2). Their past forms are as follows (with the present forms also for convenience):

	gān		**dōn**	
	present	*past*	*present*	*past*
ic	**gā**	**ēode**	**dō**	**dyde**
þū	**gǣst**	**ēodest**	**dēst**	**dydest**
hē etc	**gǣð**	**ēode**	**dēþ**	**dyde**
wē etc	**gāð**	**ēodon**	**dōþ**	**dydon**
participles	**gānde**	**gegangen**	**dōnde**	**gedōn**

✠ **Gān** is sometimes accompanied by a reflexive dative pronoun e.g. **hē ēode him of Englalande** 'he left England' (see 14.5).

Practice 14.4: give the OE for the following:

I called; he rowed; we danced; it fell; I knew; they ruled; we dreaded; she succeeded; she enticed; they hewed; it spanned; it surged.

Answers: ic hēt; hē rēow; wē hlēopon; hit fēoll; ic cnēow; hīe wēoldon; wē ondrēdon; hēo spēow; hēo spēon; hīe hēowon; hit spēonn; hit wēoll.

14.5 To return to pronouns briefly, it is worth noting in passing that OE often uses the forms of **se, sēo, ðæt** for the third person pronouns i.e. **se wæs mīn brōðor** 'he was my brother', **ic sēah ðone** 'I saw him' **ðæt wæs storm unlȳtel** 'it was no small storm'; the sense arises from using these words to mean 'that (one)'.

There are also two rather rare further personal pronouns: **wit, git** which always refer to a pair e.g. 'we two', 'you two'. They are used with plural verbs (e.g. **wit sind**, etc.) and have the following forms:

	we two	you two
nom.	**wit**	**git**
acc.	**uncet**	**incet**
gen.	**uncer**	**incer**
dat.	**unc**	**inc**

A notable use of **wit** is in expressions such as **wit Scilling** 'Scilling and I' where only the name of the person who is not speaking is given. **Uncer, incer** can be used as possessive adjectives (e.g. **mid uncrum winum**, 'with the friends of you and me, our mutual friends').

A very few OE verbs, mostly involving transition or motion, require a so-called *reflexive pronoun.* This is simply a means of referring the object of the verb back to the subject as we now do with the word '-self', for example, **se biscop wende hine** 'the bishop turned (himself)', **se fox bestæl hine** 'the fox stole (himself) away'; the pronoun may occur alone or for emphasis with the appropriate form of the adjective **self**, e.g. **hīe līcodon him selfum** 'they pleased themselves'.

A common kind of expression in NE is 'there is no beer left' or 'there were lots of people in the room' where 'there' doesn't really refer to a place but is simply a way of introducing the ideas 'no beer is left', 'lots of people were in the room'. OE sometimes uses **þǣr** 'there' as in **þǣr wæs sang ond hleahtor** 'there was singing and laughter' although just as often the simple idea is stated, as in **nis nū nān ealu** '(there) not-is now no ale'.

Vocabulary (14)

Verbs

bannan	summon	**bēatan**	beat	**blāwan**	blow
blissian	rejoice, be happy	**blōwan**	bloom	**cnāwan**	know
dragan	draw, pull	**fandian**	test, try out	**faran**	fare, go
fægnian	rejoice	**fealdan**	fold	**feallan**	fall
flōwan	flow	**fōn**	sieze, grab, get	**galan**	chant
grōwan	grow	**hātan**	call, command	**healdan**	hold
hēawan	hew, chop	**helpan**	help	**hlēapan**	leap, dance
hladan	load	**hōn**	hang	**lǣtan**	let, allow
māwan	mow	**ondrǣdan**	dread	**rǣdan**	advise
rōwan	row	**sacan**	contend	**sāwan**	sow
scacan	shake	**scieppan**	create	**slǣpan**	sleep
spannan	span, link	**spanan**	seduce, entice	**spōwan**	succeed
standan	stand	**swerian**	swear	**wadan**	walk
wealdan	rule	**weallan**	well, surge	**weaxan**	grow up
wēnan	hope, expect	**wundrian**	wonder at, be amazed		

Nouns

cēapmann (*m*)	merchant, trader	**wyrtgemang** (*n*)	mixture of spices
sceatt (*m*)	coin	**bratt** (*m*)	cloak
strand (*n*)	shore	**hlǣst** (*m*)	cargo, freight
wull (*f*)	wool	**wǣd** (*f*)	garment
gōd (*n.pl.*)	goods, commodities	**tōl** (*f*)	tool

Adjectives

elðēodisc	foreign, alien	**weorð**	valuable
silfren	(made of) silver	**wearm**	warm
missenlic	various, sundry	**þēodisc**	native

Exercises (14)

1. Translate the following into NE:

Trumhere wæs cēapmann. Hē hæfde ān micel scip þætte hē hēt hladan mid Engliscum gōdum ond þonne fōr hē mid scipmannum geond þære sǣwe on elðēodisc land, hwīlum ēast, hwīlum sūð. Þær bohton menn his hlæst wið gyldene sceattas, þā þe on Englalande swīðe weorðe wǣron. Ac Trumhere cnēow wel þæt ðā sceattas nǣron swā weorþe swā sumu elðēodisc gōd þe hē sōhte þær. Ǣrest sōhte hē elþēodiscra manna wyrtgemang; þonne gold, ond wǣda, ond wǣpnu, ond wīn, ond missenlīce metas.

2. Translate the following into OE:

Sometimes Trumhere and his men pulled the ship onto a foreign shore, and there they sat and ate until the native people came to them. They thronged around the ship, and wondered at the goods he had loaded; most often they paid with silver coins or with their own goods if they had none. These were warm cloaks, and tools, and wool, and best of all the gemstones they made in that land.

OLD ENGLISH COURSE – SECTION 15

15.1 Among the commonest verbs in OE as in NE are those which express shades of meaning with the verb's infinitive: for example, 'I must go down to the sea again' or 'I want to be alone' or 'they shall not pass', where *must, want, shall* express an attitude to the infinitives *go, be, pass*. Many of these verbs are of the preterite-present type (see 8.1) in OE, and still retain in NE some features of this class.

The commonest verbs of this type (known collectively as *modal auxiliaries*) are set out below with a brief explanation of their use. In practice, some of them overlap to some extent and it is not always clear how they differ from each other. This is equally true for NE, where the marginal difference between 'I will go' and 'I shall go' means that many speakers simply prefer one form over the other (although *he/she/it shall* are by no means as often used).

We will begin with the verb **cunnan** 'know how to':

	present	*past*
ic	cann	cūðe
ðū	canst	cūþest
hē etc.	cann	cūþe
wē etc.	cunnon	cūþon
participles:	cunnende	(unrecorded, should be ***gecunnen**)

e.g. **ic cann swimman** 'I know how to swim' from which the modern sense of 'can' (have the means, ability or power to do something) has evolved. Parallel (but without the initial 'c') to **cunnan** is the verb **unnan** 'grant, allow, bestow' e.g. **ic ann þone tūn ðǣm mynstre** 'I grant that estate to the monastery'.

⌘   The vowels of **cann, cunnon** are modelled on the type **sang, sungon**.

Practice 15.1: give the OE for the following: I know how to ride; he knew how to dive; we two know how to sing; I granted the estate to my thane.

Answers: ic cann rīdan; hē cūþe dūfan; wit cunnon singan; ic ūþe ðone tūn mīnum ðegne.

15.2 Another verb meaning 'to know' is **witan**, with the meaning of being aware of something: **ic wāt þæt þū eart blind** 'I know that you are blind'. There are separate negated forms:

	witan 'know'		nytan 'know not'	
	present	*past*	*present*	*past*
ic	**wāt**	**wiste**	**nāt**	**nyste**
þū	**wāst**	**wistest**	**nāst**	**nystest**
hē etc	**wāt**	**wiste**	**nāt**	**nyste**
wē etc	**witon**	**wiston**	**nyton**	**nyston**
participles	**witende**	**gewiten**		

✠ Where the past tense has -**st**- forms, variants with -**ss**- occur, e.g. **wissest**.

⌘ The vowels of **wāt, witon** are based on the verb type **bāt, biton**.

Practice 15.2: give the OE for the following: he knows; I don't know; we knew that this happened; I didn't know you were here; you don't know what I saw.

Answers: hē wāt; ic nāt; wē wiston þæt þis gelamp; ic nyste þæt ðū hēr wǣre; þū nāst ðætte ic sēah.

15.3 'To be allowed' or 'to have the opportunity' to do something is expressed in OE with the verb **mōtan**:

	present	*past*
ic	**mōt**	**mōste**
þū	**mōst**	**mōstest**
hē etc	**mōt**	**mōste**
wē etc	**mōton**	**mōston**

(participles are not recorded, although the present would be ***mōtende**).

Mōtan is best expressed in NE by 'may', e.g. **ic mōt rīdan** 'I may ride' where the sense is 'permission' or 'opportunity'; mere possibility is expressed with the subjunctive forms (see 16.4,5).

⌘ The vowels of **mōt, mōton** are based on the type **stōp, stōpon**.

Practice 15.3: give the OE for the following: I was allowed to drive; you two may not come with us; they have the opportunity to expel the vikings; she may set us free.

Answers: ic mōste drīfan; git ne mōton cuman mid ūs; hīe mōton þā wīcingas dræfan; hēo mōt ūs ālīesan.

15.4 **Magan** is the direct ancestor of 'may', but its meaning is rather closer to 'be able, have the power to' and can be translated with NE 'can': **ic ne mihte tæcan** "I could not teach / I was unable to teach".

	present	*past*
ic	**mæg**	**mihte**
þū	**meaht**	**mihtest**
hē etc	**mæg**	**mihte**
wē etc	**magon**	**mihton**
participle	**magende**	(unrecorded)

In poetry, **magan** can have the stronger meaning 'be powerful, avail'.

> ✳ **Where -ea- forms occur, variants with -i- occur and vice versa, e.g. miht, meahte.**

Practice 15.4: give the OE for the following: he can judge; I cannot hear; you could not walk; they were able to care for him; we can go now.

Answers: hē mæg dēman; ic ne mæg hīeran; þū ne mihtest wadan; hīe mihton hine reccan; wē magon nū gān.

15.5 Obligation is expressed in OE with the verb **sculan** 'must, shall': **ic sceal gieldan** 'I must pay' and volition with **willan** 'want to, will' which has a negated form **nyllan**:

	sculan 'must'		**willan** 'want to'		**nyllan** 'want not to'	
	present	*past*	*present*	*past*	*present*	*past*
ic	**sceal**	**scolde**	**wille**	**wolde**	**nylle**	**nolde**
þū	**scealt**	**scoldest**	**wilt**	**woldest**	**nylt**	**noldest**
hē etc	**sceal**	**scolde**	**wile**	**wolde**	**nyle**	**nolde**
wē etc	**sculon**	**scoldon**	**willaþ**	**woldon**	**nyllaþ**	**noldon**
participles			**willende**			

Sculan can seldom be translated with 'shall' which does not really convey a sense of obligation any more: **ic sceal fēran** is not 'I shall travel' but rather 'I must travel'. In the past tense, an expression such as **hē scolde bēon cyning** can mean not simply 'he had to be the king' but also 'he ought to be the king', 'he was supposed to be the king'.

Willan most often expresses a desire or intention; it is not really a preterite-present verb (e.g. pl. **willaþ** not ***willon**) but is used in ways similar to the true preterite-presents. There are instances of **wolde** having the more modern sense of 'would' rather than 'wanted to' or 'wished', e.g. **ic nyste gif ðæt wolde gelimpan** 'I did not know if that would happen'.

Practice 15.5: give the OE for the following: I had to make room; we want to praise the king; he would not buy that; they must atone; I wanted to know; you two must obey; I had to leave him behind; you must not wait; I intend to mourn.

Answers: ic scolde rȳman; wē willaþ ðone cyning herian; hē nolde þone bycgan; hīe sculon gebētan; ic wolde witan; git sculon gīeman; ic hine lǽfan scolde; þū ne scealt bīdan; ic wille cwīðan.

15.6 The verbs given in sections 15.1–5 are the commonest preterite-present verbs, but the following are no less useful:

	āgan 'possess'		**ðurfan** 'need'	
	present	*past*	*present*	*past*
ic	**āh**	**āhte**	**þearf**	**þorfte**
þū	**āhst**	**āhtest**	**þearft**	**þorftest**
hē etc	**āh**	**āhte**	**þearf**	**þorfte**
wē etc	**āgon**	**āhton**	**þurfon**	**þorfton**
participles	**āgende**	**āgen**	**þurfende**	

	gemunan 'remember'		**durran** 'dare'	
	present	*past*	*present*	*past*
ic	**geman**	**gemunde**	**dearr**	**dorste**
þū	**gemanst**	**gemundest**	**dearst**	**dorstest**
hē etc	**geman**	**gemunde**	**dearr**	**dorste**
wē etc	**gemunon**	**gemundon**	**durron**	**dorston**
participles	**gemunende**	**gemunen**	**durrende**	

āgan has a separate negative form **nāgan** i.e. **ic nāh** 'I do not possess', etc.

One final verb is **dugan** 'be of use, avail, be worthy' for which the principal recorded forms are 3rd person:

dugan 'be worthy, avail'		
hit	**dēah**	**dohte**
hīe	**dugon**	**dohton**
participle	**dugende**	

This is an impersonal verb (see 16.2).

Practice 15.6: give the OE for the following: I possessed; you needed; we dare; I dare; they remember; daring; possessed; we two remembered; that is worthy; she possesses; he dared.

Answers: ic āhte; þū ðorftest; wē durron; ic dearr; hīe gemunon; durrende; āgen ;wit gemundon; þæt dēah; hēo āh; hē dorste.

Vocabulary (15)

Nouns

unweder *(n)*	bad weather	**stormsǣ** *(m,f)*	stormy sea	**ȳþ** *(f)*	wave
īs *(n)*	ice	**snelnys** *(f)*	speed	**īeg** *(f)*	island
geteld *(n)*	tent	**rēc** *(m)*	smoke	**storm** *(m)*	storm
næss *(m)*	headland	**cynren** *(n)*	family, kin		

Verbs

oferlīþan	sail over, cross	**forlīþan**	be shipwrecked
āstīgan	rise up	**forbærnan**	burn up, burn away

Adjectives

uncūþ	unknown, unfamiliar

Conjunctions

hwæðer	whether	**swā swā**	as if, just like
īu	previously		

Exercises (15)

1. Translate the following into NE:

Ðā Trumhere fōr fram þǣm elþēodiscan lande ond lāþ ofer sǣwe ongēan Englaland, þā wæs unweder ond stormsǣ ond þā līþmenn nyston hwæðer hīe oferlīþan mihton oððe forlīþan. Hiera sum wæs forhtful ond ongann galan uncūþ galdor, ond þæt scip glād ofer ȳþum swā swā on īse. Se līþmann, se wæs īu hæftling Deniscra manna, bifode swīþe and clipode, ac his gesīþas fægnodon þæs scipes snelnysse. Sōna cōmon hīe on still wæter, þā menn and se hlæst onsunde, ond þæt scip flēat oþ sume īege.

On þǣre īege wæs lȳtel tūn, ac næs nān mann þǣr; þæs miclan hūses hrōf wæs forbærned ond scēap wunodon þǣrin. Twēgen līþmenn Trumheres rēowon on bāte wið þǣre īege, ond clipodon būton andsware. Ðonne wiston hīe ealle þæt ðā Dene hæfdon þā īege forhergod. Trumhere nyste hwǣr hīe wǣron – hīe losodon on þǣm storme – ac hē wiste þæt hīe scoldon west faran.

Ðā hīe þā ongunnon faran fram þǣre īege, þā sēah sum līðmann rēc āstīgan fram næsse; þǣr wæs lytel geteld.

2. Translate the following into OE:

They turned to the headland and looked at the tent – a single man was sitting inside; when he saw the ship he wanted to hide, but when he saw that it was not a Danish ship he cried out and rejoiced. He was loaded on board, and told them that his name was Torhta; he was a smith. Danes had taken all the people who lived there, but they had not seen his tent in which he stayed, looking for wood. His wife and children were now captives of the vikings and his father was dead – a Dane had stabbed him. Torhta wanted to avenge his family as soon as he could find a viking unprotected.

OLD ENGLISH COURSE – SECTION 16

16.1 Although it was stated above (3.3) that the infinitive is "unfinished" and so does not convey any information about tense and number, etc., there are in fact two types of infinitive in OE. The first is the type we have already met, which is used with modal auxiliary verbs, e.g. **wesan, sēon, flīeman, cnāwan,** as in **ic nyle þone cyning sēon** 'I don't want to see the king'. The second type is the so-called 'inflected infinitive' e.g. **tō wesenne, tō sēonne, tō flīemenne, tō cnāwenne,** as in **mon sende mec ðone cyning tō sēonne** 'I was sent to see the king'. This inflected infinitive form is mostly used with expressions of intention ('I was sent *in order to see* the king') and when the verb stands alone in sense: **ðæt is nū tō secgenne** 'it must now be said' **nis þæt ūs tō cnāwenne** 'that is not for us to know'.

Practice 16.1: give the inflected forms of the following: sēon; bēon; durran; flīeman; cēosan; āgan.

Answers: tō sēonne; tō bēonne; tō durrenne; tō flīemenne; tō cēosenne; tō āgenne.

16.2 There are a few verbs in OE where no subject is expressed, only the object, e.g. **mē ðyncð** '(it) seems to me', the archaic 'methinks'. Naturally, this type of expression requires a subject 'it' in NE or can be translated slightly differently, e.g. 'it seems to me' can be turned into 'I think'. These verbs are called 'impersonal' because they have no personal pronoun subject. Most have an object in the dative, (**mē spēow æt gūðe** 'I succeeded in warfare') though some use the accusative e.g. **hine nānes ðinges ne lyste** '(it) pleased him (in respect) of nothing, he desired nothing', **ðec sceamiaþ ðīnra ðēawa** '(it) shames you (in respect) of your manners, your manners shame you', **mē ðās misþyncað** '(it) displeases me (in respect) of these, these displease me'. Verbs of this type are not numerous and the few common ones given above soon become familiar.

Many verbs with no obvious, natural subject in the real world use **hit** 'it': **hit snīwð** 'it is snowing', **hit is rēnig weder** 'it is rainy weather'. (Ask yourself: what is snowing? what is rainy weather? to test this lack of a true subject.)

16.3 The irregularly formed adverbs can be summarized thus:

- where the adjective ends in -e, the adverb is identical, e.g. **blīðe** 'happy, happily'.

- where the adjective has a 'mutated' vowel (see 7.5) the adverb may not; the commonest examples are **īeðe** easy, **ēaðe** easily; **smēðe** smooth, **smūðe** smoothly; **sēfte** soft, **sōfte** softly; **swēte** sweet **swōte** sweetly.

- a few adjectives have adverbial forms based on a different root, e.g. **gōd : wel.**

Comparative and superlative forms of adverbs are regularly formed with **-or, -ost,** e.g. 'keenly' **cēne, cēnor, cēnost;** 'poorly' **earme, earmor, earmost.** A few adverbs behave differently, changing the root vowel:

	Adverb	*Comparative*	*Superlative*
'easily'	**ēaþe**	**īeð**	**ēaþost**
'distantly'	**feorr**	**fierr**	**fierrest**
'highly'	**hēah**	**hēar**	**hīehst**
'long'	**lange**	**leng**	**lengest**
'near, closely'	**nēah**	**nēar**	**nīehst**
'softly'	**sōfte**	**sēft**	**sōftost**
'formerly'	**ǣr**	**ǣr**	**ǣrest**
'late'	**sīþ**	**sīþ**	**sīþost**

A few adverbs are formed from different roots:

well	**wel**	**bet**	**betst**
		sēl	**sēlest**
badly	**yfle**	**wiers**	**wierst**
much	**micle**	**mā**	**mǣst**
little	**lȳt**	**lǣs**	**lǣst**

Practice 16.3: give the OE for the following: easily; softly; more easily; furthest; latest; most highly; most nearly; well; most; least; less.

Answers: ēaþe; sōfte; īeþ; fierrest; sīþost; hīehst; nīehst; wel; mǣst; lǣst; lǣs.

16.4 In NE we use expressions such as 'God save the king!', 'I wish I were in Barbados', 'I prefer that a book have an index' which express wishes; they differ from simple statements of fact (God saves the king, I was in Barbados, a book has an index) normally by their lack of verbal ending (e.g. save : saves). As one might expect, OE has such forms for its verbs also, one for the singular and another for the plural.

In the present tense, the singular form of the stem ends in -e (i.e. is the same as that for **ic,** except for irregular and preterite-present verbs), while the plural ends in -en: **ic wille ðæt ðū hiere** 'I wish that you hear, I want you to hear', **hē wile þæt gē cnāwen** 'he wishes that you know, he wants you to know', **hēo wile þæt hīe cumen** 'she wishes that they come, she wants them to come'.

115

In the past tense of weak verbs, again the form used with **ic** forms the singular while -en is added to the plural: **ic wolde þæt þū lufode mec** 'I wanted you to love me', **wē woldon þæt hīe ereden** 'we wanted them to plough'.

Strong verbs behave slightly differently in that the past tense form for **þū** is used in the singular, and again the plural ends in -en: **ic wolde þæt ic wǣre ðonan feorr** 'I wished that I were far from there' **hīe woldon þæt hīe fuhten** 'they wished that they could fight' or 'they wished that they had fought'.

☒ These forms of the verb are called the *subjunctive mood*, while forms used with straightforward statements of fact are called the *indicative mood*.

Practice 16.4: give the subjunctive form corresponding to the following indicative verbs: ic lufie; hē lufaþ; hē wāt; hē cnǣwþ; þū rītst; þū ride; wē cunnon; wē libbað; ic drāf; hē swealt; ic nōm.

Answers: ic lufie; hē lufie; hē wite; hē cnāwe; þū rīde; þū ride; wē cunnen; wē libben; ic drife; hē swulte; ic nōme.

16.5 The subjunctive mood has uses other than simply expressing wishes, however. It is really brought in to express anything which is in some way 'unreal' or 'non-factual', relating to intentions, wishes, desires or possibilities. Examples of the subjunctive can often be translated using the verb 'may', e.g., taking examples already given **ic wolde þæt þū lufode mec** 'I wished that you might love me', **wē woldon þæt hīe ereden** 'we wished that they might plough' **ic wille ðæt ðū hīere** 'I wish that you may hear'.

Another meaning for the subjunctive mood forms is to show purpose or a limited kind of 'futurity': **hē wearþ leorningcniht þæt hē lāreow wurde** 'he became a student in order that he might become a teacher' **ðā gefān feohtaþ oðþæt heora ān swelte** 'those opponents will fight until one of them dies'. In both these cases, the purpose (becoming a teacher, dying) are future events to which the present events (becoming a student, fighting) are leading.

16.6 The subjunctive forms for **wesan / bēon** 'to be' are not formed regularly. They are as follows:

	present		*past*
singular	**bēo**	**sīe**	**wǣre**
plural	**bēon**	**sīen**	**wǣren**

The singular form **sīe** can be used to mean 'whether it be...' in expressions such as **morgen faraþ wē sūð, sīe hāt sīe ceald** 'tomorrow we shall travel south, whether it be hot or cold' (compare archaic NE '...be it hot or cold').

Vocabulary (16)

Verbs

geþafian *(with genitive)*	agree, consent	**gefrēfran**	comfort
hungrian	go hungry	**bebycgan**	sell
befōn	seize, capture	**oferflītan**	overcome
fordōn	kill	**lædan**	lead, take, bring
āsendan	send away	**ymbclyppan**	embrace
sellan	give	**ðicgan**	accept, receive
grētan	greet	**ofslēan**	slay
ācwellan	kill	**āgieldan** *(with genitive)*	pay for
þancian *(with dative)*	thank		

Nouns

hȳþ *(f)*	harbour, port	**westdæl** *(m)*	western part
mūða *(m)*	estuary, rivermouth	**port** *(m)*	market town
segl *(m)*	sail	**mæst** *(m)*	mast
wǣfels *(n)*	cloak	**portgerēfa** *(m)*	town reeve
fæt *(n)*	container, vessel	**wīn** *(n)*	wine
fierd *(f)*	army	**cosp** *(m)*	fetter, shackle
geðrang *(n)*	crowd	**pusa** *(m)*	bag
generednes *(f)*	deliverance	**edlēan** *(n)*	reward
winescipe *(m)*	friendship	**þing** *(n)*	matter, affair
rēafere *(m)*	robber, ravager	**bana** *(m)*	killer

Adjectives

rēnig	rainy
sumes	somewhat, slightly

Exercises (16)

1. Translate the following into NE:

Torhta ǣt georne – hungrode hē þrīe dagas æfter þǣm þe þā wīcingas cōmon – ond geþafode þæs þe hē lǣdde Trumhere oþ þā hȳðe þe man ǣr sōhte on westdǣle Englalondes. Ðonne fōron hīe twēgen dagas on rēnigum wedere west, oððæt hīe cōmon on miclan mūðan and þǣrin sāwon hīe þone port. Þǣr on þǣre ēa fluton tū Denisc scipu – ōþer mid getorenum segle, ōþer būton mǣste ond sumes forbærned – and nān mann on borde.

Trumheres scip cōm sōna on port, ond hē sōhte ðone portgerēfan, his gōd tō bebycganne þe man hlōd on elþēodiscum lande. Se portgerēfa, Cūðred gehāten, nōm cyninges dæl þæs hlæstes ond bohte self sum wæfels, gylden fæt, gehroden sweord ond tū fatu wīnes. Þā gefrægn Trumhere hwæt þā scipu wæron þe mon on ēa sēah ond him andswarode Cūþred: "Þās sind Deniga scipu þe wæron on strande befongen; þā wīcingas fuhton wið cyninges fierde ac wē oferfliton hīe, fordydon sume ond ōþre læddon hider on cospum. Þā hæfdon Englisce hæftlingas on heora scipum þe nū frēo sind. Se cyning wille hīe āsendan eft hām, ælc mid sumum dæle ðæs fēos þe hīe nōmon ūs fram."

2. Translate the following into OE:

Then Torhta called out and rejoiced – he saw his wife in the crowd, hastened to her, kissed (her) and embraced (her), and the children also. These four rejoiced greatly and began to speak together.

In his bag Torhta had some silver coins with which he wanted to pay Trumhere (for) his journey and deliverance. And also for friendship he wanted to give a reward to the merchant. Trumhere agreed to accept the gift and straightaway greeted Torhta's family. However, Torhta regretted that he could not kill the viking who took away his wife and children, but she said that the ravager himself was slain in the fight. Nonetheless Cuthred said that Torhta's vengeance was the king's affair, and the king had been the viking's killer, therefore Torhta ought to be be happy. With these words Torhta was comforted, and the poor smith thanked him. He began to look for a strong horse with which to travel home.

OLD ENGLISH COURSE – SECTION 17

17.1 NE shows cause, purpose or result with adverbs such as *because, therefore, thus, so,* etc. OE forms this type of adverb using the pronoun **ðæt** (modified for case) and one of a number of prepositions. We have already seen this principle in the word **oð** 'as far as' and the phrase **oððæt** 'until'. The commonest expressions for cause ('therefore, thus') are **forþǣm** and its variants **forþȳ, þȳ, forþon**, e.g. **se cyning wæs wrāð, ond hīe forhtodon forðon ond urnon fram** 'the king was angry, and they were therefore fearful and ran away'.

For can also express 'because of': **ic swince for mīnes hlāfordes ege** 'I toil because of fear of my lord'.

⌘ **Forðǣm** is literally 'for that (reason)'.

Result is usually expressed with **forþǣm þe** (literally 'for that (reason), that') translating our word 'because': **ic nyste forðǣm ðe ic þā ungelǣred wæs** 'I did not know because I was then untaught'. Here again, **forþon ðe** is an alternative form.

Contingency is shown with the pair of words **gif ... ðonne** 'if ... then': **gif hwā befongen sīe on undǣdum, þonne swelte hē** 'if anyone be caught in wrongdoing, then let him die'. Another way of showing this is reversal of the order of subject and verb: **āhte ic ðisses rīces geweald, þū wurde flīema** 'had I control over this kingdom, you would become an exile'. Note the use of the subjunctive mood (see 16.4) with many of these expressions which are not simple statements of fact.

A kind of 'negative contingency' can be expressed with the word **būton** (**þǣm þe**) 'unless, except, but for': **ic ne sceal faran, būton þǣm þe se cyning ðafie** 'I must not go, unless the king should consent'. There is an alternative term **nefne** (or **nemne**) with the same meaning.

❖ **būton** is general, from West Saxon texts, while **nefne/nemne** are confined to Anglian texts.

Purpose may be shown with **tō þæs þe** (and its variants such as **tō þon ðæt**) 'so that': **hē rǣdde ūs tō þæs þe wē ne dwolien** 'he informed us so that we shall not make a mistake'; again, note the use of the subjunctive **dwolien** here, marking the future possibility ('we may make a mistake') rather than actuality ('we are making a mistake').

Þǣr 'there' can be used much as NE 'where' is, to act as a relative pronoun for places, e.g. **hē sēcþ tūn þǣr hē eardian mōt** 'he is looking for an estate where he may dwell'; it can also introduce possibilities, much like NE 'if', e.g. **ðǣr ic hæfde sweord on handa, þū ne mōstest libban** 'if I had a sword in my hand, you should not be allowed to live' (as in NE, there is a variant of the word order inversion above: "Had I a sword..."). The meaning of **ðǣr** is probably 'in that situation that..., in the circumstances that...'.

17.2 A useful word is **swā** 'so' which can be put to a number of uses in OE. It may translate 'as': **swā dōþ biscopas** 'as bishops do' and 'as ... as': **swā swift swā līgetu** 'as quick as lightning'. 'so' can express degree: **swā wrāð wæs hē þæt nān ne mihte hine wiþstandan** 'so angry was he that none could withstand him', or **ic eom nū swā waccra þonne hē** 'I am now so much weaker than he'. The doubled form **swā swā** means 'just as': **swā swā bēc lǣrað** 'just as books teach'.

'so' meaning 'to that degree' can be **tō þæs** (or **tō þon**): **hē wæs tō ðæs ādreht mid sārnysse þæt hē swīþe wōp** 'he was so afflicted with pain that he wept mightily' – similarly, we can sometimes say in NE 'he was *that* afflicted...'. 'such' is rendered by **swylce**: **cȳ ond swylce dēor** 'cows and such (suchlike, similar) animals'.

17.3 Although it is not much in evidence, there is a fifth case, the *instrumental*, which has left traces in OE. It is used mainly to show the means by which something is carried out. Its function has generally been taken over by the dative, and there are no separate feminine forms for it, nor plurals. It can be identified by the adjectival ending -e with an apparently dative noun, e.g. **hearde sweorde** (dative: **heardum sweorde**). One common idiom in which the use of the instrumental is necessary is expressions of accompaniment: **se cyning fōr lȳtle werode** 'the king travelled *with a small troop*', though here again it is possible to substitute **mid** and the dative.

There are special forms for 'the', 'this' in this case:

	masc.	*neut.*	*fem.*	*pl.all*
'the'/'that'	ðȳ	ðȳ, ðon	ðǣre	ðǣm
'this'	ðȳs	ðȳs	ðisse, ðisre	ðissum

These instrumental forms are used in expressions such as 'the more the merrier', e.g. **ðȳ ieldra wierþ hē ðȳ grǣdigra** 'the older he becomes, the greedier (he is)'.

Specific noun forms only rarely occur, being normally indistinguishable from the dative, but the group of nouns which form their dative with a change of stem vowel (e.g. ðæm fēt) in the instrumental still add the -e and do not mutate the stem vowel (e.g. ðȳ fōte).

17.4 A note on OE personal names is in order. Generally, OE names for the higher ranks of society (who are the people about whom we read most) are composed of two elements (dithematics), e.g. **æðele + stān** 'noble stone' (Athelstan) or **god + giefu** 'god gift' (Godiva, see below). The second element of male personal names will always be a masculine noun, and for female names a feminine noun (and likewise neuter nouns never form the second element of a personal name!). Alliteration seems to have been a desired feature particularly for royal families, with many successive generations of males and females sharing an initial (for OE poetic purposes, all vowels are considered to alliterate together).

Descriptive epithets are sometimes recorded, **Eadweard se langa** 'Edward the tall', **Eadric Strēona** 'Edric the acquisitive'.

Many personal names are recorded which are not of this type, however; they take the form of weak nouns (see 11.3) such as **Dudda, Sledda, Witta, Gōda** (masc.), **Golde, Tate, Lēofe** (fem.). Some of these may be straightforward adjectives (**gōda** 'the good one') perhaps modelled on the use of adjective nicknames (e.g. **se langa**) with the actual given name dropped, while others appear to be contractions of dithematics (**Fobba** from **Folcbeorht, Totta** from **Torhthelm**).

Some of the oldest names in the king-lists are unrepresentative of later practice: **Wōden**, for example, is the name of a heathen god (divine ancestor) and **Cerdic** appears to be a form of the Welsh name 'Caradoc'. After the Danish wars, certain types of Scandinavian personal name became common: **Gadd, Đorkel, Harold.**

Titles and ranks follow the name of the person designated, e.g. **Aidan biscop, Ēadgār cyning** (Bishop Aidan, King Edgar) although when used as nouns (rather than titles) they may precede the name: **...ond se cyning Ælfred fērde him mid** '...and the king, Alfred, travelled with them'. It is common for the title of a person with power over a given area or people to be so described: **Penda, Miercena cyning** 'Penda, king of the Mercians' (or 'King Penda of the Mercians', either translation is possible). When the grammar requires inflexion of the personal name, the title agrees with it: **Pendan cyninges** (gen.), **Stīgande biscope** (dat.).

Question: Is "Godiva" a genuine Anglo-Saxon name? Evidently not, since the legendary *Lady Godiva* was unquestionably female yet the ending -**a** forms masculine personal names. What has happened is that the lady's personal name, perhaps **Godgiefu** 'God-gift', has been recorded in a mediaeval Latin work where feminine names commonly do end in -**a**, in a more-or-less phonetic spelling of its late pronunciation "God-yi-voo". The converse change also takes place – the exalted male name **Offa** is recorded in the form 'Uffo', because in Latin the closest characteristic masculine ending is -**o**.

121

17.5 Some common adverbs of motion are formed from those of location in OE. The basic series is summarized thus:

	location at	motion away	motion towards
this place	**hēr** 'here'	**hēonan** 'hence'	**hider** 'hither'
that place	**ðǣr**	**ðonan**	**ðider**
which place?	**hwǣr**	**hwonan**	**hwider**

Others which behave similarly include:

far	**feorr**	**feorran**	**feorr**
near	**nēah**	**nēan**	**nēar**
after	**æfter**	**æftan**	-
behind	**hindan**	**hindan**	**hinder**
in front	**fore**	**foran**	**forþ**
inside	**inne/innan**	**innan**	**inn**
outside	**ūte**	**ūtan**	**ūt**
above	**uppe**	**uppan**	**upp**
above	**ufan**	**ufan**	-
below	**neoðan**	**neoþan**	**niðer**
north	**norð**	**norðan**	**norð**

(and so for **ēast, west, sūð**).

Exercises for Parts 17 and 18 are not given. By now you should be able to read moderately difficult pieces of Old English with the aid of some fairly comprehensive notes. Texts of this kind form Part III towards the end of this book.

OLD ENGLISH COURSE – SECTION 18

18.1 Conjunctions

18.2 Word formation – composition

18.3 Word formation – affixation

18.4 Word formation – derivation

18.1 Conjunctions are words which link together ideas, be they separate words or whole sentences. They are among the commonest words in use and many have already been given throughout the course. The following is a brief list of some of the most frequently met ones:

and, ond	and	**oððe ... oððe**	either ... or
ac	but, though	**ne ... ne**	neither ... nor
ðēah	(al)though	**ge ... ge**	both ... and
hūru	however	**forþȳ**	therefore, thus
nōþȳlǣs	nonetheless	**ēac**	also, in addition
furþum	moreover, even		

Whole phrases can often serve as conjunctions, for example **forþǣm þe** discussed above (17.1). Similar phrases were made with other prepositions, such as **wið ðǣm ðe** 'on condition that' or **æfter þǣm þe** 'after the time when'.

18.2 Word-formation is a vast subject for any language, but in OE there are recognizable patterns which the student will soon come to know. They fall into three main types which can be characterized by the terms *composition*, *affixation* and *derivation*.

Taking these in order, composition is the joining together of existing words to make a new <u>single word</u> such as NE 'ferryboat', 'wavelength', 'ice-cool'. OE examples are **fēðe** 'walking, gait' + **cempa** 'warrior' = **fēþecempa** 'footsoldier, infantryman' or **hyse** 'young man, youth' + **cild** 'child' = **hysecild** 'male child'. In such cases, it has to be borne in mind that **fēþecempa** is still a kind of **cempa**, and has the same gender and endings as **cempa** would normally have (**fēþecempan**, acc.sing., etc.).

Words formed in this way are called *compounds* and are very common in OE for expressing new or complex ideas, for example:

ǣfen 'evening'	+	**tīd** 'time'	**ǣfentīd** 'eventide'
ælmes 'alms'	+	**giefu** 'gift'	**ælmesgiefu** 'almsgiving'
brēost 'breast'	+	**cearu** 'worry'	**brēostcearu** 'sorrow at heart'
brim 'sea'	+	**fugel** 'bird'	**brimfugel** 'seabird'
leorning 'learning'	+	**cniht** 'boy'	**leorningcniht** 'student, disciple'

and the compounds can be adjectives as well as nouns:

brim 'sea'   +   **ceald** 'cold'   **brimceald** 'cold as the sea'
hrōf 'roof'   +   **fæst** 'firm'   **hrōffæst** 'firmly-roofed'

Compounds are not limited to two elements:

> **riht** 'direct' + **fæderen** 'paternal' + **cynn** 'kindred'
> = **rihtfæderencynn** 'direct paternal ancestry'.

Sometimes, a noun can be the second element of an adjectival compound:

hrēoh 'fierce'   +   **mōd** 'mind'   **hrēohmōd** 'cruel in thought'

Compounds are particularly popular in poetry, and may have a riddling quality whereby the referent is not specified by name:

hild 'battle'   +   **gicel** 'icicle'   **hildegicel** 'sword'

(i.e. the long, slender, pointed thing that glitters in battle)
This practice is similar to the Norse poetic puzzles called *kennings*.

The type of personal name (see 17.4) formed from two elements is in effect a compound, though to what extent OE speakers were conscious of the overall meaning in their name-giving is debatable. A name such as **Sigeberht** 'bright in victory' looks illustrious enough to have been deliberately chosen for a prince who was expected to lead his people to martial glory; but what about 'Alfred' (**Ælf** + **rǣd**) i.e. 'elf-counsel'? Could this name have been chosen for a child who was not expected to rule, and who showed intellectual leanings towards such arcane and 'elvish' matters as religion, history, physical and political geography?

18.3 Another type of word-formation is affixation, which is in effect a special type of composition in which one of the elements is not a separate word in its own right. NE examples include 'walking', 'brightness', 'kingdom' where 'walk', 'bright' and 'king' are "proper words" but '-ing', '-ness' and '-dom' are not. OE was fond of this device also.

The elements which are attached to full words are called *affixes*, those which go before the word (e.g. un-) being *prefixes* and those which come after it (e.g. -ed) *suffixes*. A full listing of all the affixes of OE with their meanings would fill a small book, but I list below many of the commoner ones, bearing in mind that those prefixes which are added to verbs will also feature in the derived nouns and adjectives.

-a   with verbs, makes masculine nouns e.g. **swica** 'traitor' **wita** 'wise man' **boda** 'herald'

ā-   with verbs **where it acts as an 'intensifier', for example hēawan 'cut'** **āhēawan** 'cut off, lop'

and-   can be added to verbs with meaning 'against' e.g. **cweðan** 'speak' **andcweðan** 'contradict'

æfter- with verbs imparts the sense 'after, behind' e.g. **cweðan** 'speak' **æftercweðan** 'repeat'

æt- with verbs to give the sense 'away' e.g. **lǣdan** 'lead' **ætlǣdan** 'lead away'

be- (1) with verbs to alter the meaning in one of three main ways:

(i) to give the sense 'round' e.g. **būgan** 'bend' **bebūgan** 'bend round'

(ii) to give a sense of deprivation e.g. **dǣlan** 'share' **bedǣlan** 'deprive' – note also **behēafdian** 'decapitate' NE '*be*head'

(iii) to make an intransitive verb transitive e.g. **sierwan** 'plot' **besierwan** 'ensnare, deceive' – note NE *be*moan, *be*straddle, etc.

(2) can be added to various adverbs and prepositions, e.g. **beforan** 'before', **behindan** 'behind', **betwēonum** 'between'.

-cund can be used to form adjectives specifying the kind or nature of the thing decribed, e.g. **godcund** 'godly, sacred' **gesīþcund** 'of the rank of retainer'

-dōm ends masculine abstract nouns e.g. **cynedōm** 'kingdom'

-end makes masculine nouns from verbs, e.g. **dēmend** 'judge', **hǣlend** 'saviour'

-ere makes masculine agent nouns from verbs, e.g. **swingan** 'flog' **swingere** 'scourge'

-estre makes feminine agent nouns e.g. **hlēapestre** 'dancer'

for- (1) with verbs can modify the sense in a bad or negative way e.g. **dēman** 'judge' **fordēman** 'condemn', **drūgian** 'dry' **fordrūgian** 'wither', **līðan** 'sail, go by sea' **forlīðan** 'be shipwrecked'.

(2) with adverbs gives the sense 'too much' e.g. **foroft** 'too often', **formonig** 'too many'

forð- with verbs gives the sense 'forwards' e.g. **cuman** 'come' **forþcuman** 'proceed'

-ful forms adjectives from nouns e.g. **forhtful** 'fearful', **egesful** 'terrible'

ge- surely the single commonest prefix in OE with many meanings. With verbs it modifies the meaning to include the result of the action e.g. **āscian** 'ask' **geāscian** 'find out' (i.e. achieve the result of asking); it can also make intransitive verbs transitive e.g. **winnan** 'fight' **gewinnan** 'win, gain'. This sense of achieving result or completion of the verb's action explains the use of **ge-** with past participles e.g. **geslægen** 'slain' (the action of slaying having been completed). Likewise with nouns such as **gelimp** 'event' (that which has happened' <**gelimpan** 'happen'). Yet the difference in meaning between verbs with and without **ge-** is not always evident e.g. **hātan** 'call' **gehātan** 'call', although there may once have been a collective sense to the prefixed forms, and this is common with the nouns e.g. **brōðor** 'brother' **gebrōðor** 'one of the brethren' **scōh** 'shoe' **gescȳ** 'pair of shoes'. This generalizing sense probably derives from the use of the conjunctions **ge...ge** 'both...and' where more than one idea is incorporated into the phrase.

-hād   makes abstract masculine nouns e.g. **mægþhād** 'maidenhood, virginity'

-ig   makes adjectives from (mainly) nouns e.g. **īsig** 'icy' **grǣdig** 'greedy'

-ing   makes masculine nouns e.g. **hōr** 'whoring' **hōring** 'fornicator'

-isc   makes adjectives, usually with mutation of the base word's vowel, e.g. **mann** 'man' **mennisc** 'human'

-lēas   makes adjectives from nouns signifying 'without', e.g. **wītelēas** 'without punishment' **witlēas** 'witless, foolish'

-lic   forms adjectives e.g. **cynelic** 'kingly' **drȳlic** 'magical'

mis-   can be added to verbs to give the sense 'wrongly' e.g. **mislimpan** 'go wrong' (note NE *mis*hap, *mis*deed)

-nes   (also **-nys**, **-nis**) makes abstract feminine nouns e.g. **beorhtnes** 'brightness' **þrīnes** 'trinity'

-o   alternative form of **-u** e.g. **hǣlo** 'health'

ofer-   can be added to verbs to mean (1) 'above, across' e.g. **oferfaran** 'travel over, cross' or (2) 'greater' e.g. **ofercuman** 'overcome', **oferflītan** 'outdo', **oferflōwan** 'overflow'.

-ol   (also **-ul**) forms adjectives e.g. **swicol** 'deceitful' **sprecul** 'talkative'

on-   indicates the beginning of an action with verbs e.g. **ongietan** 'realize' **onginnan** 'begin' (note NE *on*set); it can also make intransitive verbs transitive e.g. **onfeohtan** 'assail, attack'

-oð   forms masculine abstract nouns e.g. **huntoþ** 'hunting' **fiscoþ** 'fishing'

-scipe   forms masculine abstract nouns e.g. **gefērscipe** 'fellowship'

tō-   (1) can give the sense 'away, apart' with some verbs e.g. **tōbrecan** 'break apart' while with verbs of motion it conveys a sense of completion e.g. **tōcuman** 'come to, arrive'

(2) can be added to prepositions e.g. **tōforan** 'in front of'

-þo   forms feminine abstract nouns from adjectives, often with mutation of the vowel of the original word e.g. **strang** 'strong' **strengþo** 'strength'

-u   forms feminine abstract nouns from adjectives, with mutation of the vowel, e.g. **strengu** 'strength' **hǣlu** 'health'

un-   the commonest prefix for negation with adjectives e.g. **unearg** 'not cowardly, bold' **unscyldig** 'not guilty, innocent' and some verbs e.g. **untrumian** 'become infirm, weaken' and their derived nouns e.g. **untrumnes** 'infirmity'. When applied directly to nouns it usually modifies the meaning in a bad way e.g. **rǣd** '**advice**' **unrǣd** '**poor advice**' **þēaw** '**custom**' **unþēaw** 'evil way, bad habit' **weder** 'weather' **unweder** 'bad weather, storm'.

-ung   used to form feminine abstract nouns from verbs ending in **-ian** e.g. **eardian** 'dwell' **eardung** 'dwelling, habitation'

⌘   A Note on Gender

We have seen that "natural" gender can override strict grammatical agreement in that e.g. **þæt wīf** can have as its pronoun the feminine **sēo** rather than **hit**, despite its neuter gender.

We have also seen the use of the prefix **ge-** to form collective nouns (i.e. for groups of things, such as **gescȳ** 'pair of shoes', **gebrōðor** 'generation of brothers') which are neuter in gender.

In the latter case, it is common to find expressions such as **twēgen gebrōðor**, where the form of the word 'two' is masculine in gender, because each of the brothers is individually male.

What about mixed groups? What about sets made up of males and females? In the bible story of Adam and Eve, the prototype mixed-gender pair, having just become aware of their nakedness, Eve remarks **wit nū hēr baru standaþ** (we-two now stand here bare) and the form **baru** is neither masculine nor feminine but neuter! Probably due to its use with collective nouns and groups of things, the rule is that where genders are mixed the neuter is used.

18.4 OE features networks of often very closely related sets of words which seem to have some common thread of meaning; as an example, take the following nouns, adjectives and verbs connected with 'travelling':

fōr	*f.*	'journey'
færeld	*n.*	'way, passage'
fær	*n.*	'way, expedition'
faru	*f.*	'course, procession'
faroþ	*m.*	'shore, sea, stream'
gefara	*m.*	'travelling companion'
gefēre		'fit to travel'
faran		'to travel, set off'
fēran		'to go, travel'
geferian		'carry, convey, bring'

All the words are based on forms of **faran**: those with -a- in the root are based on the verb's present tense, those with -æ- are 'mutated' forms (see 7.5, a>æ); **fōr** is based on the preterite of the verb (see 14.1) and those with -ē- on the mutated form of this (ō>ē). Such patterning is not unique to this group however:

ferian 'convey'	**faru** 'course'	**faroþ** 'stream'
werian 'defend'	**waru** 'shelter, care'	**werod** 'bodyguard, defensive force'
derian 'harm'	**daru** 'injury, hurt'	**daroþ** 'dart, javelin'
dēman 'judge'	**dōm** 'judgement'	
fēdan 'feed'	**fōda** 'food'	

wēdan 'rage' **wōd** 'mad, angry'
brēdan 'breed' **brōd** 'brood, foetus'
blēdan 'bleed' **blōd** 'blood'

beorgan 'protect, defend' **gebeorg** 'defence' **burg** 'stronghold'
(ge)byrga (1) 'protector' (2) 'surety'

These words are all formed by derivation from the basic verbal forms. Usually the vowel correspondences noted in 7.5 are present, often acting on different vowels according to the pattern displayed in the tense system. It is quite an interesting exercise in detective skills working out what the basis is from which a set of related OE words have been derived.

See if you can work out the inter-relationships in the group below, connected with senses of 'carrying':

beran 'bear, carry, wear' **gārberend** 'spear-carrier, warrior'
byrd 'burden, responsibility' **byrd** 'birth'
byrde 'of noble birth' **gebyrde** 'innate, inborn'
gebyrdo 'parentage, family' **gebyrd** 'fate'
gebǣran 'behave, bear oneself' **bǣr** 'bier'
byrele 'cup-bearer' **bearn** 'child'
byre 'son, child' boy' **byre** 'opportunity'
bora 'bearer' **bearm** 'lap, bosom'

AFTERWORD

Having stayed with the course this far, you must have a keen interest in learning the Old English language. Where do you go from here?

Beginners' books on Old English topics are not very easy to come by – hence the need for this very course, to make the often unhelpful technical works that little bit more accessible! There are however a number of options open.

Many students go on to tackle particular literary works straightaway, such as *Ælfric's Homilies*, or the *Anglo-Saxon Chronicle*, or *Beowulf*, because it was the desire to read these works that impelled them to learn the language in the first place. It is often helpful to have a parallel text version, in which the OE is set out on one page and the NE facing it; this helps with practice in reading the texts in the original and often builds confidence. It can be a two-edged sword, though: the drawback is that the incautious or lazy among us come to rely on the NE translation, and to regard the OE as over-difficult and superfluous. I suggest that if you have worked through the lessons in this course thoroughly, you are almost certainly in a position to dispense with such aids, even if you have misgivings about reading OE straight off the page and feel you need the psychological safety-net a translation provides. But translations can be useful in quickly telling you what the original is about, in broad terms, and so can be used to help you select reading matter that is going to interest you.

Obviously, not all OE texts are in West Saxon, and a certain amount of mental adjustment may be necessary when tackling non-standard (very early, very late, poetic or dialectal) language. (*Further Steps in Old English* will introduce many of these in a fairly painless manner.) But it is important to remember that reading the *Chronicle* in translation, however good the translation may be, is reading a NE text – not the OE original. What then is the point of learning the original language, if you are going to rely on translations? Besides which, there is a great sense of achievement, even a thrill, in following the thread and capturing the sense of a narrative or poem written by an Englishman *in his own tongue* some thirty or more generations ago!

To introduce some genuine OE prose in an accessible format I have selected a handful of texts for further reading (in lieu of Exercises to sections 17 and 18), and have broken them down into phrases, carefully explaining the form and function of each as I work through them.

The purpose of these texts and their accompanying notes is to breed familiarity with the process of *parsing*, analysing the words for their form and applying this knowledge to determine their individual functions and overall relationships within the phrase, and the sentence. The practised reader carries out this process automatically and almost without thinking. Until one reaches a fair level of confidence with the prose, it is unwise to attempt verse texts, which obey a different set of rules about word order and composition!

There are today many useful works on OE grammar, and even on particular aspects such as word-order, word formation and the prehistory and development of Old English, which can be consulted to gain insight into the mechanics of the language. There are also numerous books and articles dealing with individual texts, both prose and verse, which can lead to a deeper understanding of the genius of the language than I can present in this course. I urge you to continue reading Old English, and to purchase or borrow books on specific texts which interest you: these often contain valuable commentaries on the date and dialect of composition, on the spelling and writing conventions, on their literary and cultural background, as well as the text itself and a glossary. Using them can be a real joy, and the less expensive paperback ones can be bought for less than the price of a round of drinks – they soon build into a small collection, and will form the backbone of an Old English library.

Do not neglect second-hand bookshops: in many ways, the golden age of book production on Anglo-Saxon topics was the tail end of the last and first three decades of the present century. Many works published then are very valuable for their high production standards and scrupulous scholarship. Although scholarly opinion may have moved on in respect of the details of interpretation, the edited texts retain their value to the would-be reader. Some (in fact, many) of the Anglo-Saxon texts are unlikely to be re-edited for publication in the foreseeable future, so the only opportunity you are likely to have to acquire them is via the used book market. They are also often very cheap – sturdy second-hand hardbacks usually cost less than new paperbacks.

Specialist publishers – such as *Anglo-Saxon Books* – exist to fill the gaps in the mass market, and need as much support as we can give them in order that they continue to bring out new editions of Old English texts, or re-issue ones long out of print. Nevertheless, when demand is small and reproduction both time-consuming and expensive, we have to recognize that there are a great many texts which will probably never be (re-)published.

Be sure to buy the books you are likely to want to keep – there is nothing more frustrating than waiting months to take a book out on inter-library loan and having to return it before you have finished with it. With a few exceptions, local and even major civic libraries tend not to have many Old English books on their shelves (maybe a *Beowulf* in translation or a *Sweet's Reader*) but it pays to look through the catalogue as the older libraries often have volumes in the vaults which are seldom asked for, because nobody knows they are available. The decimal shelf mark for OE texts and topics is usually 829, although sometimes they are lumped in with English language studies under the low 400s.

One immediate application for the language is to look up the meanings of local place-names – not just towns and villages, but rivers, streams and even fields may have a recorded form from Anglo-Saxon times, from a charter, the Chronicle or the Domesday survey. Even if you live in a part of the country with entirely non-English names, holidays, visits and even shopping trips can be brightened up with background knowledge of the linguistic character of the area.

Above all, find the topics that interest you and keep reading!

Part Two

OE Grammar

GLOSSARY OF GRAMMATICAL TERMS USED IN THIS BOOK

term	abbreviation	meaning
Abstract noun		Kind of <u>noun</u> which refers to an idea (e.g. redness, nationality, strength) rather than anything concrete or tangible.
Accusative	acc	<u>Case</u> associated with the direct <u>object</u>, as well as being used with certain <u>prepositions</u>
Adjective	adj	A word which describes or qualifies a <u>noun</u> (e.g. good, fast, Welsh)
Adverb	adv	A word which describes the manner in which an action is performed (e.g. well, quickly, soon, angrily) often formed from an <u>adjective</u> (good, quick, angry)
Agent noun		Kind of <u>noun</u> signifying the 'doer' of an action, e.g. the <u>verbs</u> 'find, keep, lose, weep' have agent nouns 'finder, keeper, loser, weeper'.
Case		Grammatical term denoting the way in which a word shows its function in the sentence, chiefly by the addition of endings; those used in OE are <u>nominative</u>, <u>accusative</u>, <u>genitive</u>, <u>dative</u>, <u>instrumental</u>, <u>vocative</u>.
Conjunction	conj.	Word used to join statements or ideas together (e.g. and, but, also, either).
Comparative	comp.	<u>Adjective</u> used to express a greater degree of the quality, (e.g. 'better', 'faster'.)
Dative	dat.	<u>Case</u> associated with the <u>indirect object</u> of the <u>verb</u> and with certain <u>prepositions</u>
Demonstrative	dem.	The words 'the', 'that' and 'this'.
Ending		Additional sounds/letters added to a word to show its role in the sentence, e.g. <u>case</u>, <u>gender</u>, <u>tense</u>.
Feminine	fem., f.	Grammatical <u>gender</u> associated with (but not confined to) females and abstract ideas.

133

term	abbreviation	meaning
Gender		The class to which a <u>noun</u> belongs (<u>masculine</u>, <u>feminine</u> or <u>neuter</u>), which affects its <u>endings</u> and those of <u>adjectives</u> and <u>demonstratives</u> used with it.
Genitive	gen.	<u>Case</u> denoting mainly possession, association and used with certain <u>prepositions</u>.
Imperative	imp.	Form of the <u>verb</u> associated with commands, e.g. go!, beware!, look out!
Impersonal verb	impers.	Type of verb requiring no <u>subject</u>.
Indicative	ind.	Form of the <u>verb</u> associated with statements (rather than wishes or commands).
Indirect Object	ind.obj.	Grammatical term for the person or thing indirectly affected by the action of the sentence, usually marked in NE by 'to' e.g. 'the man gave flowers to the woman', where the man is the giver (<u>subject</u>) and the flowers are the thing given (<u>object</u>), and the indirect object is the woman.
Infinitive	inf.	Unfinished form of the <u>verb</u>, not indicating any <u>person</u> or <u>tense</u> (e.g. 'to come', 'to hear').
Inflexion		System of variable <u>endings</u> added to words to show case, gender, tense, etc.
Interjection	interj.	A word or phrase such as 'yes', 'no', 'well!', 'lo and behold!', often with no real grammatical meaning but used in speech particularly as an exclamation.
Intransitive	intr	Type of <u>verb</u> where the action involves only one person or thing (the <u>subject</u>).
Masculine	masc., m.	Grammatical <u>gender</u> associated with (but not confined to) males.
Negative	neg	A word such as no, not, none.
Neuter	neut., n.	Grammatical <u>gender</u> associated with (but not confined to) inanimate objects and groups of things.
Nominative	nom.	<u>Case</u> associated with the <u>subject</u> also used with <u>comparatives</u> etc.
Noun		The name of an object (e.g. table), idea (e.g. indifference), person or place. Nouns in the last two groups in modern English often begin with a capital letter if they are specific (e.g. Alfred, London, Britain).

134

term	*abbreviation*	*meaning*
Object	obj.	The grammatical term for the person or thing to whom the <u>verb</u> is done, the affected party; it is usually in the <u>accusative</u> case.
Parts of Speech		The grammatical categories into which all words fall, e.g. noun, adjective, adverb, verb, interjection; every word must (in theory) belong to at least one of these categories.
Past Participle	past part.	That part of the <u>verb</u> used with 'have' or 'be' to form a separate past tense (e.g. 'I have done it' where 'done' is the past participle of the verb 'do').
Personal Pronoun	pers. pron.	A word standing in place of a <u>noun</u> (e.g. I, he, them) see also <u>pronoun</u>..
Plural	pl.	Number where more than one is indicated.
Possessive	poss.	A word showing possession, either an <u>adjective</u> (my, your) or a <u>pronoun</u> (mine, yours) associated with the <u>genitive</u>.
Prefix	pref.	An element (which does not usually occur as a separate word) which may be added to the beginning of a word to modify its meaning (e.g. pre- 'before' in <u>prefix</u>, un- 'not' in *unnecessary*).
Present Participle	pres.part	That part of the <u>verb</u> which is used with 'be' to form a separate way of expressing tense (e.g. 'I am going, I was going, I have been going' where 'going' is the present participle of the verb 'go').
Preposition	prep.	A word denoting a relationship between two <u>nouns,</u> e.g. spatial (above, behind, etc.), temporal (afterwards, until), directional (up, away), etc.
Preterite	pret.	Grammatical name for the past tense of the <u>verb</u>.
Preterite-Present	pret.pres.	Type of <u>verb</u> which has a present meaning but behaves as if it were a past tense form (e.g. can, must, etc.)
Pronoun	pron.	A word which stands in place of a <u>noun,</u> which may be either personal (e.g. I, us, he) or general (e.g. everyone, each).
Reflexive Pronoun	refl.pron.	A <u>pronoun</u> which refers the <u>object</u> of its sentence back to its <u>subject</u>, e.g. myself, themselves
Relative Pronoun	rel.pron.	Word which links subject or object in two separate statements, e.g. who, which, that.

term	abbreviation	meaning
Singular	sing.	Number where only one is indicated
Strong Verb	s.v.	Type of verb which changes its internal vowel to show the past tense and with a <u>past participle</u> ending -en (e.g. hide, hid, hidden).
Subject	subj.	The grammatical term for the performer of an action (the <u>verb</u>) usually in the <u>nominative</u> case.
Subjunctive	subj.	Form of the <u>verb</u> associated with wishes and uncertainties.
Suffix	suff.	An element (which does not usually occur as a separate word) which may be put at the end of a word to modify it and often converts it from one <u>part of speech</u> to another e.g. 'speech' (<u>noun</u>) 'speechless' (<u>adjective</u>), 'full' (adjective) fullness (noun) where -less, -ness are suffixes.
Superlative	superl.	<u>Adjective</u> used to express the greatest degree of the quality, e.g. 'best', 'fastest'.
Tense		<u>Ending</u> added to a <u>verb</u> to show the time in which it takes (present) or took (past) place.
Transitive	trans.	Type of <u>verb</u> involving both a <u>subject</u> and an <u>object</u>.
Verb	v.	Word denoting the action or state in a sentence (e.g. go, come, say, feel, hesitate).
Weak Verb	w.v.	Type of verb forming its past tense by adding an ending containing a 'dental' consonant [-t, -d] e.g. thanked, sent.
	*	Mark used to show words which do not occur, but which are believed to have been in use before written records began.

Summary Grammar

Here are some brief but detailed notes on OE grammar; they are aimed principally at the student who wishes to take the study of the language further and needs to have some idea of the traditional terminology used in the older reference books.

The Pronunciation of Old English

It is obvious that we cannot have direct, first-hand knowledge of the pronunciation of a language which no-one speaks any more. What we can do, however, is to make some deductions based on four sources of information:

1. the pre-history of the language, of which a surprisingly great deal is recoverable by comparison with other languages more or less closely related to OE (these include Old Saxon, Old High German, Old Norse and more distantly Gothic and the North West Germanic language recorded in the earliest runic inscriptions).

2. the subsequent history of the language, which can show the range of sounds which were likely to be distinguished in previous periods, something of their qualities and the kinds of changes they underwent.

3. OE words recorded in other languages.

4. foreign words recorded in OE texts in OE spelling rather than the original.

While there is not room here for a discussion of this vast topic (aspects of which are still hotly debated in learned circles) suffice it to say that the brief guide that follows is an attempt at a concise and middle-of-the-road description of an imagined 'typical' OE speech taking no account of regional accents or changes through time.

Orthography. The letters regularly used in printed and edited texts of OE are as follows:

a æ b c d ð e f g h i l m n o p r s t þ u w x y

and the following are rarely used:

k z

Notes on the use of the now obsolete letters æ, ð, þ will be found below. Printed texts conventionally mark long vowels and the first element of long diphthongs with a macron (‾); often the symbol 7 is used for 'and', based on a similar symbol (ꝛ) so used in OE manuscripts. Some older editions of OE texts reproduce the Anglo-Saxon 'w' as p and the 'g' as ʒ in imitation of the manuscript lettering - see below.

Punctuation in original texts was variable, some early examples showing virtually none at all, while later ones developed a system of points (· ⁒ : ? ;) similar to that in use today. Editors generally follow their own instincts as to the use of the full stop (marking the end of a sentence) versus the semi-colon (marking the end of a clause within a larger sense-unit) and the punctuation of printed editions varies accordingly. There are grounds for believing that the rigidity of the modern system would be totally alien to the Anglo-Saxon reader, especially where verse is concerned, and that the flexible punctuation used by scribes was helpful in indicating the greater range of interpretations possible.

Anglo-Saxon scribes do not seem to have marked long vowels with a macron, but some certainly used an acute accent (´) to mark the vowels of some words - perhaps an indication of metrical stress rather than length. Following late Roman practice, a macron was often used over a final **-u** to denote a missing 'm' e.g. the ending -um (**stanū** = **stanum**) or other nasal such as **-ne**, while a 'barred thorn' þ̄ was an abbreviation for *þæt*, occasionally *þa*.

Stress When pronouncing an OE word, the stress (i.e. the peak of loudness) is usually on the first syllable, e.g. *Alfred, Edgar, London* all have the same stress now as in OE; consider also how *Paris* differs in English and French mouths: the French give each syllable equal weight (pa-ri) whereas English speakers have re-modelled it on their own normal pattern (**par**-is).

The main exception to this rule of initial stress is in the matter of a few prefixes, such as the ubiquitous **ge-**, which never bear the stress so that *gewitt* 'knowledge, understanding, wit' is ye-**wit**.

Consonants Generally, the consonants of OE are pronounced much as in NE and the following can be given their normal NE pronunciation:-

$$b \quad d \quad l \quad m \quad n \quad p \quad r \quad t \quad w$$

and the following may also have their NE values:-

$$k \quad x \quad z$$

(The letters *j, q, v* were not used in OE – *j* is merely a variant of *i* and *v* of *u*; the sound of *q* was spelt *cw* e.g. *cwic* 'quick, alive' *cweorn* 'quern' *cwēn* 'queen'. But see above for printed versions of manuscript letterforms.)

Certain consonants behave differently according to their position and the sounds next to them in the word. The terms 'initial' (at the beginning of a word) and 'final' (at its end) describe positions at the "edges" of a word, while 'medial' means 'in the middle'. The concept of 'voice' plays an important part in determining pronunciation, in as much as some consonants may represent both voiced and voiceless sounds. A 'voiced' sound is one pronounced while the breath passes over and reverberates on the vocal chords, while a 'voiceless' sound lacks that feature. If this sounds complicated, practise the contrast by pronouncing the words 'ether' (with a voiceless 'th') and 'either' (with a voiced equivalent). There are other pairs of words distinguished by voicing, e.g. sip:zip; fan:van; thigh:thy (voiceless example first in each case).

f   initially and finally is voiceless (like our 'f'): *feoh* 'fee', *līf* 'life'; medially, it is usually voiced ('v'): *seofon* 'seven' *hæfde* 'had', except where it comes next to a voiceless consonant: *æfter* 'after'. Doubled (*ff*) it always has the voiceless sound: *offrian* 'offer'.

s   parallel to the above, is initially and finally voiceless('s'): *seofon* 'seven', *læs* 'less' medially voiced ('z'): *dysig* 'dozy, foolish' *ræsde* 'razed, attacked' though again voiceless when next to a voiceless consonant: *hæsp* 'hasp'. Doubled (*ss*) it is voiceless: *press* '(clothes) press'. A further notable feature is the combination *sc* which usually has the sound we spell 'sh' e.g. *scip* 'ship', *æsc* 'ash', *fiscere* 'fisher(man)'; there are a few cases where the pronunciation 'sk' applies, e.g. *ascian* 'ask'.

þ/ð   are no longer used in English (though they were passed into Icelandic where they remain in use); they are both used to write the sounds we express with 'th'. Initially and finally they are voiceless (as in 'thin'): *þorn* 'thorn', *bæþ* 'bath', medially voiced (as in 'thine'): *lāðan* 'loathe', *lāþde* 'loathed' except when next to a voiceless consonant: *gicða* 'hiccup'. Again, doubled, they are voiceless: *smiþþe* 'smithy'. (The letter Þ, þ is called 'thorn' and Ð, ð 'barred 'd'' or 'eth'. They are generally interchangeable – and are so used throughout this course – although some writers seem to have preferred one form over the other.)

h   initially is much as we use it: *heorte* 'heart', *habban* 'have'. Medially and finally, and when doubled, its pronunciation resembles the 'ch' in Scottish 'loch': *bohte* 'bought', *scōh* 'shoe', *hlehhan* 'laugh'; this medial 'h' often survives as the silent 'gh' of NE, e.g. *niht* 'night', *flyht* 'flight', *āhte* 'ought', etc.. Initially, before consonants, *h* is used to indicate a 'softer', breathier pronunciation:
– *hn*- a soft breathing before the 'n': *hnutu* 'nut'
– *hr*- a soft breathing before the 'r': *hring* 'ring'
– *hl*- a voiceless 'l' like Welsh 'll': *hlāf* 'loaf'
– *hw*- a voiceless 'w' like Scots 'wh': *hwǣr* 'where?'

g   has at least three different values:
– initially before the vowels *o, a, u, æ* and the consonants *r, l, n* it has the same value as in NE: *gold* 'gold', *gatu* 'gates', *guma* 'man', *gædrian* 'gather', *grētan* 'greet', *glæs* 'glass', *gnæt* 'gnat'.
– medially and finally it has a pronunciation similar to the voiced equivalent of 'ch' of Scottish 'loch': *sagu* 'saying', *fāg* 'hostile'; in its final position it is often softened to its voiceless variant, so that alternative spellings occur: *fāg/fāh* 'hostile', *stāg/stāh* 'climbed'.

– in the combinations *ge-, gi-, -ig* it is pronounced closer to a NE 'y': *gēar* 'year', *gield* 'yield', *blōdig* 'bloody'. (The spelling *gy-* is often a late variant of *gie-* e.g. *gyfan* = *giefan* with this sound. Otherwise it has the normal 'g' of NE e.g. *gyldan* 'gild'.)

– *-ng* represents the two consonants in 'linger', not as in 'sing' or 'singe'; therefore the cluster *-ng* consists of two separate consonants and syllables containing it behave accordingly (in terms of 'heavy syllables' – see section 9.4)

c   somewhat similarly to *g* above, has several values:

– initially before the vowels *o, a, u, æ* and the consonants *r, l, n* it has the same value as NE 'k': *corn* 'corn, *calu* 'bald', *culfre* 'culver', *cætt* 'cat', *crāwa* 'crow, *clif* 'cliff', *cnēow* 'knee'.

– in the groups *ci-, ce-, -ic* it is pronounced much as in NE 'ch': *cinn* 'chin', *cēacbān* 'cheekbone', *cirice* 'church'; there are a few cases where the 'k' sound occurs: *āscian* 'ask', *cēne* 'keen, sharp, eager'.

– *cg* may represent the NE 'g' sound when it occurs medially: *frocge* 'frog'; it may also represent the sound we represent with 'j/dg': *brycg* 'bridge', *hrycg* 'ridge, back'.

Consonants spelt double are longer variants of the single: *þone* is never confused with *þonne* in OE spelling. There are some unfamiliar consonant clusters in OE, some of which have been examined above; generally, every letter is pronounced though *sc* and *cg* need special consideration:

cn	k + n	*cniht*	youth, knight
fn	f + n	*fnæst*	blast, wind
gn	g + n	*gnagan*	gnaw
hn	soft breathing + n (see above)	*hneaw*	mean, miserly
hr	soft breathing + r (see above)	*hraðor*	rather, sooner
hl	voiceless l (see above)	*hlinc*	rising ground
hw	voiceless w (see above)	*hwettan*	whet, sharpen
wl	w + l	*wlenco*	pride
wr	w + r	*writan*	write

Vowels The vowels of OE are the hardest to determine, and have changed the most since the OE period. They can be divided into 'pure' vowels and diphthongs, both of which have long and short forms. The following is a guide to the approximate pronunciations, bearing in mind that no two dialects have exactly the same arrangement of vowels even if their consonants are identical.

Pure Vowels

a	as in	'bud' (southern)	*ā*	as in	'bard'
æ		'bat'	*ǣ*		'bad'
e		'bed'	*ē*		'bade'
i		'bid'	*ī*		'bead'
o		'body'	*ō*		'board' (no 'r')
u		'bull'	*ū*		'booed'
y		Fr. 'su'	*ȳ*		Fr. 'sur'

The *short a* is a shorter form of the vowel in *cart*, which is closer to the southern pronunciation of *cut* or to the first 'a' of '*aha!*'. The two *y* sounds can be reproduced in English by pronouncing the corresponding *i* sound and rounding the lips at the same time.

-*ī*- is often spelt -*ig*- in later documents, reflecting the 'y' pronunciation of '*g*', e.g. *bigleofa* = *bīleofa* 'food'; -*i*- followed by another vowel tends to insert a 'y' sound, which can also be spelt with -*g*- e.g. *lufi(g)end* 'affectionate, loving'.

Diphthongs These are vowels which glide from one position to another without a break, so that there is only one peak of loudness. They are conventionally spelt with two vowel letters in OE orthography, although there is still debate as to what sounds are actually being represented: apparently, those with second element *a* are glides towards the back and bottom of the mouth, and those with *o* towards the top and front. For students' purposes, the following will serve as a starting point:

ea begins with the sound of *e* and glides towards the back of the mouth, giving a sound not unlike that in 'bared, Baird'; *ēa* is similar but beginning with the vowel *ē*.

eo begins with the sound of *e* and glides towards the front (perhaps with lip rounding?) to give a sound approximating to that in 'loud' (though higher in the mouth); likewise *ēo* begins from *ē*.

ie begins with the sound of *i* and glides back to give a sound roughly like that in 'beard'; *īe* likewise from *ī*.

Script

The script in which most OE records were written is known as the Insular Hand and is based on an English reworking of an Irish version of Roman script. The basic letter forms are as follows:

a æ b c d ð e f g h i l m n o p r s t þ u w x y

a æ b c d ð e f ʒ h i l m n o p ꞃ ꞅ c þ u p x ẏ

Capitals were much less frequently used than in NE - neither sentences nor proper names necessarily began with one. The common forms are set out below:

A Æ B C D Ð E F G H I L M N O P R S T Þ U W X Y

A Æ B C D Ð E F Ᵹ h I L M N O P R S T Þ U Ƿ X Y

Variants, such as Ꞇ for T, whereby the capital is merely a larger form of the lower case letter, are quite common. The ampersand **&** is written with the character ⁊ often represented with the arabic number **7** in non-specialist extracts from OE texts. Final **m** or **n** after a vowel could be indicated with a small hooked stroke above the letter: **um** would be written ū . The common word **þæt** could be abreviated to the symbol ꝥ. The whole history of English handwriting is a vast subject, but the letter forms reproduced above are quite consistent throughout the pre-Conquest period.
OE is also recorded in its own runic characters. While the runes are a fascinating topic in themselves, they are outside the scope of the present work.

Accidence

'Accidence' is the name given to the variable forms of a word, which is to say the (usually unchanging) stem and the various possible endings. Familiarity with the accidence of a language is the key to fluency in reading and speaking. (While I was teaching myself OE from textbooks, I made tables of the various grammatical forms similar to those reproduced below from which to revise and to test myself.) In order to simplify the presentation of this information, I use a common format for all verbs and another for nouns. This enables me to set out the 'grid' once and to display the relevant information in the same format thereafter. I have used 'traditional' grammatical terminology (such as Class numbers for the verbs, etc.) so that the student who continues to study OE with the aid of the classic textbooks will not be wholly unfamiliar with the conventions and nomenclature used there.

A. Verbs

Weak Verbs

The format is as follows:

Verbal Class and Infinitive	(NE meaning)
1st sing. pres. indic	1st sing. pret.indic
2nd sing. pres. indic	2nd sing. pret.indic
3rd sing. pres. indic	3rd sing. pret.indic
all pl. pres. indic	all pl. pret.indic

Verbal Class and Infinitive	(NE meaning)
sing.pres.subj.	sing.pret.subj.
pl.pres.subj.	pl.pret.subj.
present participle	imperative singular
past participle	imperative plural
(notes)	

Weak Class I(a) **Fremman**	'perform, carry out'
fremme	**fremede**
fremest	**fremedest**
fremeð	**fremede**
fremmað	**fremedon**
fremme	**fremede**
fremmen	**fremeden**
fremmende	**freme**
gefremed	**fremmað**

All Class I(a) verbs have a short vowel and a double consonant

Weak Class I(b) **Nerian**	'save'
nerie	**nerede**
nerest	**neredest**
nereð	**nerede**
neriað	**neredon**
nerie	**nerede**
nerien	**nereden**
neri(g)ende	**nere**
genered	**neriað**

Class I(b) verbs have a short vowel followed by **-rian**

Weak Class I(c) **Dēman**	'judge'
dēme	**dēmde**
dēmest	**dēmdest**
dēmð	**dēmde**
dēmað	**dēmdon**
dēme	**dēmde**
dēmen	**dēmden**
dēmende	**dēm**
gedēmed	**dēmað**

Class I(c) verbs have either a long vowel, or a short vowel and a consonant cluster.

<u>Weak Class II **Lufian**</u>   'love'

lufie	**lufode**
lufast	**lufodest**
lufað	**lufode**
lufiað	**lufodon**
lufie	**lufode**
lufien	**lufoden**
lufiende	**lufa**
gelufod	**lufiað**

All Class II verbs end in **-ian**

<u>Weak Class III **Habban**</u>   'have'

hæbbe	**hæfde**
hafast, hæfst	**hæfdest**
hafað, hæfð	**hæfde**
habbað	**hæfdon**
hæbbe	**hæfde**
hæbben	**hæfden**
hæbbende	**hafa**
gehæfd	**habbað**

Class III verbs comprise *habban, libban, secgan, hycgan*

Strong Verbs

All the many forms of a strong verb can be deduced from the so-called 'principal parts', which are the four forms which give sufficient information for all the others (for example, the various vowel qualities) to be established.

The principal parts in the order in which grammars give them, are:

> the infinitive,
> the 3rd.sing.pret.indic.,
> the pl.pret.indic. and
> the past participle.

<u>Strong Class 1</u>

Rīdan	'ride'
rīde	**rād**
rīdest (rītst)	**ride**
rīdeð (rītt)	**rād**
rīdað	**ridon**

144

Strong Class 1 (continued)

rīde	**ride**
rīden	**riden**
rīdende	**rīd**
geriden	**rīdað**

All strong verbs with stem vowel *-ī-*

The principal parts, which are all that will be given henceforth, are therefore:

rīdan 'ride' **rād** **ridon** **geriden**

Strong Class 1

1. stem vowel *-ī*	bīdan 'wait'	bād	bidon	gebiden
2. contracted type	ðēon 'thrive'	ðāh	ðigon	geðigen

Strong Class 2

1. stem vowel *-ēo-*	bēodan 'bid'	bēad	budon	geboden
2. stem vowel *-ū-* – (aorist present)	brūcan 'use'	brēac	brucon	gebrocen
3. contracted type	flēon 'flee'	flēah	flugon	geflogen

Strong Class 3

1. stem ending nasal + consonant	bindan 'bind'	band	bundon	gebunden
2. stem ending *-l* + consonant (not *h*)	helpan 'help'	healp	hulpon	geholpen
3. stem ending *-lh, -r* + consonant, *-h* + consonant	feohtan 'fight'	feaht	fuhton	gefohten
4. stem without *-m, -n, -r, -l*	bregdan 'draw'	brægd	brugdon	gebrogden
5. stem vowel *-u-* (aorist present)	murnan 'mourn'	mearn	murnon	gemornen

Strong Class 4

1. stem vowel *-e-*	beran 'bear'	bær	bǣron	geboren
2. 'fractured' stem vowel	scieran 'cut'	scear	scēaron	gescoren
3. plural vowel in singular	niman 'take'	nōm	nōmon	genumen

Strong Class 5

1. stem vowel -e-	metan 'measure'	mæt	mǣton	gemeten
2. 'fractured' stem vowel	giefan 'give'	geaf	gafon	gegiefen
3. plural vowel in singular	etan 'eat'	ǣt	ǣton	geeten
4. stem vowel -i- + doubled consonant	biddan 'pray'	bæd	bǣdon	gebeden
5. contracted type	sēon 'see'	sēah	sǣwon	gesewen
6. contracted type	gefēon 'rejoice'	gefeah	gefǣgon	-

Strong Class 6

1. stem vowel -a-	faran 'go'	fōr	fōron	gefaren
2. stem vowel + nasal	standan 'stand'	stōd	stōdon	gestanden
3. stem vowel -e- + doubled consonant	steppan 'step'	stōp	stōpon	gestapen
4. 'fractured' stem vowel + doubled consonant	scieppan 'create'	scōp	scōpon	gescapen
5. contracted type	slēan 'strike'	slōh	slōgon	geslagen

Strong Class 7 (a)

1. stem vowel -ea-	feallan 'fall'	fēoll	fēollon	gefeallen
2. stem vowel -a-	bēatan 'beat'	bēot	bēoton	gebēaten
3. stem vowel -ā-	cnāwan 'know'	cnēow	cnēowon	gecnāwen
4. stem vowel -ō-	flōwan 'flow'	flēow	flēowon	geflōwen
5. stem vowel -a- + doubled consonant	bannan 'summon'	bēonn	bēonnon	gebannen
6. stem vowel -ē-	wēpan 'weep'	wōp	wōpon	gewōpen

Strong Class 7 (b)

1. stem vowel -ā-	hātan 'call'	hēt	hēton	gehāten
2. stem vowel -ǣ-	lǣtan 'let'	lēt	lēton	gelǣten
3. stem vowel -a- + nasal	blandan 'mix'	blēnd	blēndon	geblanden
4. contracted type	fōn 'seize'	fēng	fēngon	gefangen

B. NOUNS

Nouns will be given only in their *individual* forms, i.e. where there are only three separate endings for a noun type, only those three forms will be given. The numbered 'grid' for the nouns is as follows:

	Singular	Plural
Nominative	1	5
Accusative	2	6
Genitive	3	7
Dative	4	8

i.e. *1,2 sunu 3/7 suna 8 sunum* means that the nominative and accusative singular (positions 1 and 2) have the form '*sunu*', the genitive and dative singular, nominative, accusative and genitive plural (3, 4, 5, 6 and 7) have the form '*suna*' and the dative plural (8) has the form '*sunum*'. It is intended that this format will focus on the forms met with and allow the student to commit to memory not eight separate variants of the noun but only the minimum needed (in the case of *sunu* above, only three).

Weak Nouns (-*n* declension nouns)

M.		nama	1. nama 2/6. naman 7. namena
		'name'	8. namum
M.	(with long stem vowel)	gefā 'foe'	1. gefā 2/6. gefān 7. gefāna 8. gefām
F.		tunge	1. tunge 2/6. tungan 7. tungena
		'tongue'	8. tungum
N.		ēare 'ear'	1,2. ēare 2/6. ēaran 7. ēarena 8. ēarum

Strong Nouns

-*a* Stems

M.		stān 'stone'	1,2. stān 3. stānes 4. stāne 5,6. stānas 7. stāna 8. stānum
M.	stem in -*æ*-	dæg 'day'	1,2. dæg 3. dæges 4. dæge 5,6. dagas 7. daga 8. dagum
M.	stem in long vowel +*h*	scōh 'shoe'	1,2. scōh 3,5,6. scōs 4. scō 7. scō(n)a 8. scōm
N.	light-stemmed	scip 'ship'	1,2. scip 3. scipes 4. scipe 5,6 scipu 7. scipa 8. scipum
N.	heavy-stemmed	word 'word'	1,2,5,6. word 3. wordes 4. worde 7. worda 8. wordum
N.	stem with -*rh, -lh*	feorh 'life'	1,2,5,6. feorh 3. fēores 4. fēore 7. fēora 8. fēorum

147

-*ja* Stems

M.	stem in -*e*	ende 'end'
		1,2,4. ende 3. endes 5,6. endas 7. enda 8. endum
M.	stem in doubled consonant	hyll 'hill'
		1,2. hyll 3. hylles 4. hylle 5,6. hyllas 7. hylla 8. hyllum
M.	unique	here 'army'
		1,2. here 3. heriges 4. herige 5,6. herigas 7. heriga 8. herigum
N.	stem in -*e*	wīte 'fine'
		1,2,4. wīte 3. wītes 5,6. wītu 7. wīta 8. wītum
N.	stem in doubled consonant	cynn 'kindred'
		1,2,5,6. cynn 3. cynnes 4. cynne 7. cynna 8. cynnum

-*wa* Stems

M.	stem in -*u*	bearu 'copse'
		1,2. bearu 3. bearwes 4. bearwe 5,6. bearwas 7. bearwa 8. bearwum
M.	short vowel +*w*	ðēow 'servant'
		1,2. ðēow 3. ðeowes 4. ðeowe 5,6. ðeowas 7. ðeowa 8. ðeowum
M.	long vowel +*w*	ðēaw 'custom'
		1,2. ðēaw 3. ðēawes 4. ðēawe 5,6. ðēawas 7. ðēawa 8. ðēawum
N.	stem in -*u*	bealu 'evil'
		1,2,5,6. bealu 3. bealwes 4. bealwe 7. bealwa 8. bealwum
N.	stem in -*w*	cnēow 'knee'
		1,2,5,6. cnēow 3. cnēowes 4. cnēowe 7. cnēowa 8. cnēowum

-*ō* Stems

F.	light-stemmed	giefu 'gift'
		1. giefu 2/6. giefe 7. giefa 8. giefum (also 5,6. giefa 7. giefena)
F.	heavy-stemmed	lār 'lore'
		1. lār 2/6. lāre 7. lāra 8. lārum (also 5,6 lāra 7. lārena)

-*jō* Stems

F.	light- or heavy-stemmed	ecg 'edge'
		1 ecg 2/6. ecge 7. ecga 8. ecgum (also 5,6. ecga)

-*wō* Stems

F.	light-stemmed in -*u*	beadu 'battle'
		1. beadu 2/6. beadwe 7. beadwa 8. beadwum (also 5,6. beadwa)
F.	heavy-stemmed	mǣd 'meadow'
		1. mǣd 2/6. mǣdwe 7. mǣdwa 8. mǣdwum
F.	long vowel +*w*	stōw 'place'
		1. stōw 2/6. stōwe 7. stōwa 8. stōwum

-*i* Stems

M.	light-stemmed in -*i*	wine 'friend'	1,2,4/6. wine 3. wines 7. wina 8. winum (also 5,6. winas 7. winega)
M.	heavy-stemmed	wyrm 'insect'	1,2. wyrm 3. wyrmes 4/6. wyrme 7. wyrma 8. wyrmum
N.	light-stemmed in -*i*	spere 'spear'	1,2,4. spere 3. speres 5,6. speru 7. spera 8. sperum
N.	heavy-stemmed	wiht 'being'	1,2,5,6. wiht 3. wihtes 4. wihte 7. wihta 8. wihtum
F.	heavy-stemmed	tīd 'time'	1,2. tīd 3/6. tīde 7. tīda 8. tīdum

-*u* Stems

M.	light-stemmed in -*u*	sunu 'son'	1,2. sunu 3/7. suna 8. sunum
M.	heavy-stemmed	eard 'homeland'	1,2. eard 3/7. earda 8. eardum (also with -*a* stem endings)
F.	light-stemmed	duru 'door'	1,2. duru 3/7. dura 8. durum
F.	heavy-stemmed	hand 'hand'	1,2. hand 3/7. handa 8. handum

Monosyllabic/Athematic Declension

M.	short stem vowel	mann 'human being'	1,2. mann 3. mannes 4/6. menn 7. manna 8. mannum
M.	long stem vowel	fōt 'foot'	1,2. fōt 3. fōtes 4/6. fēt 7. fōta 8. fōtum
F.	short stem vowel	burg 'fortress'	1,2. burg 3/6. byrig 7. burga 8. burgum
F.	long stem vowel	bōc 'book'	1,2. bōc 3/6. bec 7. bōca 8 bōcum (also 3. bōce)

-*ð* Stems

M.		hæleð 'hero'	1,2,5,6. hæleð 3. hæleðes 4. hæleðe 7. hæleða 8. hæleðum (also 5,6. hæleðas)
N.		ealoð 'ale'	1,2. ealu 3, 4. ealoð 5,6. ealoðu 7. ealoða 8. ealoðum (also 1,2. ealoð)

-*ð* Stems (continued)

F.		mæg(e)ð 'girl'	1,3/6. mæg(e)ð 2. mægðe 7. mægða 8. mægðum (also -*o* stem endings)

-r Stems

M.	fæder 'father'	1/4. fæder 5,6. fæderas 7. fædera 8. fæderum (also 1/7. fæder)
M.	brōðor 'brother'	1/3,5,6. brōðor 4. brōðer 7. brōðra 8. brōðrum (also 5,6. brēðra, brōðru)
F.	sweostor 'sister'	1/6. sweostor 7. sweostra 8. sweostrum

-nd Stems

M.	stem ending in consonant	wīgend 'fighter'	1,2. wīgend 3. wīgendes 4/6. wīgende 7. wīgendra 8. wīgendum (also 5,6. wīgend, wīgendas)
M.	stem ending in vowel	fēond 'foe'	1,2. fēond 3. fēondes 4/6. fīend 7. fēonda 8. fēondum

-es/-os Stems

N.	cīld 'child'	1,2. cīld 3. cīldes 4. cīlde 5,6. cildru 7. cildra 8. cildrum (also 5,6. cild and forms without -r-)
N.	lamb 'lamb'	1,2. lamb 3. lambes 4. lambe 5,6. lambru 7. lambra 8. lambrum

C. PERSONAL PRONOUNS

	number	Nom.	Acc.	Gen.	Dat.
1st	sing.	ic	mec, mē	mīn	mē
	dual	wit	unc, uncet	uncer	unc
	pl.	wē	ūs, ūsic	ūre	ūs
2nd	sing.	ðū	ðec, ðē	ðīn	ðē
	dual	git	inc, incet	incer	inc
	pl.	gē	ēow, ēowic	ēower	ēow
3rd	sing.M.	hē	hine	his	him
	F.	hēo	hīe	hire	hire
	N.	hit	hit	his	him
	pl.	hīe	hīe	hiera	him

D. Adjectives

(1) The Strong Declension

i. light stemmed

		M.	N.	F.
sing.	Nom	cwic	cwic	cwicu
	Acc	cwicne	cwic	cwice
	Gen	cwices	cwices	cwicre
	Dat	cwicum	cwicum	cwicre
	Inst	cwice	cwice	cwicre
pl.	Nom/Acc	cwice	cwicu	cwica
	Gen	cwicra	cwicra	cwicra
	Dat/Inst	cwicum	cwicum	cwicum

ii. heavy stemmed

		M.	N.	F.
sing.	Nom	blind	blind	blind
	Acc	blindne	blind	blinde
	Gen	blindes	blindes	blindre
	Dat	blindum	blindum	blindre
	Inst	blinde	blinde	blindre
pl.	Nom/Acc	blinde	blind	blinda
	Gen	blindra	blindra	blindra
	Dat/Inst	blindum	blindum	blindum

iii. *-e* stem

		M.	N.	F.
sing.	Nom	ēce	ēce	ēce
	Acc	ēcne	ēce	ēce
	Gen	ēces	ēces	ēcre
	Dat	ēcum	ēcum	ēcre
	Inst	ēce	ēce	ēcre
pl.	Nom/Acc	ēce	ēce	ēca
	Gen	ēcra	ēcra	ēcra
	Dat/Inst	ēcum	ēcum	ēcum

151

iv. -*u* stem

		M.	N.	F.
sing.	Nom	nearu	nearu	nearu
	Acc	nearone	nearu	nearwe
	Gen	nearwes	nearwes	nearore
	Dat	nearwum	nearwum	nearore
	Inst	nearwe	nearwe	nearore
pl.	Nom/Acc	nearwe	nearu	nearwa
	Gen	nearora	nearora	nearora
	Dat/Inst	nearwum	nearwum	nearwum

(2) The Weak Declension

i. light stemmed

		M.	N.	F.
sing.	Nom	cwica	cwice	cwice
	Acc	cwican	cwice	cwican
	Gen	cwican	cwican	cwican
	Dat	cwican	cwican	cwican
	Inst	cwican	cwican	cwican
pl.	Nom/Acc	cwican	cwican	cwican
	Gen	cwicena	cwicena	cwicena
	Dat/Inst	cwicum	cwicum	cwicum

ii. heavy stemmed

		M.	N.	F.
sing.	Nom	blinda	blinde	blinde
	Acc	blindan	blinde	blindan
	Gen	blindan	blindan	blindan
	Dat	blindan	blindan	blindan
	Inst	blindan	blindan	blindan
pl.	Nom/Acc	blindan	blindan	blindan
	Gen	blindena	blindena	blindena
	Dat/Inst	blindum	blindum	blindum

iii. *-e* stem

		M.	N.	F.
sing.	Nom	ēca	ēce	ēce
	Acc	ēcaṇ	ēce	ēcan
	Gen	ēcan	ēcan	ēcan
	Dat	ēcan	ēcan	ēcan
	Inst	ēcan	ēcan	ēcan
pl.	Nom/Acc	ēcan	ēcan	ēcan
	Gen	ēcena	ēcena	ēcena
	Dat/Inst	ēcum	ēcum	ēcum

iv. *-u* stem

		M.	N.	F.
sing.	Nom	nearwa	nearwe	nearwe
	Acc	nearwan	nearwe	nearwan
	Gen	nearwan	nearwan	nearwan
	Dat	nearwan	nearwan	nearwan
	Inst	nearwan	nearwan	nearwan
pl.	Nom/Acc	nearwan	nearwan	nearwan
	Gen	nearwena	nearwena	nearwena
	Dat/Inst	nearwum	nearwum	nearwum

Part Three

OE Texts

SELECTED TEXTS IN OLD ENGLISH

The notes to these texts are cross-referred to appropriate section(s) of the Course for ease of reference; where there is more than one section indicated usually this is due to my having discussed the grammatical form first and then given further notes on usage later. Naturally, not every word in the texts appears in the course, so section references will often be for the purpose of identifying the ending (or vowel in the case of strong verbs). Frequent words such as *þā, and, hīe* are only cross-referred in full the first few times of their occurence; however, the number, case and gender of *hīe* is always given. Nouns referred to in the notes are normally given in their nominative singular form and verbs in the infinitive. The text is broken down into logical, manageable phrases for analysis and translation. In the second and subsequent texts the cross-referencing is progressively less comprehensive as the reader's confidence increases and the glossary definitions are not repeated in the notes.

Notes

Spelling normalizations have been undertaken in the interest of clarity; they include replacing original -**y**- with -**i**-, -**ī**- with -**ie**- and -**an** with -**on**.

'<' before a word means 'from';
'>' means 'becomes';
material in square brackets '[...]' is included to clarify the syntax or to supply additional information.

1. Engla Tocyme

The Arrival of the English

(From the Old English version of Bede's Ecclesiastical History of the English People.)

Ðā wæs ymb fēower hund wintra and nigon and fēowertig fram ūres drihtnes menniscnysse þæt Martiānus cāsere rīce onfēng and vii gēar hæfde. Se wæs siexta ēac fēowertigum fram Agustō þām cāsere. Ðā Angleþēod and Seaxna wæs gelaðod fram þām foresprecenan cyninge, and on Brytene cōm on þrim miclum scipum, and on ēastdǣle þisses ēalondes eardungstōwe onfēng þurh ðæs ilcan cyninges bebod, þe hīe hider gelaðode, þæt hīe sceoldon for heora ēðle compian and feohtan. And hīe sōna compodon wið heora gewinnan, þe hīe oft ǣr norðan onhergodon; and Seaxan þā sige geslōgon, þā sendon hie hām ǣrendracan and hēton secgan þisses landes wæstmbǣrnysse and Brytta yrgþo. And hīe þā sōna hider sendon māran sciphere strengrena wigena; and wæs unoferswīðendlic werod, þā hīe tōgædre geþēodde wǣron. And him Bryttas sealdon and gēafon eardungstōwe betwuh him, þæt hīe for sibbe and for hǣlo heora ēðles campoden and wunnen wið heora fēondum, and hīe him andleofne and āre forgēafen for heora gewinne.

Cōmon hīe of þrim folcum ðām strangestum Germānie, þæt is of Seaxum and of Angle and of Gēatum. Of Gēata fruman sindon Cantware and Wihtsǣtan; þæt is sēo ðēod þe Wiht þæt ēalond oneardað. Of Seaxum, þæt is of ðām lande þe mon hāteð Ealdseaxan, cōmon Ēastseaxan and Sūðseaxan and Westseaxan. Of Engle cōmon Ēastengle and Middelengle and Mierce and eall Norðhymbra cynn; is þæt land ðe Angulus is genemned, betwuh Gēatum and Seaxum; and is sægd of ðǣre tīde þe hīe ðanon gewiton oð tōdæge þæt hit wēste wunige. Wǣron ǣrest heora lāttēowas and heretogan twēgen gebrōðru, Hengest and Horsa. Hīe wǣron Wihtgilses suna, þæs fæder wæs Wōden nemned, of ðæs strȳnde monigra mǣgða cyningcynn fruman lǣdde. Ne wæs ðā ielding tō þon þæt hīe hēapmǣlum cōmon māran weorod of þām þēodum þe wē ǣr gemynegodon. And þæt folc ðe hider cōm ongan weaxan and miclian tō þon swīðe þæt hīe wǣron on miclum ege þām selfum landbigengum ðe hīe ǣr hider laðedon and cīgdon.

Æfter þissum hīe ðā geweredon tō sumre tīde wið Pehtum, þā hīe ǣr ðurh gefeoht feor ādrifon. And þā wǣron Seaxan sēcende intingan and tōwyrde heora gedāles wið Bryttas, cȳðdon him openlīce and sǣgdon, nemne hīe him māran andleofne sealden, þæt hīe woldon him sylfe niman and hergian, þǣr hīe hit findan mihton. And sōna ðā bēotunge dǣdum lǣston; bærndon and hergodon and slōgon fram ēastsǣ oð westsǣ, and him nǣnig wiðstōd. Ne wæs ungelīc wræcc þām ðe īu Chaldēas bærndon Hierusalēme weallas and ðā cynelican getimbru mid fȳre fornōmon for ðæs godes folces synnum. Swā þonne hēr fram þǣre ārlēasan ðēode, hwæðere rihte godes dōme, nēah ceastra gehwylce and land forhergode wǣron. Hruron and fēollon cynelīcu getimbru somod and ānlīpie, and gehwǣr sācerdas and mæsseprēostas betwuh wibedum wǣron slægene and cwielmde; biscopas mid folcum būton ǣnigre āre scēawunge ætgædre mid īserne and līge fornumene wǣron. And ne wæs sēo bebyrignys sealde þām ðe swā hrēowlīce ācwealde wǣron. And monige ðǣre earmen lāfe on wēstenum fangene wǣron and hēapmǣlum sticode. Sume for hungre heora fēondum on hand ēodon and ēcne þēowdōm gehēton wið ðǣm þe him mon andleofne forgēafe; sume ofer sǣ sorgiende gewiton; sume forhtiende on ēðle gebidon and þearfende līf in wuda and in wēstenum and on hēam clifum sorgiende mōde symle dydon.

Text	Notes & Translation
Ðā	then adverb of time (8.3)
wæs	(it) was 3rd.sing.pret.indic. <*wesan* 'be' (10.6)
ymb	after preposition meaning 'after' in expressions of time, governing the accusative (4.4)
fēower	four numeral (4.3)
hund	hundreds noun neut.acc.pl. (after *ymb*) (4.3, 14.3)
wintra	(of) years noun neut.gen.pl. showing relationship to *hund*; *winter* can have the general meaning 'year' as well as the more specific 'winter'. (6.1, 14.2)
ond nigon	and nine conj. 'and'; numeral (4.3)
ond fēowertig	and forty conj. 'and'; numeral (4.3)
fram ūres drihtnes menniscnysse	from our lord's incarnation *fram* prep. governing the dative 'from, since' (4.6); *ūres* poss. masc.gen.sing. (5.3) agreeing with *drihtnes* noun masc.gen.sing. <*drihten* 'lord' (6.1); *menniscnysse* noun fem.dat.sing. <*menniscnys* ('man+ish+ness' = humanity), in this case 'incarnation'(4.5).
þæt	that conj.(7.1)

Text	Notes & Translation
Martiānus cāsere	Caesar Martianus *Martiānus* (personal name) followed by his rank or title *cāsere* 'Caesar' (masc.nom. sing.) subject – this is normal OE practice (17.4)
rīce onfēng	acquired power *rīce* noun neut.acc.sing. (2.1)< *rīce* 'kingdom, power' object of *onfēng* 3rd sing.pret.ind.<*onfōn* 'receive, acquire' < *on* + *fōn* (14.4)
ond vii	and seven conj. 'and'; *vii*, Roman numeral for *seofon*, numeral (4.3)
gēar hæfde.	years (he) held (it). *gēar* noun neut.acc.pl. adverb of time (11.6); *hæfde* 3rd. sing. pret.ind. <*habban* 'have, hold' (9.3)
Se wæs	He was *se* pron. nom.sing.masc.(14.5), subject of *wæs* (see above)
siexta ēac fēowertigum	(the) forty sixth *siexta* ordinal numeral (12.4), *ēac* 'also, as well'; *fēowertigum* numeral (4.3) inst. pl.(17.3); ['sixth also with forty' is a clumsy way of expressing 'forty sixth']
fram Agustō	from Augustus *fram* prep. (see above); *Agustō* personal name dat.sing. after *fram*, retaining its Latin ending (this is not uncommon in texts translated from a Latin original – *Martiānus* above does likewise).
Þām cāsere.	the Caesar *þām* dem. dat.sing.masc.(4.5), agreeing with *cāsere* dat. sing. masc., dative after *fram* (4.6).
Ðā	Then adverb of time (8.3)
Angelþēod	(the) English nation noun nom.sing.fem. <*Angel* 'Angle' + *þēod* 'race, nation'

Text	Notes & Translation
ond Seaxna	and (that) of (the) Saxons conj. 'and'; *Seaxna* noun gen.pl.masc.(6.2); [*þēod* has to be understood here]
wæs gelaðod	was invited *wæs* (see above); *gelaðod* past part. <*gelaðian* 'invite' (9.2)
fram	by prep. with dative, here meaning 'by'
þām foresprecenan cyninge	the aforementioned king *þām* dem. dat.sing.masc. (4.5) agreeing with *cyninge* dat.sing. after *fram* <*cyning* 'king' (4.5); *foresprecenan* adj. dat.sing.masc. weak after *þām* (12.1) <*foresprecen* past. part. <*foresprecan* 'speak before, mention in advance'. [The king, *Wyrtgeorn* = Vortigern, had been mentioned in a previous chapter.]
and on Brytene cōm	and came into Britain conj.'and'; *on* prep. with acc. 'into' (11.6); *Brytene* noun acc.sing.fem. (after *on*) <*Bryten* 'Britain'; *cōm* 3ʳᵈ.sing.pret.ind. <*cuman* 'come' (12.5)
on þrim miclum scipum	in three great ships *on* prep. With dat. 'in' (4.6); *þrim* numeral dat.pl.neut.(14.3); *miclum* adj. dat.pl.neut. (4.5) agreeing with *scipum* noun dat.pl.neut. after *on* (4.6) <*scip* 'ship'
and on ēastdǣle	and in (the) eastern part conj.'and'; *on* prep. with dat. 'in' (4.6); *ēastdǣle* noun dat.sing.masc. (after *on*) (4.5)<*ēast* 'east' + *dǣl* deal, portion, part'
þisses ēalondes	of this island *þisses* dem. gen.sing.neut. (6.1) agreeing with *ēalondes* noun gen.sing.neut. (14.2) <*ēalond* 'island' <*ēa* 'river' + *land* 'land'
eardungstōwe onfēng	received a place in which to live *eardungstōwe* noun acc.sing.fem. (2.1) <*eardungstōw* 'dwelling place' <*eardung* 'dwelling, habitation' <*eardian* 'dwell' + *stōw* 'location, site', acc. as object of *onfēng* verb 3rd sing.pret.ind. <*onfōn* (see above).

Text	Notes & Translation
þurh þæs ilcan cyninges bebod	by that same king's command *þurh* prep. with acc. 'through, by means of' (4.4); *þæs* dem. gen.sing.masc. (6.1); *ilcan* adj. gen.sing.masc. weak with *þæs* (12.1); *cyninges* noun gen.sing.masc. <*cyning* 'king' (6.1); *bebod* noun acc.sing.neut. (2.1), acc.after *þurh*
þe hīe hider gelaðode	who invited them here *þe* rel.pron. (7.1); *hīe* pron. acc.pl. object of *gelaðode*, 3rd sing.pret.ind.<*gelaðian* 'invite' (9.1); *hider* adverb of motion 'hither, to this place' (17.5)
þæt hīe scoldon	(so) that they should *þæt* conj. (7.1); *hīe* pers.pron. nom.pl. (3.1) subject of *scoldon* 3rd.pl.pret.ind. <*sculan* 'be obliged, shall' (15.5)
for heora ēðle	for their homeland *for* prep. with dat. 'for, on behalf of' (4.6); *heora* poss.pron.(5.3); *ēðle* noun dat.sing.masc. <*ēðel* 'homeland' (4.5) dative after *for*.[*heora* = the Britons']
compian and feohtan	wage war and fight. *compian* verb. inf. (3.3) 'wage war'; *feohtan* verb inf.(3.3) 'fight'
And hīe sōna compodon	And they straightaway waged war conj. '*and*'; *hīe* pron. nom.pl. (3.1) subject of *compodon* 3rd pl.pret.ind. <*compian* 'wage war' (9.1); *sōna* adv. 'straightaway, soon, immediately' (10.3) [*hīe* = the Angles and Saxons]
wið heora gewinnan	against their enemies *wið* prep. with acc. 'against' (4.4); *heora* (as above); *gewinnan* noun acc.pl.masc. <*gewinna* 'adversary, enemy', acc. after *wið*.[*heora* = the Britons'].
þe hīe oft ǣr norþan onhergodon	who had previously often attacked them from the north *þe* rel.pron.(7.1); *hīe* pron. acc.pl. (3.4), object of *onhergodon*, 3rd pl.pret.ind. <*onhergian* 'attack'<*on* 'on(to)' + *hergian* 'harry' (9.1); *oft* adverb of time 'often'; *ǣr* adv. of time 'before'; *norþan* adv. of motion (17.5)[*hīe* = the Britons]

Text

Notes & Translation

**and Seaxan þā
sige geslōgon**

and when (the) Saxons won the victory
conj. 'and'; *Seaxan* noun nom.pl.masc. (6.2) subject of
geslōgon, 3rd pl.pret.ind. < *geslēan* 'gain by fighting'
<*slēan* 'strike' (14.1); *þā* conj. 'when' (8.3); *sige* noun
acc.sing.masc. *sige* "victory" object of *geslōgon*

**þā sendon
hīe hām ǣrendracan**

then they sent messengers home
þā conj. 'then' (8.3); *sendon* verb 3rd pl.pret.ind.
<*sendan* 'send' (10.2); *hīe* pron. nom.pl. (3.1) subject
of *sendon*; *hām* adv. 'home'; *ǣrendracan* noun
acc.pl.masc. <*ǣrendraca* 'messenger' (11.3) <*ǣrend*
'message, errand', object of *sendon*.

and hēton secgan

and told (them) to speak
conj. 'and'; *hēton* verb 3rd pl.pret.ind. < *hātan* 'call,
tell, command' (14.4); *secgan* verb inf. 'speak' (3.3)

**þisses landes
wæstmbǣrnysse**

of the fruitfulness of this land
þisses dem.gen.sing.neut. (6.1) agreeing with *landes*
noun gen.sing.neut. <*land* 'land' (6.1); *wæstmbǣrnysse*
noun gen.sing.fem. <*wæstmbǣrnys* 'fertility,
fruitfulness' <*wæstm* 'fruit' + *bǣr* 'bearing' + *nys*
'-ness' (6.1)

and Brytta yrgþo

and of the Britons' worthlessness.
conj. 'and'; *Brytta* noun gen.pl.masc. <*Bryttas* 'the
Britons' (6.1); *yrgþo* noun gen.sing.fem. <*yrgþo*
'worthlessness' (9.6) <*earg* 'slack'

**And hīe þā sōna
hider sendon**

And then they straightaway sent here
conj. 'and'; *hīe* pron. nom.pl. subject of *sendon* (as
above); *þā* conj. 'thereafter' [*hīe* = the Saxons at home
who heard the message]; *hider* as above.

māran sciphere

a greater ship-borne force
māran adj.comp.acc.sing.masc. weak (13.4), agreeing
with *sciphere*, acc.sing. masc. (6.2) <*scip* 'ship' + *here*
'military force', object of *sendon*.

strengrena wigena

of stronger warriors
strengrena adj. comp. gen.pl.masc. <*strang* 'strong'
(13.1), agreeing with *wigena* noun gen.pl.masc.<*wiga*
'warrior' (11.3)

Text	Notes & Translation
and wæs unoferswīðendlic werod	and (it) was an invincible force *and wæs* (see above); *unoferswīðendlic* adj. nom.sing.neut. 'invincible' <*oferswīþend* (13.5) 'conquering' <*oferswīðan* 'overcome' (10.5), agreeing with *werod* noun nom.sing.neut.
þā hīe tōgædere geþēodde wæron	when they were united together *þā* adv. 'when' (8.3); *hīe* pron. nom.pl.; *tōgædere* adv. 'together'; *geþēodde* past. part. (9.2) <*geþēodan* 'join forces, unite peoples' <*þēod* 'nation, people'; *wæron* 3rd.pl.pret.ind. <*wesan* 'be' (10.6) [*hīe* = the existing Saxon forces and the newly-arrived ones]
And him Bryttas sealdon and gēafon	And to them the Britons handed over and gave *him* pron. dat.pl. (4.5); *Bryttas* noun nom.pl.masc. 'Britons', subject of *sealdon* verb 3rd pl.pret.ind. <*sellan* 'hand over' (10.2) *gēafon* verb 3rd pl.pret.ind. <*giefan* (13.2)
eardungstōwe betwuh him	a dwelling place among them *eardungstōwe* noun acc.sing.fem. (see above) object of *sealdon, gēafon* 'dwelling place'; *betwuh* prep. with dat. 'between, among'; *him* pron. dat.pl. [*betwuh him* = among the Britons]
þæt hīe	(so) that they *þæt* conj. 'that' (7.1); *hīe* pron. nom.pl.
for sibbe and for hǣlo	for (the) peace and well-being *for* prep. with dat. (4.6) 'for'; *sibbe* noun dat.sing.fem. <*sibb* 'peace, friendship' (4.5), *hǣlo* dat.sing.fem. <*hǣlo* 'well-being' (9.6), both dat. after *for*.
heora ēðles	of their homeland *heora* poss.pron. (5.3); *ēðles* noun gen.sing.masc. <*ēþel* 'homeland'
campoden and wunnen	should wage war and strive 3rd pl.pret.subj. <*campian*, 'wage war' (16.4,16.5) *winnan* 'fight, strive' (16.4,16.5)

Text	Notes & Translation
wið heora fēondum	against their enemies *wið* prep. with dat. 'against' (4.6); *heora* poss.pron.; *fēondum* noun dat.pl.masc. <*fēond* 'enemy' (7.4), dat. after *wið*. [*heora* = 'their' the Saxons' and the Britons']
and hīe him andleofne and āre forgēafen	and they should grant them sustenance and honour *hīe* pron. nom.pl.; *him* pron. dat.pl.; *andleofne* noun acc.sing.fem. <*andleofen* 'sustenance' (2.1), object of *forgēafen*; *āre* noun acc.sing.fem. <*ār* 'honour' (2.1) object of *forgēafen* 3rd pl.pret.subj. <*forgiefan* 'allow, grant' <*giefan* 'give' (13.2) [*hīe* = the Britons, *him* = the Saxons]
for heora gewinne	because of their trouble *for* prep. with dat. 'because of' (17.1); *heora* poss.pron.; *gewinne* noun dat.sing.neut. <*gewinn* 'hardship, struggle, strife' (4.5)
Cōmon hīe	They came *cōmon* 3rd pl.pret.ind. <*cuman* 'come' (12.5); *hīe* pers.pron. nom.pl. subject of *cōmon*
of þrim folcum	from three peoples *of* prep. with dat. 'from, off' (4.6); *þrim* dat. numeral (14.3); *folcum* noun dat.pl.neut. <*folc* 'nation, people', dat. after *of* (4.6).
ðām strangestum	the strongest (ones) *ðām* dem. dat.pl.neut. (4.5); *strangestum* adj. superl. dat.pl.neut. weak after *ðām* (12.1), dat. agreeing with *folcum*.
Germānie	of Germany noun gen.sing retaining Latin inflexion = *Germaniae*
þæt is of Seaxum	which is (to say) from (the) Saxons *þæt* rel.pron.(7.1); *is* 3rd sing.pres.ind. <*wesan* 'be' (5.2); *of* prep. with dat. 'from' (4.6); *Seaxum* noun dat.pl.masc. <*Seaxe* 'Saxons' (6.2)
and of Angle	and from (the) Angeln *of* prep. with dat. 'from' (4.6); *Angle* noun dat.sing.masc. (=Angeln, the home of the Angles) (6.2)

Text	Notes & Translation
and of Gēatum	and from (the) Jutes *Gēatum* noun dat.pl.masc.; [this spelling is a later rationalization of Bede's *Iutis* >'Jutes']
And of Gēata fruman	And from the Jutes' source *Gēata* noun gen.pl.masc. (see above); *fruman* noun dat.sing.masc. <*fruma* 'source, progenitor'
sindon Cantware	are the people of Kent *sindon* 3rd pl.pres.ind. <*wesan* 'be'; *Cantware* noun nom.pl.fem. 'inhabitants of Kent' [perhaps <Romano-British *Cantuarii*], subject of *sindon*
ond Wihtsǣtan	and the Wight settlers *Wihtsǣtan* noun nom.pl.masc. <*Wiht* 'Vectis, the Isle of Wight' + *sǣtan* nom.pl. <*sǣta* 'settler' (11.3)
þæt is sēo ðēod	which is (to say) that people *þæt is* (see above); *sēo* dem. nom.sing.fem.agreeing with *ðēod* noun nom.sing.fem.
þe Wiht þæt ēalond oneardað	which inhabits the Isle of Wight. *þe* rel.pron. (7.1); *Wiht* (see above); *þæt* dem.acc.sing.neut. agreeing with *ēalond* noun acc.sing.neut. 'island' (2.1) object of *oneardað* 3rd sing.pres.ind. <*oneardian* 'inhabit' <*on* 'on' +*eardian* 'dwell'
Of Seaxum	From (the) Saxons *Seaxum* noun dat.pl.masc. <*Seaxe* 'Saxons'
þæt is of ðām lande	which is (to say) from that land *þæt is* (see above); *ðām* dem. dat.sing.neut. agreeing with *lande* dat.sing.neut.<*land* 'land'
ðe mon hāteð	which is called
Ealdseaxan	(the) Old Saxons *ðe* rel.pron.; *mon* indef.pron.; *hāteð* 3rd sing.pres.ind.<*hātan* 'call'; *Ealdseaxan* noun nom.pl.masc.<*eald* 'old' + *seaxan* 'Saxons'
cōmon	came 3rd pl.pret.ind. <*cuman* 'come'
ēastseaxan	(the) East Saxons i.e. men of Essex nom.pl.masc. <*ēast* 'east' +*seaxan* 'Saxons'

Text | Notes & Translation

and Sūþseaxan

and (the) South Saxons i.e. men of Sussex
nom.pl.masc. <*sūþ* 'south' + *seaxan* 'Saxons'

and Westseaxan

and (the) West Saxons. i.e. men of Wessex
nom.pl.masc.<*west* 'west'+*seaxan* 'Saxons'

Of Engle cōmon

From Angeln came the East Angles

Ēastengle

Engle noun dat.sing.masc., dat. after *of*, *ēastengle*
<*ēast* 'east' + *engle* 'Angles' nom.pl.masc.; *cōmon*
(see above)

and Middelengle

and Middle Angles
Middelengle <*middel* 'middle' + *engle* 'Angles'
nom.pl.masc.

and Mierce

and Mercians
Mierce nom.pl.masc. 'Mercians' <*mearc* 'border' (6.2)

**and eall
Norðhymbra cynn**

and all the Northumbrian nation
eall adj. nom.sing.neut. agreeing with *cynn* noun
nom.sing.neut.; *Norðhymbra* noun gen.pl.masc.
<*Norðhymbre* <*norð* 'north' + *hymbre* 'men of the
Humber'.

Is þæt land

(It) is that land
is 3rd sing.pres.ind. <*wesan* 'be'; *þæt* dem.
nom.sing.neut. agreeing with *land* noun nom.sing.neut.
[this sentence defines the meaning of *Engle* above]

**þe Angulus is
nemned**

which is called 'Angulus'
þe rel.pron.; *Angulus* place name in Latin guise,
nom.sing.masc.; *nemned* past part. <*nemnan* 'name'
(9.2) although unusually without the prefix *ge-*

**betwuh Gēatum
and Seaxum**

between (the) Jutes and Saxons
betwuh prep. with dat. 'between' (4.6); *Gēatum*,
Seaxum both dat.pl.masc. after *betwuh*

and is sægd

and (it) is said
sægd past part. <*secgan* 'say' again without the prefix
ge- (9.2, 10.2)

of ðǣre tīde

from that time
of prep. with dat. 'from'; *ðǣre* dem. dat.sing.fem.
agreeing with *tīde* noun dat.sing.fem. <*tīd* 'time' (4.5)

Text	Notes & Translation
þe hīe ðanon gewiton	when they left there *þe* rel.pron. (7.1); *hīe* pers.pron nom.pl.; *ðanon* adv. of motion (= *ðonan*) (17.5); *gewiton* 3rd pl.pret.ind. <*gewītan* 'go away, leave' (10.5) [*hīe* = the Angles]
oð tōdæge	until today *oð* prep. with acc. 'until'; *tōdæge* adv. of time <*tō* 'to' + *dæge* 'day' (dat. after *tō*) 'today'
þæt hit wēste wunige	that it remains waste. *þæt* conj.; *hit* pron. nom.sing. neut. (= *þæt land*); *wēste* adj. nom.sing.neut. (4.2) agreeing with *hit*; *wunige* 3rd sing.pres. subj. <*wunian* 'remain' (7.3) [subjunctive because the writer is only reporting what may be, not what he knows to be true]
Wǣron ǣrest heora lāttēowas and heretogan	At first their leaders and military commanders were *wǣron* 3rd pl. pret.ind. < *wesan* 'be' (10.5); *ǣrest* adv. of time 'at first' (16.3); *heora* poss. pron. (5.3); *lāttēowas* noun nom.pl.masc. (1.2) <*lāttēow* 'leader'; *heretogan* noun. nom.pl.masc. (11.3) <*heretoga* (<*here* 'military force') [*heora* may refer to all the Germanic peoples named, or perhaps more naturally only to the *Angle* mentioned previously]
twēgen gebrōðru	two brothers *twēgen* numeral nom.pl.masc. (4.3); *gebrōðru* noun nom.pl. neut. <*ge* (collective prefix) + *brōðor* 'brother' (10.1)
Hengest and Horsa	Hengest and Horsa. Personal names nom.sing. masc.; *hengest* is a normal word for a stallion while *horsa* appears to be based on *hors* 'horse'. [There may be some symbolism here since many dynastic foundation myths feature a pair of brothers with names which are linked in sense.]
Hīe wǣron Wihtgilses suna	They were the sons of Wihtgils *hīe* pers.pron. nom.pl.; *wǣron* (as above); *Wihtgilses* personal name gen.sing.masc. *suna* noun nom.pl.masc. <*sunu* 'son'

Text	Notes & Translation

**þæs fæder wæs
Witta hāten**

whose father was called Witta

þæs rel.pron. (7.1); *fæder* noun nom.sing.masc.; *wæs* (as above); *Witta* personal name nom.sing.masc. (11.3,17.4); *hāten* past part. <*hātan* 'call' again without the prefix *ge-*

**þæs fæder wæs
Wihta hāten**

whose father was called Wihta

Wihta personal name nom.sing.masc.

**þæs fæder wæs
Wōden hāten**

whose father was called Woden

Wōden divine name [for the god of inspiration and magic who stands at the head of many Anglo-Saxon genealogies.]

of ðæs strȳnde

from whose stock

ðæs rel.pron. (7.1); *of* prep. with dat. 'from'; *strȳnde* noun dat.sing.fem. <*strȳnd* 'stock, succession' dat. after *of* (4.6)

**monigra mǣgða
cyningcynn**

the royal family of many a people

monigra adj. gen.pl.fem. (6.1) agreeing with *mǣgða* noun gen.pl.fem. <*mǣgð* 'nation, tribe' (6.1); *cyningcynn* noun nom.sing.neut. 'royal family'<*cyning* 'king' + *cynn* 'kin,family'

fruman lǣdde

took (its) source.

fruman noun acc.sing.masc. <*fruma* 'beginning, source' (11.3) object of *lǣdde* 3rd sing.pret.ind. <*lǣdan* 'lead, draw, take'

Ne wæs ðā ielding

Then (there) was no delay

ne neg. particle (2.3); *wæs* (as above); *ðā* adv. of time (8.3); *ielding* noun nom.sing.fem. 'delay' <*eald* 'old, advanced in time' subject of *wæs*

tō þon þæt

to the effect that

conj. (17.1)

**hīe hēapmǣlum
cōmon**

they came in crowds,

hīe pers.pron. nom.pl.; *hēapmǣlum* adv. of degree (10.3) <*hēap* 'crowd'; *cōmon* (as above) [*hīe* = defined below]

169

Text	Notes & Translation
māran werod	greater forces *māran* adj.comp. nom.pl.neut weak (13.4) agreeing with *werod* noun nom.pl.neut. (1.2)
of þām þēodum	from those nations *of* (as above); *þām* dem. dat.pl.fem. agreeing with *þēodum* noun dat.pl.fem. <*þēod* 'nation'
þe wē ǣr gemynegodon	which we have previously mentioned. *þe* rel.pron. (7.1); *wē* pers.pron. (3.1); *ǣr* adv. of time (16.3); *gemynegodon* 1st pl.pret.ind. <*gemynegian* 'call to mind, remember, mention' [*wē* = the writer and his readers]
And þæt folc	And the army *þæt* dem. nom.sing.neut. (1.2) agreeing with *folc* noun nom.sing.neut. [*folc* has definite military overtones, unlike the NE 'folk']
ðe hider cōm	which came here *ðe* rel.pron; *hider* adv. of motion (17.5); *cōm* 3rd sing.pret.ind. <*cuman* 'come'
ongan weaxan	began to grow *ongan* verb 3rd sing.pret.ind. <*onginnan* 'begin' (12.3); *weaxan* verb inf..
and miclian	and to increase *miclian* verb inf. < *micel* 'great'
tō þon swīþe þæt	so strongly that *tō þon þæt* 'to that degree that' (17.2); *swīþe* adv. of degree <*swīþ* 'strong'
hīe wǣron	they were *hīe* pers.pron nom.pl.; *wǣron* (as above) [*hīe* = the army]
on miclum ege	as a great (source of) fear *on* prep. with dat. 'on, in, as' (4.6); *miclum* adj. dat.sing.masc. agreeing with *ege* noun dat.sing.masc. <*ege* 'fear', dative after *on*

Text	Notes & Translation
þām selfum landbigengum	to the selfsame inhabitants of the land *þām* dem. dat.pl.masc.; *selfum* adj. dat.pl. masc. weak (after *þām*)(12.1) agreeing with *landbigengum* noun. dat.pl.masc. <*landbigenga* 'inhabitant of the land'
ðe hīe ǣr hider laðodon ond cīgdon	who had previously invited them and called them here. *ðe* rel.pron.; *hīe* pers.pron. acc.pl. object of the following verbs; *ǣr* adv. of time (16.3); *hider* adv. of motion (17.5); *laðodon* verb 3rd pl. pret.ind. <*laðian* 'invite' (9.2); *cīgdon* verb 3rd pl.pret.ind. <*cīgan* 'summon, call' (9.2)
Æfter þissum hīe ðā geweredon	After these (events) they then united in defence *æfter* prep. with dat.(4.6) 'after'; *þissum* pron. dat.pl.neut.; *hīe* pers.pron.nom.pl.; *ðā* adv. of time (8.3); *geweredon* verb 3rd pl.pret.ind. <*gewerian* 'unite in defence' <*ge* collective prefix + *werian* 'defend' (9.1) [*þissum* = pl.neut.referring to 'these (events)' just recounted]
tō sumre tīde	at a certain moment *tō* prep. with dat. 'to, at' (4.6); *sumre* adj. dat.sing.fem. strong (dat. after *tō*) agreeing with *tīde* dat.sing.fem. <*tīd* 'point in time'
wið Pehtum	with (the) Picts *wið* prep. with dat. (4.6) 'with'; *Pehtum* dat.pl.masc. <*Peht* 'Pict' [this is not the usual meaning of *wið*, which normally takes the accusative]
þā hīe ǣr	whom they previously *þā* rel.pron. acc.pl. (7.1); *hīe* pers.pron. nom.pl.; *ǣr* adv. 'formerly, previously' (16.3)
ðurh gefeoht feor ādrifon	had driven far off by fighting *ðurh* prep. with acc. 'through, by means of' (4.4) *gefeoht* noun acc.sing.neut. (2.1); *feor* adv. of motion (17.5); *ādrifon* verb 3rd pl.pret.ind. <*ādrīfan* 'drive off' (10.5)

Text	Notes & Translation
And ðā wǣron Seaxan sēcende	And then (the) Saxons began to look for *ðā* adv. of time (8.3); *wǣron* (as above); *Seaxan* noun nom.pl.masc. (6.2); *sēcende* verb pres.part. <*sēcan* 'seek' (13.5)
intingan and tōwyrde	a cause and an opportunity *intangan* noun acc.sing.masc. <*intinga* 'cause' (11.3); *tōwyrde* noun acc.sing.fem. <*tōwyrd* 'opportunity, occasion', both acc. as objects of *wǣron sēcende*
heora gedāles wið Bryttas	for their separation from (the) Britons; *heora* poss.adj. (5.3); *gedāles* noun gen.sing.neut. <*gedāl* 'separation, division', gen.with the meaning 'in respect of' (14.2); *wið* prep. with acc. 'against'; *Bryttas* noun acc.pl.masc.acc. after *wið*.
cȳðdon him openlice	(they) declared to them openly *cȳðdon* 3rd pl.pret.ind. <*cȳððan* 'reveal, declare, make known' (9.1); *him* pers.pron. dat.pl., ind. obj. of *cȳðdon*; *openlice* adv. <*openlic* 'open, plain'(10.3)
and sægdon	and (they) said *sægdon* 3rd pl.pret.ind. <*secgan* 'say'
nemne hīe him mǣran andleofne sealden	unless they were to give them more food *nemne* conj. 'except, but for, unless' (17.1); *hīe* pers.pron. nom.pl.masc. subject of *sealden*; *him* pers.pron. dat.pl. ind.obj. of *sealden; mǣran* adj. acc.sing.fem.weak (12.1) agreeing with *andleofne* noun acc.sing.fem. <*andleofen* 'food, sustenance, wages', obj.of *sealden* 3rd pl.pret.subj. <*sellan* 'give'
þæt hīe woldon him selfe niman and hergian	that they themselves intended to seize (it) and harry *þæt* conj. (7.1); *hīe* pers. pron. nom. pl. masc.; *woldon* 3rd pl.pret.ind. *willan* 'will, intend' (15.5); *him selfe* refl.pron. nom.pl. masc. (14.5) *niman* and *hergian* verb infs.
þǣr hīe hit findan mihton	wherever they could find it *þǣr* adv. of position 'there, wherever' (17.1); *hīe* pers.pron. nom.pl.masc.; *hit* pers.pron.acc.sing.neut., object of *findan* verb inf.; *mihton* 3rd pl.pret.ind. <*magan* (15.4) [*hit*= presumably the *andleofen* they were owed]

Text	Notes & Translation
And sōna ðā bēotunge dǣdum lǣston	And they straightaway made good their words with actions *sōna* adv. of time 'immediately, straightaway' *ðā* dem. acc.sing.fem. (2.1) agreeing with *bēotunge* noun acc.sing.fem. <*bēotung* 'threat, promise'; *dǣdum* noun dat.pl.fem. <*dǣd* 'deed' (17.3); *lǣston* verb 3rd pl.pret.ind.<*lǣstan* 'carry out, perform, make good (a threat or promise)' (9.1)
bærndon and hergodon and slōgon	(they) burnt and harried and slew verbs 3rd pl.pret.ind <*bærnan* 'burn'(9.1), *hergian* 'harry'(9.1), *slēan* 'slay'(14.1)
fram ēastsǣ oð westsǣ	from the eastern sea to the western *fram* prep. with dat. 'from' (4.6); *ēastsǣ* noun dat.sing.masc. <*ēastsǣ* 'eastern sea' (9.6); *oð* prep. with acc. 'as far as' (4.4); *westsǣ* noun acc.sing.masc. 'western sea' (9.6) [the *Ēastsǣ* is the North Sea and English Channel, the *Westsǣ* is the Irish Sea]
and him nǣnig wiðstōd	and none could withstand them. *him* pers.pron. dat.pl.masc. (4.5); *nǣnig* pron.nom.sing. 'none' (8.5); *wiðstōd* verb 3rd sing.pret.ind. <*wiðstandan* 'withstand'
Ne wæs ungelīc wræcc	(That) was not a dissimilar vengeance *ne* adv. of negation 'not' (2.3); *wæs* as above; *ungelīc* adj. nom.sing.neut. (4.1) <*un-* 'not' + *gelīc* 'alike, similar' agreeing with *wræcc* noun nom.sing.neut.
þām ðe īu	to that one, when previously *þām* pron. dat. sing. neut. (dat. after *gelīc*) 'that one' (11.2); *ðe* rel.pron. (7.1); *īu* adv.of time 'formerly, of old'
Chaldēas bærndon Hierusalēme weallas	(the) Chaldeans burnt the walls of Jerusalem *Chaldēas* noun nom.pl.masc. 'Chaldeans' subj. of *bærndon* verb 3rd pl.pret.ind. < *bærnan* 'burn' (9.1); *Hierusalēme* noun gen.sing.fem. (possibly modelled on the Latin gen. sing. Hierusalemæ); *weallas* acc.pl.masc. (obj. of *bærndon*) (1.2)

<u>Text</u>	<u>Notes & Translation</u>
and ðā cynelīcan getimbru mid fȳre fornōmon	and devastated the royal buildings with fire *ðā* dem. acc.pl.neut. agreeing with *getimbru*; *cynelīcan* adj. acc.pl.neut. weak (12.1) after *ðā*; *getimbru* noun acc.pl.neut. <*getimber* 'building' obj. of *fornōmon* (1.2); *mid* prep. with dat. 'with' (4.6); *fȳre* noun dat.sing.neut. <*fȳr* 'fire' (4.5); *fornōmon* verb 3rd pl.pret.ind. <*forniman* 'destroy, devastate, overcome' (12.5)
for ðæs godes folces synnum	because of the sins of that people of God *for* prep. with dat. 'for' (4.6); *ðæs* dem. gen.sing.neut. (6.1) agreeing with *folces*; *godes* noun gen.sing.masc. <*god* 'God' (6.1); *folces* noun gen.sing.neut. <*folc* 'nation, folk' (6.1); *synnum* noun dat.pl.fem. <*synn* 'sin' (4.5) (dat. after *for*)
Swā þonne hēr	Likewise here, then, adverbs 'so, thus', 'then, in that case', 'here' [*hēr* = in Britain]
·fram þǣre ārlēasan ðēode	because of that impious nation *fram* prep. with dat. 'in respect of, because of' (4.6); *þǣre* dem. dat.sing.fem. (4.5) agreeing with *ðēode*; *ārlēasan* adj. dat.sing.fem. weak (12.1) (after *þǣre*) agreeing with *ðēode* noun dat.sing.fem. <*ðēod* 'nation, tribe' (dat. after *fram*)
hwæðere rihte godes dōme	yet justly by God's judgement *hwæðere* conj. 'yet, nevertheless'; *rihte* adv. <adj.*riht* 'right, correct' (10.3); *godes* as above; *dōme* noun dat.sing.masc. <*dōm* 'doom, judgement' (17.3, 4.5)
nēah ceastra gehwylca and land forhergode wǣron	nearly all fortresses and regions were ravaged *nēah* adv. of degree 'nearly'; *ceastra* noun nom.pl.fem. <*ceaster* 'fortress, stronghold' (1.4); *gehwylca* adj. nom.pl.fem. (4.1, 8.5) 'every'; *land* noun nom.pl.neut. (1.4) <*land* 'land, area, region'; *forhergode* adj. nom.pl. neut.(4.1), past participle (9.2) <*forhergian* 'ravage'; *wǣron* as above.

Text	Notes & Translation
Hruron and fēollon cynelīcu getimbru	Royal buildings tumbled and fell *hruron* verb 3rd pl.pret.ind. <*hrēosan* 'fall, perish' (11.4,); *fēollon* verb 3rd pl.pret.ind. <*feallan* 'fall' (14.4); *cynelīcu* adj. nom.pl.neut. agreeing with *getimbru* noun nom.pl.neut. subject of both preceding verbs
somod and ānlīpie	together and singly adverbs
and gehwǣr sācerdas and mæsseprēostas betwuh wībedum wǣron slægene and cwielmde	and everywhere priests and clergymen were slain and murdered among heathen altars; *gehwǣr* adv. of place 'everywhere' (8.5); *sācerdas, mæsseprēostas* nouns nom.pl.masc. (1.2) 'priests, clergymen'; *betwuh* prep. with dat. 'between, among' (4.6); *wībedum* noun dat.pl.masc. <*wībed* '(heathen) altar' (4.5); *wǣron* as above; *slægene* adj. nom.pl.masc. (agreeing with *sācerdas, mæsseprēostas*) (11.5) past part. <*slēan* (14.1) 'slay'; *cwielmde* adj. nom.pl.masc. (agreeing with *sācerdas, mæsseprēostas*) past part. (9.2) <*cwielman* 'kill' <*cwealm* 'killing, murder' (7.5)
biscopas mid folcum	bishops with (their) peoples *biscopas* noun nom.sing.masc. (1.2); *mid* prep. with dat. 'with' (4.6); *folcum* noun dat.pl.neut. [this phrase is parallel to *sācerdas and mæsseprēostas* above]
būton ǣnigre āre scēawunge	without regard to any mercy *būton* prep. with dat. 'without' (4.6); *ǣnigre* adj. gen.sing.fem. <*ǣnig* 'any' (6.1); *āre* noun gen.sing.fem. <*ār* 'honour, mercy' (6.1); *scēawunge* noun dat.sing.fem. (dat. after *būton*) <*scēawung* 'respect, regard'
ætgædere mid īserne and līge fornumene wǣron.	were destroyed with fire and iron together. *ætgædere* adv. 'together'; *mid* prep. with dat. 'with, by means of' (4.6); *īserne* noun dat.sing.neut. (4.5); *līge* noun dat. sing.neut. (4.5); *fornumene* adj. nom.pl. masc. (agreeing with *biscopas*) past part. (11.5) < *forniman* 'destroy' (12.5); *wǣron* as above.

Text

Notes & Translation

And ne wæs sēo bebyrignes sealde

And burial was not given
ne adv. of negation (2.3); *wæs* as above; *sēo* dem. nom.sing.fem.; *bebyrignes* noun nom.sing.fem. 'burial'; *sealde* adj. nom.sing.fem past part. (9.2,10.2) <*sellan* 'give'

þām þe swā hrēowlīce ācwealde wǣron

to those who had been so cruelly killed
þām þe rel.pron. dat. as indirect obj. of *sealde* (7.2); *swā* adv. of degree 'so' (17.2); *hrēowlīce* adv. <*hrēow* 'cruel' (10.3); *ācwealde* adj. nom.pl. past part <*ācwellan* 'strike down kill'; *wǣron* as above.

And monige ðǣre earman lāfe on wēstenum fangene wǣron

And many (ones) of the wretched remnant were caught in deserted places
monige adj. nom.pl.masc. (12.2, 14.2); *ðǣre* dem. gen.sing.fem. agreeing with *lāfe* (14.2); *earman* adj. gen.sing.fem. weak after *ðǣre* (12.1); *lāfe* noun gen.sing.fem. <*lāf* 'remnant, remainder'; *on* prep. with dat. 'on, in' (4.6); *wēstenum* noun dat.pl.neut. <*wēsten* 'wasteland, deserted place' <*wēste* 'waste, barren'; *fangene* adj. nom.pl. agreeing with *monige* past part. <*fōn* 'take, seize, capture' (11.5,14.4); *wǣron* as above.

and hēapmǣlum sticode

stabbed in large numbers
hēapmǣlum adv. of degree 'wholesale, in large numbers'; *sticode* adj. nom.pl.masc. agreeing with *monige* past part. <*stician* 'stab' (9.2)

Sume for hungre heora fēondum on hand ēodon

Because of hunger, some gave themselves up to their enemies
sume pron. nom.pl.masc. 'some (ones)'; *for* prep. with dat. 'because of' (4.6); *hungre* noun dat.sing.masc. (4.5) dat. after *for*; *heora* poss.adj. (5.3); *fēondum* noun dat.pl.masc. (11.2, 10.4); *on* prep. with acc. 'into' *hand* noun acc.sing.fem. with *on*; *ēodon* verb 3rd pl. pret.ind. <*gān* (14.4) [*on hand gān* 'to go into the hand(s) of' means to surrender oneself into someone's power]

Text

Notes & Translation

and ēcne þēowdōm gehēton

and promised everlasting service
ēcne adj. acc.sing.masc. (4.1) agreeing with *þēowdōm* noun acc.sing.masc., object of *gehēton* verb 3rd pl.pret.ind. <*gehātan* 'promise, vow' <*hātan* 'call out, declare' (14.4)

wið ðon þe him mon andleofne forgēafe

provided that they should be given food
wið ðon þe conj. 'on condition that, provided that' <*wið* 'in exchange for'; *him* pers.pron.dat.pl.masc.; *mon* indefinite pronoun (8.5); *andleofne* noun acc.sing.fem. obj. of *forgēafe* verb 3rd sing. pret.subj. <*forgiefan* 'give up, hand over' (13.2, 16.4, 16.5)[subjunctive because they did so on condition that they *should be* given food]

Sume ofer sǣ sorgiende gewiton

Some passed in sorrow across (the) sea
sume as above; *ofer* prep. with acc. 'over, across' (4.4); *sǣ* noun acc.sing.masc. (acc. after *ofer*) (9.6); *sorgiende* pres.part. <*sorgian* 'be sorrowful, mourn' (13.5); *gewiton* verb 3rd pl.pret.ind. <*gewītan* 'go, pass, travel' (10.5)

sume forhtiende on ēðle gebidon

some stayed cowering in (their) homeland
sume as above; *forhtiende* pres.part. <*forhtian* 'be afraid' (13.5); *on* prep. with dat. 'on, in' (4.6); *ēðle* noun dat.sing.masc. (dat. after *on*) <*ēðel* 'homeland' (4.5); *gebidon* verb 3rd pl.pret.ind. <*gebīdan* 'wait, abide' (10.5)

and þearfende līf in wuda and in wēstenum

and a poverty-stricken life in woodland and wasteland
þearfende adj. acc.sing.neut < pres.part < *þearfan* 'be needy, be in poverty' (13.5); *līf* noun acc.sing.neut.; *in* prep. with dat. 'in, on'; *wuda* noun dat.sing.masc. (dat. after *in*) <*wudu* 'woodland' (9.5); *wēstenum* noun dat.pl.neut. <*wēsten* 'wasteland'

and on hēam clifum sorgiende mōde symle dydon

and on high cliffs with a sorrowing heart (they) carried on ever after.
on prep.with dat. 'on, in'; *hēam* adj. dat.pl.neut (4.2) agreeing with *clifum* noun dat.pl.neut. *clif* 'cliff'; *sorgiende* adj. dat.sing.masc. <pres.part as above; *mōde* noun dat. sing. masc. <*mōd* 'heart, mind' (17.3); *symle* adv. of time 'always'; *dydon* verb 3rd pl.pret.ind. <*dōn* 'do, carry out' (14.4)

2. Deniga Hergung

The Anglo-Saxon Chronicle
Entry for AD997

From Plummer's edition of the *Anglo-Saxon Chronicle*.

Hēr on ðissum gēare fērde se here ābūtan Defnanscīre intō Sæfernmūðan ond þǣr gehergodon ǣgðer ge on Cornwēalum ge on Norðwēalum ond on Defenum, ond ēodon him þā ūp æt Wecedport and þǣr micel yfel worhton on bærnette and on manslihtum. Ond æfter þām wendon eft ābūtan Penwihtsteort on ðā sūðhealfe ond wendon þā intō Tamermūðan ond ēodon þā ūp oðþæt hīe cōmon tō Hlidaforda ond ælc ðing bærndon ond slōgon þæt hīe gemētton ond Ordulfes mynster æt Tæfingsctoce forbærndon ond unāsecgendlīce herehūðe mid him tō scipum brōhton.

Text	Notes & Translation
Hēr	Here [annals are set out serially, so this means 'at this point in the record' – most ASC entries begin with *hēr*]
on ðissum gēare	in this year *on* prep. with dat. 'in, on'; *ðissum* dem. dat.sing. neut. agreeing with *gēare* noun dat.sing.neut.
fērde se here	the invading force travelled *fērde* 3rd sing.pret.ind. <*fēran* 'travel, go along'; *se* dem. nom.sing.masc. agreeing with *here* noun nom.sing.masc. subject of *fērde* [the *here* is a Viking fleet and army mentioned in previous annals]
ābūtan Defnanscīre	around Devonshire *ābūtan* prep. with acc. 'about, around'; *Defnanscīre* noun acc.sing.fem <*Defnan* 'men of Devon' + *scīr* 'shire, division'
intō Sæfernmūðan	into the mouth of the Severn *intō* prep. with dat. 'to, into, against'; *Sæfernmūðan* noun dat.sing.masc. <*Sæfern* 'the Severn' (British *Sābrinā*) + *mūða* 'rivermouth'

<u>Text</u>	<u>Notes & Translation</u>
ond ðǣr gehergodon	and harried there *ðǣr* adv. 'there, at that place'; *gehergodon* 3rd pl.pret.ind. <*gehergian* 'harry, ravage' [the forms of this verb with and without the prefix *ge-* do not appear to have substantially different meanings]
ǣgðer ge on Cornwēalum ge on Norðwēalum	both in Cornwall and Wales *ǣgðer* conj. a reduced form of *ǣghwæðer* 'either, both' often occurring with *ge... ge...* conj. 'both ... and ...' *on* prep.with dat. 'on, against'; *Cornwēalum*, noun dat.pl.masc. <*Corn-* 'Cornish' (<British *Cornovii*) + *walh* 'Briton, servant' *Norðwēalum* noun dat.pl.masc. 'North Welsh' [*walh* was a generic Germanic name for a Celtic-speaker, here distinguished by the tribal name *Cornovii* and the geographical denomination 'north']
and on Defenum	and in Devon *Defenum* noun dat.pl.masc.
and ēodon him	and went *ēodon* 3rd pl.pret.ind. <*gān* 'go'; *him* refl.pron. (14.4)
þā ūp æt Wecedport	then up to Watchet *þā* adv. 'then'; *ūp* adv. 'up'; *æt* prep. with acc. 'towards, to'; *Wecedport* noun acc.sing.masc. <*port* 'town, port' [*æt* only rarely takes the accusative]
ond þǣr micel yfel worhton	and wrought great evil there *micel* adj. acc.sing. neut. agreeing with *yfel* noun acc.sing.neut.; *worhton* 3rd pl.pret.ind. <*wyrcan* 'make, bring about'
on bærnette and on manslihtum	in burning and slaying men *on* prep. with dat. 'on, in'; *bærnette* noun dat.sing. neut. (dat.after *on*) <*bærnet* <*bærnan* 'burn, set fire to'; *manslihtum* noun dat.pl.masc. <*mansliht* 'manslaughter, murder'
Ond æfter ðām	and after those (things) *æfter* prep.with dat. 'after'; *ðām* pron. dat.pl.masc. (14.5) 'those'

179

Text	Notes & Translation
wendon eft ābūtan Penwihtsteort	(they) turned back round Land's End *wendon* 3rd pl.pret.ind. <*wendan* 'turn'; *eft* adv. 'after, back, again'; *Penwihtsteort* noun acc.sing.masc. 'the Penwith Peninsula' <*steort* 'start, beginning, tail' [the Penwith Peninsula, the westernmost part of Cornwall]
on ðā sūðhealfe	onto the southern side *on* prep.with acc. 'onto, into'; *ðā* dem. acc.sing.fem. agreeing with *sūðhealfe* noun acc.sing.fem. <*sūð* 'south' + *healf* 'half, side'
ond wendon þā intō Tamermūðan	and then turned into the mouth of the Tamar *wendon* as above; *Tamermūðan* noun dat.sing.masc. as above
ond ēodon þā ūp oðþæt hīe cōmon tō Hlidaforda	and travelled up until they came to Lydford *ēodon* as above; *oðþæt* conj. 'until'; *cōmon* 3rd pl.pret. ind. <*cuman* 'come'(12.5); *tō* prep.with dat. 'to'; *Hlidaforda* noun dat.sing. masc.(9.5)
ond ǣlc ðing bærndon ond slōgon þæt hīe gemētton	and (they) burnt and slew every thing they came across *ǣlc* adj. acc.sing. agreeing with *ðing* noun acc.sing.neut., obj. of *bærndon* 3rd pl.pret. ind. <*bærnan* 'burn, set fire to' and *slōgon* 3rd pl.pret.ind. <*slēan* 'slay'; *þæt* rel.pron. acc.sing.neut. (7.1) obj. of *gemētton* 3rd pl.pret.ind. <*mētan* 'meet, encounter'
ond Ordulfes mynster forbærndon	and burnt down Ordulf's minster *Ordulfes* noun gen.sing.masc. <*Ordulf* (<*ord* 'spearpoint' + *wulf* 'wolf') (17.4); *mynster* noun acc.sing.neut. obj. of *forbærndon* 3rd pl.pret.ind. <*forbærnan* 'burn down'
æt Tæfingstoce	at Tavistock *æt* prep.with dat. 'at'; *Tæfingstoce* noun dat.sing.neut.
ond unāsecgendlīce herehūþe mid him tō scipum brōhton	and brought untold plunder with them to (their) ships *unāsecgendlīce* adj. acc.sing.fem. agreeing with *herehūþe* noun acc.sing.fem. obj. of *brōhton* 3rd pl.pret.ind. <*bringan* 'bring, fetch'(10.2); *mid* prep.with dat. 'with'; *him* pers.pron.dat.pl.masc. 'them'; *tō* prep.with dat. 'to'; *scipum* noun dat.pl.neut. <*scip* 'ship'

3. Lǣcedōmas

A Remedy for Blains and Another for Poisoning

From Cockayne's edition of the *Leechdoms*. (Don't try these at home!)

Wið ðā blegene genim nigon ǣgra ond sēoð hīe fæste, ond nim þā geolcan ond dō þæt hwīte āweg, ond mera ðā geolcan on ānre pannan, ond wring þæt wōs ūt þurh ǣnne clāð, ond nim eall swā fela dropena wīnes swā ðāra ǣgra bēo, and eall swā fela dropena unhālgodes eles, ond eall swā fela huniges dropena, ond of finoles moran eall swā fela dropena, genim ðonne ond dō hit eall tōsomne ond wring ūt ðurh ǣnne clāð ond sele ðām menn etan. Him bið sōna sel.

Gif mon ðung ete, āþecge buteran ond drince – se ðung gewīt on ðā buteran. Eft wið ðone, stande on hēafde, āslēge him mon fela scearpena on þām scancan, þonne gewīt ūt þæt ātter þurh þā scearpan.

Text	Notes & Translation
Wið ðā blegene	Against the blain *wið* prep.with acc. 'against'; *ðā* dem. acc.sing.fem. agreeing with *blegene* noun acc.sing.fem. <*blegen* 'blain, sore, boil'
genim nigon ǣgra	take nine eggs together *genim* verb 2nd sing.imp. <*geniman* 'take, bring together' (6.4); *nigon* 'nine' with partitive gen. (14.2) *ǣgra* gen.pl.neut. <*ǣg* 'egg' (10.4)
ond sēoð hīe fæste	and hard-boil them *sēoð* verb 2nd sing.imp. <*sēoðan* 'boil'; *fæste* adv. <*fæst* 'fast, hard, firm'; *hīe* pers.pron. acc.pl.neut.
ond nim ðā geolcan	and take the yolks *nim* verb 2nd sing.imp. <*niman* 'take, remove'; *ðā* dem. acc.pl.masc. agreeing with *geolcan* noun acc.pl.masc. <*geolca* 'yolk'
ond dō þæt hwīte āweg	and remove the white *dō* verb 2nd sing.imp. <*dōn* 'do, put'; *þæt* dem. acc.sing. neut. agreeing with *hwīte* noun acc.sing.neut. 'white (part)' (12.2); *āweg* adv. 'away'

Text	Notes & Translation
ond mera ðā geolcan on ānre pannan	and purify the yolks in one pan *mera* verb 2nd sing.imp. <*merian* 'cleanse'; *ðā geolcan* as above; *on* prep.with dat. 'in'; *ānre* num. dat.sing.fem. agreeing with *pannan* noun acc.sing.fem <*panne* 'pan, vessel'
ond wring þæt wōs ūt þurh ænne clāð	and wring out the liquid through one cloth *wring* verb 2nd sing.imp. <*wringan* 'wring, twist'; *þæt* dem. acc.sing.neut. agreeing with *wōs* noun acc.sing. neut.; *ūt* adv. 'out'; *þurh* prep.with acc. 'through'; *ænne* num. acc.sing.masc. agreeing with *clāð* noun acc.sing. masc.
ond nim eall swā fela dropena wīnes swā ðāra ægra bēo	and take as many drops of wine as there are eggs *nim* as above; *eall* adv. 'all, entirely'; *swā...swā* conj. as...as; *fela* adj. 'many' (14.2); *dropena* gen.pl.masc. <*dropa* 'drop, drip'; *wīnes* gen.sing.neut. <*wīn* 'wine'; *ðāra* dem. gen.pl.neut. agreeing with *ægra* as above; *bēo* 3rd sing.pres.subj. <*bēon* 'be' [...and take all as many (of) drops of wine as (it may) be of the eggs]
ond eall swā fela dropena unhālgodes eles	and as many drops of unhallowed wine *ond eall swā fela dropena* as above; *unhālgodes* adj. gen.sing.neut. <*unhālgod* 'unhallowed, unconsecrated' past part <*hālgian* 'hallow, consecrate' agreeing with *eles* noun gen.sing.neut. <*ele* 'oil'
ond eall swā fela huniges dropena	and as many drops of honey *ond eall swā fela dropena* as above; *huniges* noun gen. sing. neut. <*hunig* 'honey'
ond of finoles moran eall swā fela dropena	and from the root of fennel as many drops *of* prep.with dat. 'from'; *finoles* noun gen.sing.masc. <*finol* 'fennel'; *moran* noun dat.sing.fem. <*more* 'root, tuber' (dat. after *of*); *eall swā fela dropena* as above
genim ðonne ond dō hit eall tōsomne	then take (these things) and put it all together *genim* as above; *ðonne* adv. 'then'; *dō* as above; *hit* pers. pron. acc.sing.neut.; *eall* adj. acc.sing.neut. agreeing with *hit*; *tōsomne* adv. 'together'
ond wring ūt þurh ænne clāð	and wring (it) out through one cloth as above

Text	Notes & Translation
ond sele ðām menn etan	and give (it) to the person to eat *sele* verb 2nd sing.imp. <*sellan* 'give'; *ðām* dem. dat.sing.masc. agreeing with *menn* noun dat.sing.masc. <*mann* 'person'; *etan* verb inf.
Him bið sōna sēl	To him (it) shall be immediately well *him* pers.pron.dat.sing.masc. (masc. agreeing with *mann*); *bið* 3rd sing.pres.ind. <*bēon* 'be'; *sōna* adv. 'straightaway'; *sel* adj. nom.sing.neut. 'healthy, well, sound' and hence 'cured'
Gif mon ðung ete	If someone should eat a poisonous plant *gif* conj. 'if'; *mon* indef.pron. 'someone, anyone' (8.5); *ðung* acc.sing.masc. obj. of *ete* verb 3rd sing.pres.subj. <*etan* 'eat' [*ðung* is sometimes identified with the plant 'wolfsbane']
āðecge buteran	(let him) take butter *āðecge* verb 3rd sing.pres.subj. <*āðecgan* 'receive, take'; *buteran* noun acc.sing.fem. <*butere* 'butter'
and drince	and (let him) drink *drince* 3rd sing.pres.subj. <*drincan* 'drink' [not an injunction to drink butter, but rather to take butter and (strong?) drink together]
se þung gewīt on þā buteran	the poisonous matter passes into the butter *se* dem. nom.sing.masc. agreeing with *þung* noun nom.sing.masc. subject of *gewīt* 3rd sing.pres.ind. <*gewītan* 'pass, travel, go'; *on* prep.with acc. 'into'; *þā* dem. acc.sing.fem. agreeing with *buteran* noun acc.sing.fem.
Eft wið ðone	Again, against that *eft* adv. 'again'; *wið* prep.with acc. 'against'; *ðone* pron. acc.sing.masc. (14.5)
stande on hēafde āslēge him mon	(let him) stand on (his) head, (let) someone strike him *stande* verb 3rd sing.pres.subj. <*standan* 'stand'; *on* prep.with dat. 'on'; *hēafde* noun dat.sing.neut. <*hēafod* 'head'; *āslēge* verb 3rd sing.pres.subj. <*āslēan* 'strike'; *him* pers.pron. dat.sing.masc.; *mon* as above

<u>Text</u>	<u>Notes & Translation</u>
fela scearpena on þām scancan	many cuts on the leg *fela* as above; *scearpena* noun gen.pl.fem. <*scearpe* 'cut, graze, scoring'; *on* as above; *þām* dat.sing.masc. agreeing with *scancan* noun dat.sing.masc. <*scanca* 'shank, leg'
þonne gewīt ūt þæt ātter ðurh ðā scearpan.	then the poison passes out through the cuts. *þonne* as above; *gewīt* as above; *ūt* as above; *þæt* dem. nom.sing.neut. agreeing with *ātter* noun nom.sing.neut.; *ðurh* prep.with acc. 'through'; *ðā* dem. acc.pl.fem. agreeing with *scearpan* noun acc.pl.fem.

4. Ines Dōmas

Two Extracts from the Laws of King Inc

Be Ines dōmum. xliiij. Ic, Ine, mid Godes giefe Westseaxena cyning, mid geðeahte ond mid lāre Cēnredes mīnes fæder ond Heddes mīnes biscopes ond ēorcenwaldes mīnes biscopes, mid eallum mīnum ealdormonnum ond þæm ieldstum witum mīnre ðēode ond ēac micelre gesomnunge Godes ðēowa, wæs smēagende be ðære hǣlo ūrra sāwla ond be ðǣm staþole ūres rīces, ðætte riht ǣw ond rihte cynedōmas ðurh ūre folc gefæstnode ond getrymede wǣren, þætte nǣnig ealdormanna ne ūs undergeðēodedra æfter þām wǣre āwendende ðās ūre dōmas.

Be gefeohtum. l. Gif hwā gefeohte on cyninges hūse sīe hē scyldig ealles his ierfes ond sīe on cyninges dōme hwæðer hē līf āge oþþe nāge. Gif hwā on mynstre gefeohte, cxx scillinga gebēte. Gif hwā on ealdormonnes hūse gefeohte oððe on ōðres geðungenes witan, lx scillinga gebēte hē ond ōþer lx geselle tō wīte. Gif ðonne on gafolgeldan hūse oððe on gebūres gefeohte cxx scillinga tō wīte geselle and ðām gebūre vi scillinga. Ond þēah hit sīe on middum felda gefohten, cxx scillinga tō wīte sīe āgiefen. Gif ðonne on gebēorscipe hie geciden ond ōðer hiora mid geðylde hit forbere, geselle se ōðer xxx scillinga tō wīte.

Text	Notes & Translation
Be Ines dōmum	Concerning the judgements of (King) Ine *be* prep.with dat. 'by, about, concerning'; *Ines* noun gen.sing. masc. <*Ine* [personal name]; *dōmum* noun dat.pl.masc. <*dōm* 'judgement' (dat. after *be*).
xliiij.	44 [the numbering is due to these laws' inclusion in the law code of King Alfred]
Ic, Ine, mid Godes giefe Westseaxena cyning	I, Ine, King of the West Saxons by God's favour *ic* pers.pron. 1st sing.nom.; *mid* prep.with dat. 'with'; *Godes* noun gen.sing.masc. <*God* 'God'; *giefe* noun dat.sing.fem. <*giefu* 'gift, favour, grace'; *Westseaxena* noun gen.pl.masc. <*Westseaxe* 'West Saxons'; *cyning* noun nom.sing.masc.
mid geðeahte ond mid lāre	with (the) consideration and (the) instruction *mid* prep.with dat.; *geðeahte* noun dat.sing.neut. <*geðeaht; lāre* noun dat.sing.fem. <*lār.*

185

Text	Notes & Translation
Cēnredes mīnes fæder	of Cenred, my father, *Cēnredes* noun gen.sing.masc. *<Cēnred* [personal name]; *mīnes* poss.adj. gen.sing.masc. agreeing with *fæder* noun gen.sing.masc. (10.1)
ond Heddes mīnes biscopes	and of Hedde, my bishop, *Heddes* noun gen.sing.masc. *<Hedde* (6.2) [personal name]; *mīnes* as above; *biscopes* noun gen.sing.masc. *<biscop*
ond Eorcenwaldes mīnes biscopes	and of Eorcenwald, my bishop, *Eorcenwaldes* noun gen.sing.masc. *<Eorcenwald* [personal name]
mid eallum mīnum ealdormonnum	with all my governors *mid* prep.with dat.; *eallum* adj. dat.pl.masc. *<eall*; *mīnum* poss.adj. dat.pl.masc.; *ealdormonnum* noun dat.pl.masc. *<ealdormonn* [an *ealdormonn* was a provincial governor and the highest ranking official of secular administration]
and þām ieldstum witum mīnre ðēode	and the most senior advisers of my people *þām* dem. dat.pl.masc.; *ieldstum* adj. dat.pl.masc. superlative of *eald; witum* noun dat.pl.masc *<wita* 'wise man, adviser' (all dat. after *mid*); *mīnre* poss.adj. gen.sing.fem. agreeing with *ðēode* noun gen.sing.fem. *<ðēod* [the *witan* (pl. of *wita*) was the circle of royal advisers and counsellors to whom the king could turn for expert opinion]
ond ēac micelre gesomnunge Godes ðēowa	and also a great gathering of God's servants *ēac* conj.; *micelre* adj. dat.sing.fem. *<micel; gesomnunge* noun dat.sing.fem. *<gesomnung; Godes* as above; *ðēowa* noun gen.pl.masc. *<ðēow*
wæs smēagende be ðǣre hǣlo ūrra sāwla	thought about the well-being of our souls *wæs* as above; *smēagende* verb pres.part.(13.5) *<smēagan; be* prep.with dat.; *ðǣre* dem. dat.sing.fem. agreeing with *hǣlo* noun dat.sing.fem. (9.6); *ūrra* poss.adj. gen.pl.fem. agreeing with *sāwla* gen.pl.fem. *<sāwol* [the subject of *wæs smēagende* is *ic* several lines earlier]

186

Text

Notes & Translation

ond be ðǣm staþole ūres rīces

and about the foundation of our kingdom
be as above; *ðǣm* dem.dat.sing.masc. agreeing with
staþole dat.sing.masc. <*staþol*; *ūres* poss.adj.
gen.sing.neut. agreeing with *rīces* noun gen.sing.neut.
<*rīce* (6.2)

þætte riht ǣw ond rihte cynedōmas

so that just law and just royal judgements
þætte conj. 'so that'; *riht* adj. nom.sing.fem. agreeing
with *ǣw* noun nom.sing.fem.; *rihte* adj. nom.pl.masc.
<*riht* agreeing with *cynedōmas* noun nom.pl.masc.

ðurh ūre folc gefæstnode and getrymede wǣren

should be made firm and strong throughout our people
ðurh prep.with acc.; *ūre* poss.adj. nom.sing.neut.
agreeing with *folc* noun nom.sing.neut.; *gefæstnode* adj.
nom.sing.neut. <past part. <*fæstnian*; *getrymede* adj.
nom.sing.neut. <past part. <*trymman*; *wǣren* verb 3rd
pl.pret.subj. (16.4,5,6).

þætte nǣnig ealdormonna

so that none of (the) governors
þætte as above; *nǣnig* pron. nom.sing.masc in partitive
gen. (14.2) with *ealdormonna* noun gen.pl.masc.

ne ūs undergeðēodedra

nor of those subject to us
ne conj. 'nor'; *ūs* pers.pron. dat.pl.1st; *undergeðēodedra*
adj. used substantively (12.2) gen.pl.masc. <past part.
<*undergeðēodan* 'subdue, rule over'

æfter þām wǣre āwendende ðās ūre dōmas

after them should change these, our judgements
æfter prep.with dat.; *þām* pron. dat.pl.masc. (14.5); *wǣre*
verb 3rd sing.pret.subj.; *āwendende* pres.part <*āwendan*;
ðās pron. acc.pl.masc.; *ūre* poss.adj. acc.pl.masc.
agreeing with *dōmas* noun acc.pl.masc. <*dōm*

Be gefeohtum. l.

Concerning fighting. 50.
be prep.with dat.; *gefeohtum* noun dat.pl.neut. <*gefeoht*;
'50' is the number of the law

gif hwā gefeohte on cyninges hūse

if anyone should fight in (the) king's house
gif conj. 'if'; *hwā* pron.(8.5); *gefeohte* verb 3rd
sing.pres.subj. <*gefeohtan*; *on* prep.with dat.; *cyninges*
noun gen.sing.masc. <*cyning*; *hūse* noun dat.sing.neut.
<*hūs*.

Text	Notes & Translation
sīe hē scyldig ealles his īerfes	let him be liable (to the extent) of all his property *sīe* verb 3rd sing.pres.subj.(16.6); *hē* pers.pron. nom.sing.masc 3rd; *scyldig* adj. nom.sing masc.; *ealles* adj. gen.sing.neut. <*eall*; *his* poss.adj. gen.sing.neut. agreeing with *īerfes* noun gen.sing.neut. <*īerfe*
ond sīe on cyninges dōme hwæðer hē līf āge oþþe nāge	and let it be in the king's decision whether he may have life or not *sīe* as above; *on cyninges* as above; *dōme* noun dat.sing.masc.; *hwæðer* conj. 'whether'; *hē* as above; *līf* noun acc.sing.neut.; *āge* verb 3rd sing.pres.subj. <*āgan*; *oþþe* conj. 'or'; *nāge* verb <*ne + āge* as above.
Gif hwā on mynstre gefeohte cxx scillinga gebēte	If anyone should fight in a minster, let him atone (with)120 shillings *gif hwā on* as above; *mynstre* noun dat.sing.neut. <*mynster*; *gefeohte* as above; *cxx* num. '120'; *scillinga* noun gen.pl.masc. partitive gen.; *gebēte* verb 3rd sing.pres.subj. <*gebētan*
Gif hwā on ealdormonnes hūse gefeohte	If anyone should fight in a governor's house as above except *ealdormonnes* noun gen.sing.masc.
oððe on ōðres geðungenes witan lx scillinga gebēte hē	or (that of) another high-ranking adviser, let him atone (with) 60 shillings *ōðres* adj. gen.sing.masc. agreeing with *witan*; *geðungenes* adj. gen.sing.masc. <*geðungen* ; *witan* noun gen.sing. masc. <*wita*; *lx* num. (=*siextig*) 'sixty'.
ond ōþer lx geselle tō wīte	and let him give another 60 as a punishment *ōþer* adj. acc.sing.neut. agreeing with *lx* num. '60' (14.3, note); *geselle* verb 3rd sing.pres.subj. <*gesellan*; *tō* prep.with dat.; *wīte* noun dat.sing.neut. <*wīte*
Gif ðonne on gafolgeldan hūse oððe on gebūres gefeohte	If (he) should fight in a tax-payer's house or a farmer's *gif* conj.; *ðonne* adv. 'then'; *gafolgeldan* noun gen.sing. masc. <*gafolgelda* 'tribute-giver, tax-payer'; *gebūres* noun gen.sing.masc. <*gebūr* 'farmer' [both *gafolgelda* and *gebūr* are ranks of freeman]

Text	Notes & Translation
cxx scillinga tō wīte gescllc ond þām gebūre vi scillinga	let him pay 120 shillings as a fine and 6 shillings to the farmer *þām* dem. dat.sing.masc. agreeing with *gebūre* dat.sing.masc. <*gebūr*; *cxx* (=*hund twintig*) 'one hundred and twenty'; *vi* num. '6'
Ond þēah hit sīe on middum felda gefohten	And even though it be fought in the middle of open country *þēah* conj.; *hit* pers.pron. nom.sing.masc. (= *þæt gefeoht*); *sīe* as above; *on* prep.with dat.; *middum* adj. dat.sing. masc. agreeing with *felda* noun dat.sing.masc (9.5); *gefohten* past part. <*feohtan* (12.3)
cxx scillinga tō wīte sīe āgiefen	let 120 shillings be given as a fine *āgiefen* past part. <*āgiefan*
Gif ðonne on gebēorscipe hīe gecīden	If they then may quarrel at a drinking-bout *gif ðonne* as above; *on* as above; *gebēorscipe* noun dat.sing.masc.; *gecīden* verb 3rd pl.pres.subj. <*gecīdan*
ond ōðer hiora mid geðylde hit forbere,	and (one or) other of them should endure it patiently *ōðer* pron. nom.sing.masc.; *hiora* pron. gen.pl. (partitive gen.); *mid* prep.with dat.; *geðylde* noun dat.sing.fem <*geðyld*; *hit* pron. acc.sing.neut (= the quarrelling); *forbere* verb 3rd sing.pres.subj. <*forberan*
geselle se ōðer xxx scillinga tō wīte.	let the other one give 30 shillings as a fine. *xxx* num. (=*ðrītig*) 'thirty'

Glossary to the Selected Texts

Excluded are the personal pronouns, forms of *se* and *ðes,* and *þe*. Alphabetically, *æ* follows *a* and *ð* follows *t*; words beginning *ge-* are included under *g*.

The following abbreviations are used:

adj.	adjective		*num.*	numeral
adv.	adverb		*pl.*	plural
f.	feminine noun		*poss.adj.*	possessive adjective
m.	masculine noun		*prep.*	preposition
n.	neuter noun		*v.*	verb

ābūtan	prep.	about, around		*æt*	prep.	(1) with dat. 'at'
ācwellan	v.	kill				(2) with acc. 'to'
ādrīfan	v.	drive off		*ætgædre*	adv.	together
āgan	v.	have		*ēw*	f.	law
āgiefan	v.	give up, hand over		*bærnan*	v.	burn, set fire
ān	num.	one		*bærnet*	n.	burning
and	conj.	and		*be*	prep.	with dat. 'by,
andlēofen	f.	food, reward,				concerning, about'
		sustenance		*bebod*	n.	command, behest
Angle	m.pl.	Angles, English		*bebyrignys*	f.	burial
Angleþēod	f.	Anglian folk,		*bēon*	v.	be
		English nation		*bēotung*	f.	threat, promise
Angulus	m.	Angeln		*betwuh*	prep.	between
ānlīpie	adv.	singly		*biscop*	m.	bishop
ār	f.	honour		*blegen*	f.	blain, sore, boil
ārlēas	adj.	impious, lacking		*bringan*	v.	bring, fetch
		honour		*Bryttas*	m.pl.	Britons
āslēan	v.	strike, beat		*Bryten*	f.	Britain
ātter	n.	poison		*butere*	f.	butter
āðecgan	v.	get, receive		*būton*	prep.	with dat. 'without'
āweg	adv.	away		*Cantware*	m.pl.	Kentish folk
āwendan	v.	change, alter		*cāsere*	m.	Caesar
æfter	prep.	with dat. 'after'		*ceaster*	f.	fort, stronghold
ēg	n.	egg		*Chāldeas*	m.pl.	Chaldeans
ēgðer	conj.	either, both		*cīgan*	v.	call, summon
ēlc	adj.	each, every		*clāð*	m.	cloth
ēnig	adj.	any		*clif*	n.	cliff
ēr	adv.	previously		*compian*	v.	fight, campaign
ērendraca	m.	messenger		*Cornwēalas*	m.pl.	Cornish men
ērest	adv.	at first		*cuman*	v.	come

cwielman	v.	kill
cynedōm	m.	kingly judgement, legal decision
cynelīc	adj.	royal, kingly
cyning	m.	king
cyningcynn	n.	royal family
cynn	n.	(1) kin, family (2) race
cȳðan	v.	declare, make known
dǣd	f.	deed, action
Defnanscīr	f.	Devonshire
Defenan	m.pl.	men of Devon
dōm	m.	judgement
dōn	v.	(1) do, carry out (2) put, take
drihten	m.	lord
drincan	v.	drink
dropa	m.	drop, drip
ēac	conj.	also, besides
eald	adj.	old
ealdormonn	m.	provincial governor
Ealdseaxan	m.pl.	Old Saxons
eall	adj.	all
ēalond	n.	island
eardungstōw	f.	dwelling-place
earm	adj.	poor
ēastdǣl	m.	eastern part
Ēastengle	m.pl.	East Angles
Ēastsǣ	m.	North Sea
Ēastseaxan	m.pl.	East Saxons
ēce	adj.	eternal, everlasting
eft	adv.	(1) back (2) again
ege	m.	fear, dread
ele	n.	oil
Engle	m.pl.	Angles (= Angle)
etan	v.	eat
ēðel	m.	homeland
fæder	m.	father
fæst	adj.	hard, firm
fæstnian	v.	make firm
feallan	v.	fall
fela	adj.	many
feld	m.	open country
feohtan	v.	fight
fēond	m.	enemy
feor	adv.	far
fēower	num.	four
fēowertig	num.	forty
fēran	v.	travel, go along
findan	v.	find
finol	m.	fennel
folc	n.	(1) nation, people (2) military force
fōn	v.	take, seize, capture
for	prep.	with dat. 'for'
forbærnan	v.	burn down, destroy with fire
forberan	v.	forbear, endure, tolerate
foresprecen	adj.	above-mentioned, aforesaid
forgiefan	v.	give up, hand over
forhergian	v.	harry, ravage
forhtian	v.	be afraid, fear
forniman	v.	destroy, devastate, overcome
fram	prep.	with dat. 'from'
fruma	m.	source, origin
fȳr	n.	fire
gafolgelda	m.	tax-payer, freeman
gān	v.	go
ge ... ge	conj.	both ... and
gēar	n.	year
Geatas	m.pl.	Geats, Jutes
gebēorscipe	m.	drinking-bout, party
gebētan	v.	atone, compensate
gebīdan	v.	stay, remain, abide
gebrōðru	n.pl.	brothers
gebūr	m.	farmer, freeman

191

gecīdan	v.	trade insults, quarrel	*hātan*	v.	(1) call, speak out (2) bid, order
gedāl	n.	separation, division	*hǣlo*	f.	health, well-being
			hēafod	n.	head
gefeoht	n.	fighting, battle	*hēah*	adj.	high
gefeohtan	v.	fight	*hēapmǣlum*	adv.	in large numbers
gehātan	v.	promise	*hēr*	adv.	(1) here
gehergian	v.	harry			(2) at this point (in the annals)
gehwǣr	adv.	everywhere			
gehwylc	pron.	each, every	*here*	m.	army, invading force
gemētan	v.	meet, come across, encounter			
			herehūð	f.	spoils of war, plunder
gemynegian	v.	remember, mention, call to mind	*heretoga*	m.	warlord, military leader
geniman	v.	collect, bring together	*hergian*	v.	harry, ravage
			hider	adv.	hither, to this place
geolca	m.	yolk	*Hlidaford*	m.	Lydford
gesellan	v.	hand over, pay	*hrēosan*	v.	fall
geslēan	v.	win by fighting	*hrēowlīce*	adv.	cruelly
gesomnung	f.	assembly, gathering	*hund*	num., n.	hundred
			hunger	m.	hunger, starvation
getimber	n.	building	*hunig*	n.	honey
geðeaht	n.	consideration, deliberation	*hūs*	n.	house, dwelling
			hwā	pron.	someone, anyone
geðēodan	v.	join forces, unite	*hwæðer*	conj.	whether
geðungen	adj.	high-ranking, noble	*hwæðere*	conj.	however, nevertheless
geðyld	f.	patience, forbearance	*hwīte*	n.	white part, albumen
gewerian	v.	unite in defence	*ielding*	f.	delay
gewinn	n.	strife, hardship	*ierfe*	n.	property, possessions
gewinna	m.	adversary			
gewītan	v.	go, move, pass	*intinga*	m.	cause
giefan	v.	give	*ilca*	adj.	same
giefu	f.	gift, favour, grace	*in*	prep.	(1) with acc. 'into' (2) with dat. 'in'
gif	conj.	if			
god	m.	God	*intō*	prep.	with dat. 'into, to'
habban	v.	have	*īsern*	n.	iron
hām	adv.	home	*īu*	adv.	once, previously
hand	f.	(1) hand (2) power	*lāf*	f.	remnant, remainder

land	n.	land
landbigenga	m.	inhabitant of a land
lār	f.	lore, knowledge, instruction
lātteōw	m.	leader
laðian	v.	invite
lǣdan	v.	lead, draw, take
lǣstan	v.	make good a vow
līf	n.	life
līg	n.	fire, blaze
magan	v.	be able
man	pron.	one, someone
mann	m.	human being, person
mansliht	m.	manslaughter, murder, killing
māra	adj.	more, greater
mǣgð	f.	kindred, folk, tribe
mæssepreost	m.	priest
menniscnys	f.	humanity
merian	v.	(1) test (2) cleanse
micel	adj.	great, large
miclian	v.	grow, get bigger
mid	prep.	with dat. 'with, by means of'
midd	adj.	middle, central
Middelengle	m.pl.	Middle Angles
Mierce	m.pl.	Mercians
mīn	poss. adj.	my
mōd	m.	heart, mind
mon	pron.	someone, anyone
monig	adj.	many
more	f.	root
mūða	m.	rivermouth, estuary
mynster	n.	minster, monastery
nǣnig	pron.	none, no
nēah	adv.	almost, nearly
nemnan	v.	name
nemne	conj.	unless
nigon	num.	nine
niman	v.	take, capture
norðan	adv.	from the north

Norðhymbre	m.pl.	Northumbrians
Norðwēalas	m.pl.	Welsh
of	prep.	with dat. 'off, from
ofer	prep.	with acc. 'over, across, beyond'
oft	adv.	often
on	prep.	(1) with acc. 'into, onto' (2) with dat. 'in, on'
oneardian	v.	dwell in, inhabit
onfōn	v.	acquire, receive
onginnan	v.	begin, start
onhergian	v.	harry against, ravage
openlīce	adv.	openly, plainly
oð	prep.	with acc. 'until, up to'
ōðer	adj.	(1) other, another (2) second
oþþæt	conj.	until
panne	f.	pan, vessel
Penwihtsteort	m.	Penwith peninsula, Land's End
rīce	n.	(1) kingdom (2) rule
riht	adj.	right, true, just
rihte	adv.	rightly
sācerd	m.	clergyman
sāwol	f.	soul, spirit
Sæfernmūða	m.	mouth of the Severn
scanca	m.	leg
scearpe	f.	cut, scoring
scēawung	f.	respect, regard
scilling	m.	shilling, silver coin
scip	n.	ship
sciphere	m.	seaborne army
scīr	f.	shire, division
sculan	v.	have to, be obliged to
scyldig	adj.	liable, owing
Seaxe	m.pl.	Saxons
sēcan	v.	seek, look for
secgan	v.	say, tell

sēl	adj.	sound, cured, well	*tōwyrd*	f.	opportunity,
self	adj.	self, same			occasion
sellan	v.	give, hand over	*trymman*	v.	make strong,
sendan	v.	send			support
seofon	num.	seven	*twēgen*	num.	two
sēoðan	v.	boil	*twintig*	num.	twenty
sibb	f.	peace	*ðā*	adv.	then
siexta	num.	sixth	*ðanon*	adv.	thence, from there
siextig	num.	sixty	*ðǣr*	adv.	(1) there
sige	n.	victory			(2) wherever
slēan	v.	(1) strike	*ðæt*	conj.	that
		(2) strike down,	*ðætte*	conj.	so that
		slay	*ðēah*	conj.	(even) though
smēagan	v.	think, consider,	*ðearfan*	v.	be needy
		reflect	*ðēod*	f.	nation, tribe
somod	adv.	together	*ðēow*	m.	servant
sōna	adv.	immediately	*ðēowdōm*	m.	bondage, servitude
sorgian	v.	sorrow, be sad	*ðing*	n.	thing, item
standan	v.	stand	*ðonne*	adv.	(1) then (2) than
staþol	m.	foundation,	*ðrēo*	num.	three
		establishment,	*ðrītig*	num.	thirty
		security	*ðung*	m.	poisonous plant
stician	v.	stab, knife	*ðurh*	prep.	with acc. 'through'
strang	adj.	strong	*unāsecgendlic*	adj.	uncountable, untold
strȳnd	f.	stock, lineage	*undergeðēodan*	v.	subdue, rule
sum	pron.	some(one)	*ungelīc*	adj.	unlike, dissimilar
sunu	m.	son	*unhālgod*	adj.	unconsecrated
sūðhealf	f.	southern side	*unoferswīð-*		
Sūðseaxan	m.pl.	South Saxons	*endlīc*	adj.	irresistible'
swā		(1) conj. 'so'	*ūp*	adv.	'up'
		(2) adv. 'so'	*ūre*	poss. adj.	'our'
swīðe	adv.	(1) very	*ūt*	adv.	'out'
		(2) greatly, strongly	*wæstmbǣrnys*	f.	'fruitfulness'
symle	adv.	ever, always	*weall*	m.	'wall'
synn	f.	sin	*weaxan*	v.	'grow, get bigger'
Tamermūða	m.	mouth of the Tamar	*Wecedport*	m.	'Watchet'
Tæfingstoc	n.	Tavistock	*wendan*	v.	'turn, go'
tīd	f.	time	*werod*	n.	(1) 'bodyguard'
tō	prep.	with dat. 'to'			(2) 'military force'
tō ðon ðæt	adv.	so that	*wesan*	v.	'to be'
tōdæge	adv.	today	*wēste*	adj.	'waste, barren'
tōgædre	adv.	together	*wēsten*	n.	'wasteland'
tōsomne	adv.	together	*Westsǣ*	m.	'Irish Sea'

194

Westseaxan	m.pl.	West Saxons
wībed	m.	heathen altar
wiga	m.	warrior
Wiht	n.	(Isle of) Wight
Wihtsǣtan	m.pl.	Wight-settlers
willan	v.	will, wish, intend, mean
wīn	n.	wine
winnan	v.	fight, strive
winter	n.	winter, year
wita	m.	(1) wise man, sage (2) counsellor
wīte	n.	punishment
wið	prep.	(1) with acc. 'against' (2) with dat. 'against, along with'
wið ðǣm ðe	conj.	in exchange for, provided that
wiðstandan	v.	withstand
wǣs	n.	juice, liquid
wræcc	n.	vengeance
wringan	v.	twist, wring
wudu	m.	woods, woodland
wunian	v.	remain, stay
wyrcan	v.	make, bring about
yfel	n.	evil, terrible deeds
ymb	prep.	with acc. 'after'
yrgðo	f.	laxity, cowardice, worthlessness

ADDITIONAL TEXTS IN OLD ENGLISH

Included below are additional texts. The texts given earlier under *Selected Texts* are repeated here for the convenience of those who wish to follow the texts while listening to the audiotape *Ærgeweorc: Old English Verse and Prose*. The *Glossary of Words used in the Course* does not contain all the words found in these additional texts.

1. Deor

Welund him be wurman wræces cunnade, anhydig eorl earfoþa dreag, hæfde him to gesiþþe sorge ond longaþ, wintercealde wræce; wean oft onfond, siþþan hine Niðhad on nede legde, swoncre seonobende on syllan monn.

þæs ofereode, þisses swa mæg.

Beadohilde ne wæs hyre broþra deaþ on sefan swa sar swa hyre sylfre þing, þæt heo gearolice ongieten hæfde þæt heo eacen wæs; æfre ne meahte þriste geþencan, hu ymb þæt sceolde.

þæs ofereode, þisses swa mæg.

We þæt Mæðhilde monge gefrugnon wurdon grundlease Geates frige, þæt hi seo sorglufu slæp ealle binom.

þæs ofereode, þisses swa mæg.

Ðeodric ahte þritig wintra Mæringa burg; þæt wæs monegum cuþ.

þæs ofereode, þisses swa mæg.

We geascodan Eormanrices wylfenne geþoht; ahte wide folc Gotena rices.

þæt wæs grim cyning.

Sæt secg monig sorgum gebunden, wean on wenan, wyscte geneahhe þæt þæs cynerices ofercumen wære.

þæs ofereode, þisses swa mæg.

Siteð sorgcearig, sælum bidæled, on sefan sweorceð, sylfum þinceð þæt sy endeleas earfoða dæl.

Mæg þonne geþencan, þæt geond þas woruld witig dryhten wendeþ geneahhe, eorle monegum are gesceawað, wislicne blæd, sumum weana dæl.

þæt ic bi me sylfum secgan wille, þæt ic hwile wæs Heodeninga scop, dryhtne dyre.

Me wæs Deor noma.

Ahte ic fela wintra folgað tilne, holdne hlaford, oþþæt Heorrenda nu, leoðcræftig monn londryht geþah, þæt me eorla hleo ær gesealde.

þæs ofereode, þisses swa mæg.

2. Beowulf –The Funeral of Scyld Scefing

Him ða Scyld gewat to gescæphwile felahror feran on frean wære.

Hi hyne þa ætbæron to brimes faroðe, swæse gesiþas, swa he selfa bæd, þenden wordum weold wine Scyldinga, leof landfruma lange ahte.

Þær æt hyðe stod hringedstefna, isig ond utfus, æþelinges fær.

Aledon þa leofne þeoden, beaga bryttan, on bearm scipes, mærne be mæste.

Þær wæs madma fela of feorwegum, frætwa, gelæded; ne hyrde ic cymlicor ceol gegyrwan hildewæpnum ond heaðowædum, billum ond byrnum; him on bearme læg madma mænigo, þa him mid scoldon on flodes æht feor gewitan.

Nalæs hi hine læssan lacum teodan, þeodgestreonum, þon þa dydon þe hine æt frumsceafte forð onsendon ænne ofer yðe umborwesende.

þa gyt hie him asetton segen geldenne heah ofer heafod, leton holm beran, geafon on garsecg; him wæs geomor sefa, murnende mod.

Men ne cunnon secgan to soðe, selerædende, hæleð under heofenum, hwa þæm hlæste onfeng.

3. Engla Tocyme (The Arrival of the English)

Ða wæs ymb feower hund wintra and nigon and feowertig fram ures drihtnes menniscnysse þæt Martianus casere rice onfeng and vii gear hæfde. Se wæs siexta eac feowertigum fram Agusto þam casere. Ða Angleþeod and Seaxna wæs gelaðod fram þam foresprecenan cyninge, and on Brytene com on þrim miclum scipum, and on eastdæle þisses ealondes eardungstowe onfeng þurh ðæs ilcan cyninges bebod, þe hie hider gelaðode, þæt hie sceoldon for heora eðle compian and feohtan. And hie sona compodon wið heora gewinnan, þe hie oft ær norðan onhergodon; and Seaxan þa sige geslogon, þa sendon hie ham ærendracan and heton secgan þisses landes wæstmbærnysse and Brytta yrgþo. And hie þa sona hider sendon maran sciphere strengrena wigena; and wæs unoferswiðendlic werod, þa hie togædre geþeodde wæron. And him Bryttas sealdon and geafon eardungstowe betwuh him, þæt hie for sibbe and for hælo heora eðles campoden and wunnen wið heora feondum, and hie him andleofne and are forgeafen for heora gewinne.

Comon hie of þrim folcum ðam strangestum Germanie, þæt is of Seaxum and of Angle and of Geatum. Of Geata fruman sindon Cantware and Wihtsætan; þæt is seo ðeod þe Wiht þæt ealond oneardað. Of Seaxum, þæt isof ðam lande þe mon hateð Ealdseaxan, comon Eastseaxan and Suðseaxan and Westseaxan. Of Engle comon Eastengle and Middelengle and Mierce and eall Norðhymbra cynn; is þæt land ðe Angulus is genemned, betwuh Geatum and Seaxum; and is sægd of ðære tide þe hie ðanon gewiton oð todæg þæt hit weste wunige. Wæron ærest heora latteowas and heretogan twegen gebroðru, Hengest and Horsa. Hie wæron Wihtgilses suna, þæs fæder wæs Woden nemned, of ðæs strynde monigra mægða cyningcynn fruman lædde. Ne wæs ða ielding to þon þæt hie heapmælum comon maran weorod of þam þeodum þe we ær gemynegodon. And þæt folc ðe hider com ongan weaxan and miclian to þon swiðe þæt hie wæron on miclum ege þam selfum landbigengum ðe hie ær hider laðedon and cigdon.

Æfter þissum hie ða geweredon to sumre tide wið Pehtum, þa hie ær ðurh gefeoht feor adrifon. And þa wæron Seaxan secende intingan and towyrde heora gedales wið Bryttas, cyðdon him openlice and sægdon, nemne hie him maran andleofne sealden, þæt hie woldon him sylfe niman and hergian, þær hie hit findan mihton. And sona ða beotunge dædum læston; bærndon and hergodon and slogon fram eastsæ oð westsæ, and him nænig wiðstod. Ne wæs ungelic wræcc þam ðe iu Chaldeas bærndon Hierusaleme weallas and ða cynelican getimbru mid fyre fornomon for ðæs godes folces synnum. Swa þonne her fram þære arleasan ðeode, hwæðere rihte godes dome, neah ceastra gehwylce and land forhergode wæron. Hruron and feollon cynelicu getimbru somod and anlipie, and gehwær sacerdas and mæssepreostas betwuh wibedum wæron slægene and cwielmde; biscopas mid folcum buton ænigre are sceawunge ætgædre mid iserne and lige fornumene wæron. And ne wæs seo bebyrignys sealde þam ðe swa hreowlice acwealde wæron. And monige ðære earmen lafe on westenum fangene wæron and heapmælum sticode. Sume for hungre heora feondum on hand eodon and ecne þeowdom geheton wið ðæm þe him mon andleofne forgeafe; sume ofer sæ sorgiende gewiton; sume forhtiende on eðle gebidon and þearfende lif in wuda and in westenum and on heam clifum sorgiende mode symle dydon.

4. Ines Domas

Be Ines domum. xliiij. Ic, Ine, mid Godes giefe Westseaxena cyning, mid geðeahte ond mid lare Cenredes mines fæder ond Heddes mines biscopes ond Eorcenwaldes mines biscopes, mid eallum minum ealdormonnum ond þæm ieldstum witum minre ðeode ond eac micelre gesomnunge Godes ðeowa, wæs smeagende be ðære hælo urra sawla ond be ðæm staþole ures rices, ðætte riht æw ond rihte cynedomas ðurh ure folc gefæstnode ond getrymede wæren, þætte nænig ealdormanna ne us undergeðeodedra æfter þam wære awendende ðaus ure domas.

Be gefeohtum. l. Gif hwa gefeohte on cyninges huse sie he scyldig ealles his ierfes ond sie on cyninges dome hwæðer he lif age oþþe nage. Gif hwa on mynstre gefeohte, cxx scillinga gebete. Gif hwa on ealdormonnes huse gefeohte oððe on oðres geðungenes witan, lx scillinga gebete he ond oþer lx geselle to wite. Gif ðonne on gafolgeldan huse oððe on gebures gefeohte cxx scillinga to wite geselle and ðam gebure vi scillinga. Ond þeah hit sie on middum felda gefohten, cxx scillinga to wite sie agiefen. Gif ðonne on gebeorscipe hie geciden ond oðer hiora mid geðylde hit forbere, geselle se oðer xxx scillinga to wite.

5. Deniga Hergung (The Danes' Harrying)

Her on ðissum geare ferde se here abutan Defnanscire into Sæfernmuðan ond þær gehergodon ægðer ge on Cornwealum ge on Norðwealum ond on Defenum, ond eodon him þa up æt Wecedport and þær micel yfel worhton on bærnette and on manslihtum. Ond æfter þam wendon eft abutan Penwihtsteort on ða suðhealfe ond wendon þa into Tamermuðan ond eodon þa up oðþæt hie comon to Hlidaforda ond ælc ðing bærndon ond slogon þæt hie gemetton ond Ordulfes mynster æt Tæfingsctoce forbærndon ond unasecgendlice herehuðe mid him to scipum brohton.

6. Durham

Is ðeos burch breome geond Breotenrice, steppa gestaðolad, stanas ymbutan wundrum gewæxen.
Weor ymbeornad, ea yðum stronge, and ðer inne wunað feola fisca kyn on floda gemonge.
And ðær gewexen is wudafæstern micel: wuniad in ðem wycum wilda deor monige, in deope dalum deora ungerim.
Is in ðere byri eac bearnum gecyðed ðe arfesta eadig Cudberch and ðes clene cyninges heafud, Osuualdes, Engle leo, and Aidan biscop, Eadberch and Eadfrið, æðele geferes.
Is ðer inne midd heom æðelwold biscop and breoma bocera Beda, and Boisil abbot, ðe clene Cudberte on gecheðe lerde lustum, and he his lara wel genom. Eardiæð æt ðem eadige in in ðem minstre unarimeda reliquia, ðær monia wundrum gewurðað, ðes ðe writ seggeð, midd ðene drihnes wer domes bideð.

7. The Ordeal (B. Be ðon ðe ordales weddigaþ)

GIF hwa ordales weddige, ðonne cume he, þrim nihtum ær, to þam mæssepreoste þe hit halgian scyle, and fede hine sylfne, mid hlafe and mid wætre and sealte and wyrtum ær he to gan scyle, and gestonde him mæssan þæra þreora daga ælcne, and offrige to and ga to husle ðy dæge þe he to ðam ordale gan scyle, and swerige ðonne þone að þæt he sy mid folcryhte unscyldig ðære tihtlan, ær he to ðam ordale ga.
And gif hit sy wæter, ðæt he gedufe oþre healfe elne on þam rape. Gif hit sy isenordal, beon ðreo niht ær mon þa hond undo.

8. Wið Dweorh (Against a Dwarf)

Wið dweorh man sceal niman VII lytle oflætan, swylce man mid ofrað, and writan þas naman on ælcre oflætan: Maximianus, Malchus, Iohannes, Martimianus, Dionisius, Constantinus, Serafion.
þænne eft þæt galdor, þæt her æfter cweð, man sceal singan, ærest on þæt wynstre eare, þænne on þæt swiðre eare, þænne bufan þæs mannes moldan.
And ga þænne an mædenman to and ho hit on his sweoran, and do man swa þry dagas; him bið sona sel.

Her com in gangan, in spiderwiht, hæfde him his haman on handa, cwæð þæt þu his hæncgest wære, legde þe his teage an sweoran.

Ongunnan him of þæm lande liþan; sona swa hy of þæm lande coman, þa ongunnan him ða liþu colian.

þa com in gangan dweores sweostar; þa geændade heo and aðas swor ðæt næfre þis ðæm adlegan derian ne moste, ne þæm þe þis galdor begytan mihte, oððe þe þis galdor ongalan cuþe.   Amen. Fiað.

9. Wið Wennum (Against a Wen)

Wenne, wenne, wenchichenne, her ne scealt þu timbrien, ne nenne tun habben, ac þu scealt north eonene to þan nihgan berhge, þer þu hauest, ermig, enne broþer. He þe sceal legge leaf et heafde.

Under fot wolues, under ueþer earnes, under earnes clea, a þu geweornie.

Clinge þu alswa col on heorþe, scring þu alswa scerne awage, and weorne alswa weter on anbre.

Swa litel þu gewurþe alswa linsetcorn, and miccli lesse alswa anes handwurmes hupeban, and alswa litel þu gewurþe þet þu nawiht gewurþe.

10. Wið Wæterælfadle (For the Water-Elf Disease)

Gif mon biþ on wæterælfadle, þonne beoþ him þa handnæglas wonne and þa eagan tearige and wile locian niþer.

Do him þis to læcedome: eoforþrote, cassuc, fone nioþoweard, eowberge, elehtre, eolone, merscmealwan crop, fenminte, dile, lilie, attorlaþe, polleie, marubie, docce, ellen, felterre, wermod, streawbergean leaf, consolde.

ofgeot mid ealaþ, do hæligwæter to, sing þis gealdor ofer þriwa: Ic benne awrat betest beadowræda, swa benne ne burnon, ne burston, ne fundian, ne feologan, ne hoppettan, ne wund waxsian, ne dolh diopian; ac him self healde halewæge, ne ace þe þon ma, þe eorþan on earce ace.

Sing þis manegum siþum: Eorþe þe onbere eallum hire mihtum and mægenum.

þas galdor mon mæg singan on wunde.

11. The Nine Herbs Charm

Gemyne ðu, mucgwyrt, hwæt þu ameldodest, hwæt þu renadest æt Regenmelde.

Una þu hattest, yldost wyrta.

ðu miht wið III and wið XXX, þu miht wiþ attre and wið onflyge, þu miht wiþ þam laþan ðe geond lond færð.

Ond þu, wegbræde, wyrta modor, eastan openo, innan mihtigu; ofer ðe crætu curran, ofer ðe cwene reodan, ofer ðe bryde bryodedon, ofer þe fearras fnærdon.

Eallum þu þon wiðstode and wiðstunedest; swa ðu wiðstonde attre and onflyge and þæm laðan þe geond lond fereð.

Stune hætte þeos wyrt, heo on stane geweox; stond heo wið attre, stunað heo wærce.

Stiðe heo hatte, wiðstunað heo attre, wreceð heo wraðan, weorpeð ut attor.

þis is seo wyrt seo wiþ wyrm gefeaht, þeos mæg wið attre, heo mæg wið onflyge, heo mæg wið ðam laþan ðe geond lond fereþ.

Fleoh þu nu, attorlaðe, seo læsse ða maran, seo mare þa læssan, oððæt him beigra bot sy.

Gemyne þu, mægðe, hwæt þu ameldodest, hwæt ðu geændadest æt Alorforda; þæt næfre for gefloge feorh ne gesealde syþðan him mon mægðan to mete gegyrede.

þis is seo wyrt ðe wergulu hatte; ðas onsænde seolh ofer sæs hrygc ondan attres oþres to bote.

Ðas VIIII magon wið nygon attrum.

Wyrm com snican, toslat he man; ða genam Woden VIIII wuldortanas, sloh ða þa næddran, þæt heo on VIIII tofleah.

þær geændade æppel and attor, þæt heo næfre ne wolde on hus bugan.

Fille and finule, felamihtigu twa, þa wyrte gesceop witig drihten, halig on heofonum, þa he hongode; sette and sænde on VII worulde earmum and eadigum eallum to bote.

Stond heo wið wærce, stunað heo wið attre, seo mæg wið III and wið XXX, wið feondes hond and wið færbregde, wið malscrunge manra wihta.

Nu magon þas VIIII wyrta wið nygon wuldorgeflogenum, wið VIIII attrum and wið nygon onflygnum, wið ðy readan attre, wið ðy runlan attre, wið ðy hwitan attre, wið ðy wedenan attre, wið ðy geolwan attre, wið ðy grenan attre, wið ðy wonnan attre, wið ðy wedenan attre, wið ðy brunan attre, wið ðy basewan attre, wið Wyrmgeblæd, wið wætergeblæd, wið þorngeblæd, wið þystelgeblæd, wið ysgeblæd, wið attorgeblæd, gif ænig attor cume eastan fleogan oððe ænig norðan cume oððe ænig westan ofer werðeode.

Crist stod ofer adle ængan cundes.

Ic ana wat ea rinnende þær þa nygon nædran nean behealdað; motan ealle weoda nu wyrtum aspringan, sæs toslupan, eal sealt wæter, ðonne ic þis attor of ðe geblawe.

Mugcwyrt, wegbrade þe eastan open sy, lombescyrse, attorlaðan, mageðan, netelan, wudusuræppel, fille and finul, ealde sapan.

Gewyrc ða wyrta to duste, mængc wiþ þa sapan and wið þæs æpples gor.

Wyrc slypan of wætere and of axsan, genim finol, wyl on þære slyppan and beþe mid æggemongc, þonne he þa sealfe on do, ge ær ge æfter.

Sing þæt galdor on ælcre þara wyrta, III ær he hy wyrce and on þone æppel ealswa; ond singe þon men in þone muð and in þa earan buta and on ða wunde þæt ilce gealdor, ær he þa sealfe on do.

12. Læcedomas

Wið ða blegene genim nigon ægra ond seoð hie fæste, ond nim þa geolcan ond do þæt hwite aweg, ond mera ða geolcan on anre pannan, ond wring þæt wos ut þurh ænne clað, ond nim eall swa fela dropena wines swa ðara ægra beo, and eall swa fela dropena unhalgodes eles, ond eall swa fela huniges dropena, ond of finoles moran eall swa fela dropena, genim ðonne ond do hit eall tosomne ond wring ut ðurh ænne clað ond sele ðam menn etan. Him bið sona sel.

Gif mon ðung ete, aþecge buteran ond drince – se ðung gewit on ða buteran. Eft wið ðone, stande on heafde, aslege him mon fela scearpena on þam scancan, þonne gewit ut þæt atter þurh þa scearpan.

13. Beowulf's Greeting

Beowulf maðelode on him byrne scan, searonet seowed smiþes orþancum: Wæs þu, Hroðgar, hal.
Ic eom Higelaces mæg ond magoðegn; hæbbe ic mærða fela ongunnen on geogoþe.
Me wearð Grendles þing on minre eþeltyrf undyrne cuð; secgað sæliðend þæt þæs sele stande, reced selesta, rinca gehwylcum idel ond unnyt, siððan æfenleoht under heofenes hador beholen weorþeð.
þa me þæt gelærdon leode mine þa selestan, snotere ceorlas, þeoden Hroðgar, þæt ic þe sohte, forþan hie mægenes cræft minne cuþon, selfe ofersawon, ða ic of searwum cwom, fah from feondum.
þær ic fife geband, yðde eotena cyn ond on yðum slog niceras nihtes, nearoþearfe dreah, wræc Wedera nið wean ahsodon, forgrand gramum, ond nu wið Grendel sceal, wið þam aglæcan, ana gehegan ðing wið þyrse.
Ic þe nu ða, brego Beorhtdena, biddan wille, eodor Scyldinga, anre bene, þæt ðu me ne forwyrne, wigendra hleo, freowine folca, nu ic þus feorran com, þæt ic mote ana ond minra eorla gedryht, þes hearda heap, Heorot fælsian.
Hæbbe ic eac geahsod þæt se æglæca for his wonhydum wæpna ne recceð.
Ic þæt þonne forhicge swa me Higelac sie, min mondrihten, modes bliðe, þæt ic sweord bere oþðe sidne scyld, geolorand to guþe, ac ic mid grape sceal fon wið feonde ond ymb feorh sacan, lað wið laþum; ðær gelyfan sceal dryhtnes dome se þe hine deað nimeð.
Wen ic þæt he wille, gif he wealdan mot, in þæm guðsele Geotena leode etan unforhte, swa he oft dyde, mægen Hreðmanna.
Na þu minne þearft hafalan hydan, ac he me habban wile dreore fahne, gif mec deað nimeð.
Byreð blodig wæl, byrgean þenceð, eteð angenga unmurnlice, mearcað morhopu; no ðu ymb mines ne þearft lices feorme leng sorgian.
Onsend Higelace, gif mec hild nime, beaduscruda betst, þæt mine breost wereð, hrægla selest; þæt is Hrædlan laf, Welandes geweorc.
Gæð a wyrd swa hio scel.

14. The Battle of Brunanburh

Her Æþelstan cyning, eorla dryhten,
beorna beahgifa and his broþor eac,
eadmund æþeling, ealdorlangne tir
geslogon æt sæcce sweorda ecgum
ymbe Brunanburh. Bordweal clufan,
heowan heaþolinde hamora lafan,
afaran eeadweardes swa him geæþele wæs
from cneomægum þæt hi æt campe oft
wiþ laþra gehwæne land ealgodon,
hord and hamas. Hettend crungun,
Sceottta leoda and scipflotan
fæge feollan, feld dænnede
secga swate siðþan sunne up
on morgentid, mære tungol,
glad ofer grundas, godes condel beorht,
eces drihtnes, oð sio æþele gesceaft
sah to setle. Þær læg secg mænig
garum ageted, guma norþerna
ofer scild scoten swilce Scittisc eac
werig, wiges sæd. Wesseaxe forð
ondlongne dæg eoredcistum
on last legdun laþum þeodum,
heowan herefleman hindan þearle
mecum mylenscearpan. Myrce ne wyrndon
heardes hondplegan hæleþa nanum
þæra þe mid Anlafe ofer æra gebland
on lides bosme land gesohtun,
fæge to gefeohte. Fife lægun
on þam campstede cyningas giunge,
sweordum aswefede, swilce seofene eac
eorlas Anlafes unrim heriges,
flotan and Scotta. Þær geflemed wearð
Norðmanna bregu, nede gebeded,
to lides stefne litle werode;
cread cnear on flot, cyning ut gewat
on fealene flod, feorh generede.
Swilce þær eac se froda mid fleame com
on his cyþþe norð Costontinu
har hilderinc, hreman ne þorfte
mæca gemanan, he wæs his mæga sceard
freonda gefylled on folcstede,

beslagen æt sæcce and his sunu forlet
on wælstowe wunden forgrunden,
giiungne æt guðe. Gelpan ne þorfte
beorn blandenfeax bilgeslihtes,
eald inwidda, ne Anlaf þy ma;
mid heora herelafum hlehhan ne þorftun
þæt heo beaduweorca beteran wurdun
on campstede cumbolgehnastes,
garmittinge, gumena gemotes,
wæpengewrixles, þæs hi on wælfelda
wiþ eadweardes afaran plegodan.
Gewitan him þa Norþmen nægledcnearrum,
dreorig daraða laf on Dinges mere
ofer deop wæter Difelin secan,
eft Iraland æwiscmode.
Swilce þa gebroþer begen ætsamne,
cyning and æþeling cyþþe sohton,
Wesseaxna land wiges hremige.
Letan him behindan hræw bryttian
saluwigpadan þone sweartan hræfn
hyrnednebban and þane hasewanpadan
earn æftan hwit, æses brucan
grædigne guðhafoc and þæt græge deor
wulf on wealde. Ne wearð wæl mare
on þis eiglande æfre gieta
folces gefylled beforan þissum
sweordes ecgum þæs þe us secgaþ bec,
ealde uðwitan, siþþan eastan hider
Engle and Seaxe up becoman
ofer brad brimu Brytene sohtan,
wlance wigsmiþas, Wealas ofercoman,
earlas arhwate eard begeatan.

15. Blagkmon by Adrian Pilgrim

He wæs broðor min blacmon þeoden
æðele ealdor anrades hyges
þeah he a swa rihte ricsode swa he meahte
him wiðsawon suhtrigan earge
grimme leodmagas gryrefah geþrang.
Heard wæs hæleðe hildþracu on morum.
Oðwand þonan eodor ær æfen com
brego mid wigheape west to garsecge

leofa wealdend þurh laðne cræft
wraðe gefliemed forþ to elþeode
on wægflotum twæm wilgiefa mid cempum
þa drefde lagu dædcene flocc.
Fram streamstæðe feorr stormwind geslog
brimliðendra scipu on brantum wætrum
Þæt wæs micel wundor þæt wæpenwigan
on ærmergen iegclifu sawon
scimgerihte ofer sciene flod
gimstan on flote þe god us geheold.
Her we awunodon hearra mid þegnum
brego mid beadorincum blacmon cynebald
her on mænige mædwum ond beorgum
weold þus gleawe wintra twentig
ure þengel þegnboren manna
norðanhymbrum þe him neah wunodon
eallum his niedmagum nu gesundum.
Peohtas hræðre pæhton urne æðeling
tunstede gestodon treowlease on niht
folcgeweriend þus feond ofslog
hæðencynnes hetelic yfeldæda
þa mind bangare of burge gefleah.

Þenden sunne nu sincþ under snawbeorghliþ
blawaþ blæstas bittere ofer hæðe
geomore ic begnornie his grimne deaþ.
Runstafas on rodstane rihthlafordes naman
blacmon gecyðaþ cynecunnes leoht
he wæs broðor min bealocwealme genumen
metod a gehealde on heofone his þeow
hlaford mænige mildne bealdor
dryhten on swegle to domdæge giefe
iegfolce friðu frea ælmihtig
a buton ende eallwealdend cyning.

This verse was the 1995 winning entry for the
biennial Cædmon Prize run by The English Companions.

Battle of Maldon

…brocen wurde.
Hēt þā hyssa hwǣne hors forlǣtan,
feor āfȳsan and forð gangan,
hicgan tō handum and t[ō] hige gōdum.
Þ[ā] þæt Offan mǣg ǣrest onfunde
þæt se eorl nolde yrhðo geþolian,
hē lēt him þā of handon lēofne flēogan
hafoc wið þæs holtes, and tō þǣre hilde stōp;
be þām man mihte oncnāwan þæt se cniht nolde
wācian æt [þ]ā m w[ī]g e þā hē tō wǣpnum fēng.
Ēac him wolde Ēadrīc his ealdre gelǣstan,
frēan tō gefeohte: ongan þā forð beran
gār tō gūþe – hē hæfde gōd geþanc
þā hwīle þe hē mid handum healdan mihte
bord and brād swurd; bēot hē gelǣste
þa hē ætforan his frēan feohtan sceolde.
Ðā þǣr Byrhtnōð ongan beornas trymian:
rād and rǣdde, rincum tǣhte
hū hī sceoldon standan and þone stede healdan,
and bæd þæt hyra randan rihte hēoldon
fæste mid folman, and ne forhtedon nā.
Þā hē hæfde þæt folc fægere getrymmed,
hē līhte þā mid lēodon þǣr him lēofost wæs
þǣr hē his heorðwerod holdost wiste.
Þā stōd on stæðe, stīðlīce clypode
Wīcinga ār, wordum mǣlde.
Sē on bēot ābēadbrimlīþendra
ǣrænde tō þām eorle þǣr hē on ōfre stōd:
«Mē sendon tō þē sǣmen snelle,
hēton ðē secgan þæt þū mōst sendan raðe
bēagas wið gebeorge, and ēow betere is
þæt gē þisne gārrǣs mid gafole forgyldon
þon wē swā hearde [hi]lde dǣlon.
Ne þurfe wē ūs spillan gif gē spēdaþ tō þām:
wē willað wið þām golde grið fæstnian;
gyf þū þat gerǣdest, þe hēr rīcost eart,
þæt þū þīne lēoda lȳsan wille,
syllan sǣmannum on hyra sylfra dōm
fēoh wið frēode and niman frið æt ūs,

wē willaþ mid þām sceattum ūs tō scype gangan,
on flot fēran and ēow friþes healdan.»
Byrhtnōð maþelode, bord hafenode,
wand wācne æsc, wordum mǣlde,
yrre and ānrǣd āg eaf him andsware:
"Gehȳrst þū sǣlida, hwæt þis folc segeð?
Hī willað ēow tō gafole gāras syllan,
ǣttrynne ord and ealde swurd,
þā heregeatu þe ēow æt hilde ne dēah!
Brimmanna boda, ābēod eft ongēan,
sege þīnum lēodum miccle lāþre spell,
þæt hēr stynt unforcūð eorl mid his werode
þe wile gealgean ēþel þysne,
Æþelredes eard, ealdres mīnes
folc and foldan. Feallan sceolon
hæþene æt hilde! Tō hēanlic mē þinceð
þæt gē mid ūrum sceattum tō scype gangon
unbefohtene nū gē þus feor hider
on ūrne eard in becōmon;
ne sceole ge swā sōfte sinc gegangan:
ūs sceal ord and ecg ǣr gesēman,
grim gūðplega, ǣr [w]ē gofol syllon!"
Hēt þā bord beran, beornas gangan
þæt hī on þām ēasteðe ealle stōdon.
Ne mihte þǣr for wætere werod tō þām ōðrum
þǣr cōm flōwende flōd æfter ebban;
lucon lagustrēamas; tō lang hit him þūhte
hwænne hī tōgædere gāras bēron.
Hī þǣr Pantan strēam mid prasse bestōdon,
Ēastseaxena ord and se æschere;
ne mihte hyra ǣnig ōþrum derian
būton hwā þurh flānes flyht fyl genāme.
Se flōd ūt gewāt – þā flotan stōdon gearowe,
Wīcinga fela, wīges georne.
Hēt þā hæleða hlēo healdan þā bricge
wigan wīgheardne sē wæs hāten Wulfstān,
cāfne mid his cynne; þæt wæs Cēolan sunu
þe ðone forman man mid his francan ofscēat
þe þǣr baldlīcost on þā bricge stōp.
Þǣr stōdon mid Wulfstāne wigan unforhte,

Ælfere and Maccus, mōdige twēgen,
þā noldon æt þām forda flēam gewyrcan,
ac hī fæstlīce wið ðā fȳnd weredon
þā hwīle þe hī wǣpna wealdan mōston
Þā hī þæt ongēaton and georne gesāwon
þæt hī þǣr bricgweardas bitere fundon,
ongunnon lytegian þā lāðe gystas,
bǣdon þæt hī upgangan āgan mōston,
ofer þone ford faran, fēþan lǣdan.
Ðā se eorl ongan for his ofermōde
ālȳfan landes tō fela lāþere ðēode;
ongan ceallian þā ofer cald wæter
Byrhtelmes bearn; beornas gehlyston:
"Nū ēow is gerȳmed, gāð ricene tō ūs,
guman tō gūþe! God āna wāt
hwā þǣre wælstōwe wealdan mōte."
Wōdon þā wælwulfas, for wætere ne murnon,
Wicinga werod west ofer Pantan
ofer scir wæter scyldas wēgon;
lidmen tō lande linde bǣron.
þǣr ongēan gramum gearowe stōdon
Byrhtnōð mid beornum: hē mid bordum hēt
wyrcan þone wihagan and þæt werod healdan
fæste wið fēondum. Þā wæs f[e]ohte nēh,
tir æt getohte; wæs sēo tid cumen
þæt þǣr fǣge men feallan sceoldon.
Þǣr wearð hrēam āhafen, hremmas wundon,
earn ǣses georn – wæs on eorþan cyrm!
Hī lēton þā of folman fēolhearde speru
[grimme] gegrundene gāras flēogan.
Bogan wǣron bysige; bord ord onfēng;
biter wæs se beadurǣs. Beornas fēollon,
on gehwæðere hand hyssas lāgon.
Wund wear[ð] Wulfmǣr, wælrǣste gecēas;
Byrhtnōðes mǣg, hē mid billum wearð,
his swustersunu, swiðe forhēawen.
Þǣr wær[ð] Wicingum wiþerlēan āgyfen:
gehȳrde ic þæt Ēadweard ānne slōge
swiðe mid his swurde – swenges ne wyrnde –
þæt him æt fōtum fēoll fǣge cempa.

Þæs him his ðēoden þanc gesǣde
þām būrþēne þā hē byre hæfde.
Swā stemnetton stiðhicgende
hysas æt hilde, hogodon georne
hwā þǣr mid orde ǣrost mihte
on fǣgean men feorh gewinnan,
wigan mid wǣpnum. Wæl fēol on eorðan;
stōdon stædefæste. Stihte hī Byrhtnōð,
bæd þæt hyssa gehwylc hogode tō wīge
þe on Denon wolde dōm gefeohtan.
Wōd þā wīges heard, wǣpen ūp āhōf,
bord tō gebeorge, and wið þæs beornes stōp;
ēode swā ānrǣd eorl tō þām ceorl,
ǣgþer hyra ōðrum yfeles hogode
Sende ðā se sǣrinc sūþerne gār
þæt gewundod wearð wigena hlāford:
hē scēaf þā mid ðām scylde, þæt se sceaft tōbærst
and þæt spere sprengde þæt hit sprang ongēan.
Gegremod wearð se gūðrinc: hē mid gāre stang
wlancne Wicing þe him þā wunde forgeaf.
Frōd wæs se fyrdrinc: hē lēt his francan wadan
þurh ðæs hysses hals – hand wisode
þæt hē on þām fǣrsceaðan feorh gerǣhte.
Ðā hē ōþerne ofstlīce scēat
þæt sēo byrne tōbærst: hē wæs on brēostum wund
þurh ðā hringlocan; him æt heortan stōd
ǣtterne ord. Se eorl wæs þē bliþra:
hlōh þā mōdi man, sǣde Metode þanc
ðæs dægweorces þe him Drihten forgeaf.
Forlēt þā drenga sum daroð of handa
flēogan of folman þæt sē tō forð gewāt
þurh ðone æþelan Æþelredes þegen.
Him be healfe stōd hyse unweaxen,
cniht on gecampe: sē full cāflīce
brǣd of þām beorne blōdigne gār:
Wulfstānes bearn, Wulfmǣr se geonga,
forlēt forheardne faran eft ongēan;
ord in gewōd þæt sē on eorþan læg
þe his þēoden ǣr þearle gerǣhte.
Ēode þā gesyrwed secg tō þām eorle:

hē wolde þæs beornes bēagas gefecgan,
rēaf and hringas and gerēnod swurd. .
Đā Byrhtnōð bræd bill of scēðe,
brād and brūneccg and on þā byrnan slōh.
Tō raþe hine gelette lidmanna sum
þā hē þæs eorles earm āmyrde.
Fēoll þā tō foldan fealohilte swurd,
ne mihte hē gehealdan heardne mēce,
wǣpnes wealdan. Þā gȳt þæt word gecwæð
hār hilderinc: hyssas bylde,
bæd gangan forð gōde gefēran.
Ne mihte þā on fōtum leng fæste gest[a]ndan.
Hē tō heofenum wlāt,[hæleð gemǣlde:]
"Geþance þē, ðēoda Waldend,
ealra þǣra wynna þe ic on worulde gebād.
Nū ic āh, milde Metod, mǣste þearfe
þæt þū minum gāste gōdes geunne,
þæt min sawul tō ðē siðian mōte
on þin geweald, Þēoden engla,
mid friþe ferian. Ic eom frymdi tō þē
þæt hī helsceaðan hȳnan ne mōton!"
Đā hine hēowon hǣðene scealcas,
and bēgen þā beornas þe him big stōdon,
Ælfnōð and Wulmǣr, [þæt hī on wæle] lāgon
ðā onemn hyra frēan feorh gesealdon.
Hī bugon þā fram beaduwe þe þǣr bēon noldon!
Þǣr wurdon Oddan bearn ǣrest on flēame,
Godrīc fram gūþe, and þone gōdan forlēt
þe him mænigne oft mēar gesealde;
hē gehlēop þone eoh þe āhte his hlāford,
on þām gerǣdum þe hit riht ne wæs.
And his brōðru mid himbēgen ær[n]don,
God[w]ine and Godwīg; gūþe ne gȳmdon
ac wendon fram þām wige and þone wudu sōhton;
flugon on þæt fæsten and hyra fēore burgon,
and manna mā þonne hitǣ nig mǣð wǣre,
gyf hī þā geearnunga ealle gemundon
þe hē him tō duguþe gedōn hæfde.
Swā him Offa on dæg ǣr āsǣde
on þām meþelstede þā hē gemōt hæfde,

210

þæt þǣr mōdelīce manega sprǣcon
þe eft æt þ[ea]r[f]e þolian noldon.
Þā wearð āfeallen þæs folces ealdor,
Æþelredes eorl; ealle gesāwon
heorðgenēatas þæt hyra heorra læg.
Þā ðǣr wendon forð wlance þegenas,
unearge men, efston georne:
hī woldon þā ealle ōðer twēga,
lif forlǣtun oððe lēofne gewrecan.
Swā hī bylde forð bearn Ælfrīces,
wiga wintrum geong, wordum mǣlde;
Ælfwine þā cwæð, hē on ellen sprǣc:
"Gemun[a] þā mǣla þe wē oft æt meodo sprǣcon
þonne wē on bence bēot āhōfon,
hæleð on healle, ymbe heard gewinn.
Nū mæg cunnian hwā cēne sȳ!
Ic wylle mine æþelo eallum gecȳþan,
þæt ic wæs on Myrcon miccles cynnes;
wæs min ealda fæder Ealhelm hāten,
wis ealdorman, woruldgesǣlig.
Ne sceolon mē on þǣre þēode þegenas ætwitan
þæt ic of ðisse fyrde fēran wille,
eard gesēcan nū min ealdor ligeð
forhēawen æt hilde. Mē is þæt hearma mǣst —
hē wæsǣ g[ð]er min mǣgand min hlāford."
Þā hē forð ēode; fæhðe gemunde
þæt hē mid orde ānne gerǣhte
flotan on þām folce þæt sē on foldan læg
forwegen mid his wǣpne. Ongan þā winas manian
frȳnd and gefēran þæt hī forð ēodon.
Offa gemǣlde, æscholt āscēoc:
"Hwæt, þū, Ælfwine, hafast ealle gemanode
þegenas tō þearfe. Nū ūre þēoden lið,
eorl on eorðan, ūs is eallum þearf
þæt ūre ǣghwylc ōþerne bylde,
wigan tō wīge, þā hwile þe hē wǣpen mæge
habban and healdan, heardne mēce,
gār and gōd swurd. Ūs Godrīc hæfð,
earh Oddan bearn, ealle beswicene.
Wēnde þæs formoni man, þā hē on mēare rād,

on wlancan þām wicge, þæt wǣre hit ūre hlāford;
forþan wearð hēr on felda folc tōtwǣmed,
scyldburh tōbrocen – ābrēoðe his angin
þæt hē hēr swā manigne man āflȳmde!"
Lēofsunu gemǣlde and his linde āhōf,
bord tō gebeorge. Hē þām beorne oncwæð:
"Ic þæt gehāte þæt ic heonon nelle
flēon fōtes trym, ac wille furðor gān,
wrecan on gewinne minne winedrihten.
Ne þurfon mē embe Stūrmere stedefæste hælæð
wordum ætwitan, nū min wine gecranc,
þæt ic hlāfordlēas hām siðie,
wende fram wīge, ac mē sceal wǣpen niman,
ord and iren!" Hē ful yrre wōd,
feaht fæstlīce – flēam hē forhogode!
Dunnere þā cwæð, daroð ācwehte,
unorne ceorl, ofer eall clypode,
bæd þæt beorna gehwylc Byrhtnōð wrǣce:
"Ne mæg nā wandian sē þe wrecan þenceð
frēan on folce, nē for fēore murnan!"
þā hī forð ēodon, fēores hī ne rōhton.
Ongunnon þā hiredmen heardlice feohtan,
grame gārberend, and God bǣdon
þæt hī mōston gewrecan hyra winedrihten
and on hyra fēondum fyl gewyrcan.
Him se gȳsel ongan geornlīċe fylstan:
hē wæs on Norðhymbron heardes cynnes,
Ecglāfes bearn. Him wæs Æscferð nama;
hē ne wandode nā æt þām wīġplegan
ac hē fȳsde forð flān genēhe;
hwilon hē on bord scēat, hwilon beorn tǣsde;
ǣfre embe stunde hē sealde sume wunde
þā hwile ðe hē wǣpna wealdan mōste.
Þā gȳt on orde stōd Ēadweard se langa,
gearo and geornful; gylpwordum spræc
þæt hē nolde flēogan fōtmǣl landes,
ofer bæc būgan, þā his betera leg.
Hē bræc þone bordweall and wið þā beornas feaht
oð þæt hē his sincgyfan on þām sǣmannum
wurðlīce wrec ǣr hē on wæle lǣge.

Swā dyde Æþerīc, æþele gefēra,
fūs and forðgeorn, feaht eornoste,
Sibyrhtes brōðor, and swiðe mænig ōþer.
Clufon cellod bord – cēne hī weredon!
Bærst bordes lærig and sēo byrne sang
gryrelēoða sum. Þā æt gūðe slōh
Offa þone sǣlidan, þæt hē on eorðan fēoll;
and ðǣr Gaddes mǣg grund gesōhte:
raðe wearð æt hilde Offa forhēawen;
hē hæfde ðēah geforþod þæt hē his frēan gehēt
swā hē bēotode ǣr wið his bēahgifan
þæt hī sceoldon bēgen on burh ridan,
hāle tō hāme, oððe on here crin[c]gan,
on wælstōwe wundum sweltan;
hē læg ðeēenlīce ðēodne gehende.
Ðā wearð borda gebræc! Brimmen wōdon,
gūðe gegremode; gār oft þurhwōd
fǣges feorhhūs. For[ð] ðā ēode Wistān,
Þurstānes suna, wið þās secgas feaht.
Hē wæs on geþrang hyra þrēora bana
ǣr him Wīgel[m]es bearn on þām wæle lǣge.
Þǣr wæs stið gemōt; stōdon fæste
wigan on gewinne. Wīgend cruncon,
wundum wērige; wæl fēol on eorþan.
Ōswold and Ēadwold ealle hwile
bēgen þā gebrōþru beornas trymedon;
hyra winemāgas wordon bǣdon
þæt hī þǣr æt ðearfe þolian sceoldon,
unwāclīce wǣpna nēotan.
Byrhtwold maþelode, bord hafenode;
sē wæs eald genēat; æsc ācwehte.
Hē ful baldlīce beornas lǣrde:
"Hige sceal þē heardra, heorte þē cēnre,
mōd sceal þē māre þe ūre mægen lȳtlað.
Hēr lið ūre ealdor eall forhēawen,
gōd on grēote: ā mæg gnornian
sē ðe nū fram þis wīgplegan wendan þenceð!
Ic eom frōd fēores; fram ic ne wille,
ac ic mē be healfe minum hlāforde,
be swā lēofan men, licgan þence."

Swā hī Æþelgāres bearn ealle bylde,
Godrīċ tō gūþe; oft hē gār forlēt,
wælspere windan on þā Wicingas.
Swā hē on þām folce fyrmest ēode,
hēow and hȳnde o[ð] þæt hē on hilde gecranc.
Næs þæt nā se Godric þe ðā gū[ð]e forbēah! . . . .

Part Four

Key to Exercises

KEY TO EXERCISES IN OLD ENGLISH

Section 1

1. (a) this man is riding (b) the sun is shining (c) this horse bites (d) the night is growing dark (e) these men are coming (f) the ship awaits
2. (a) ðā menn rīdað (b) se cyning wadeð (c) se mōna scīnð (d) hors bītað (e) ðēos bryd wadeð (f) tunglu scīnað.

Section 2

1. (a) this man is riding the horse (b) this man rides those horses (c) this horse bites men (d) the king hears a tale but the king does not love tales (e) either the nobleman or the king lives in this house(f) the bishops await the king (g) the thanes are giving oaths (h) the king is awaiting these boats (i) this bride loves gifts and praise (j) grief and strife afflict that people.
2. (a) se cyning lufað lāre (b) se ðegn lufað ðis hors (c) ðā līðmenn ābīdað ðæt scip (d) sēo brȳd lufað ðis hūs (e) menn oneardiað ðis land (f) se biscop oneardað ðæt rīce (g) sēo brȳd lufað giefa (h) se æðeling sēcð glōfe (i) biscopas ne lufiað ne ceare ne sace (j) līðmann ne wadeð ne rīdeð hors.

Section 3

1. (a) these men are making that knowledge known (b) the prince is travelling (c) the bishops are judging (d) thanes obey the king (e) we are burning the tree (f) I hear words and obey them (g) the herdsmen feed sheep (h) the king is driving the bishop out (i) a healer has remedies (j) you are making room for a boat (k) doctors heal.
2. (a) ic lǣre ðis bearn (b) ðā æðelingas dǣlað ðæt rīce (c) wē gīemað ðās word (d) gē hīerað tale (e) ðā biscopas wēnað (f) ðū gīemst ðone biscop (g) hīe dǣlað ðone hlāf ond fēdað hine (h) ic ālīese hīe (i) hīe flīemað ðone here (j) ðū nīedest mec (k) folc cwīðeð.

Section 4

1. (a) strife afflicts kings in England (b) two powerful kings and twelve thanes are coming (c) that minster is famed throughout England (d) the bishop feeds poor men (e) sailors travel by ships (f) green trees do not burn at all (g) they mourn and heal me with good remedies.
2. (a) mǣre mann hæfð longsum lof (b) earme menn lǣfað lȳtele lāfe (c) ðā ðegnas flīemað ðone here mid hiera sweordum – hīe fērað ongean ðā scipu (d) sēo stōw is betwēonan ðǣm hyllum fore ðā trēow (e) grēne æceras and tile sind on ðissum

217

lande (f) se hierde is be ðǣm stānum ofer ðone æcer (g) ne cyningas ne biscopas ne fērað ðurh þæt land.

Section 5

1. (a) the sailor entrusts his ship to the thane (b) the baker is neither old nor poor (c) hateful men shall never be happy (d) my house is between those hills (e) your house is not high, but it is wide and spacious (f) this word is doubtful – I shall not declare it (g) without a remedy these men will soon be dead.

2. (a) sēo benn is sār and hē is sēoc (b) hwatne mann ne flīemþ se here (c) hēo cymð tō him tō brȳde ond lufaþ hine (d) nis þæt wīf fāh ne flāh (e) glæd mann hæfþ scip, sweord ond wīf (f) ne se cyning ne his þegn ne ālīesþ ðā wīcingas (g) on Englalande, ðā æceras sind brāde and þæt brim is nearu.

Section 6

1. Dudda is a farmer in the land of the Mercians; his son is called Dunnere. Either the farmer or his son will plough the fields on their estate. The farmer's son is very strong – he fells trees with his axe, But Dudda is not strong at all – he is old and unwell and seldom ploughs. His wife is dead, but Dunnere loves him and most often ploughs. Their farm is small but they have sheep for wool and as food. Why does Dudda not plough? Because he is old and sick. Why does Dunnere plough? Because he is young and strong.

2. Berhtwulfes eard is on ēastenglum. Ylfe ādreccað hine, cweðeð hē, ac Swǣppa his wine wereð hine wið hīe mid galdrum. His word sind fremfulu ond þā ylfe sind forhtfule. Galdor bið lāþlic þǣm ylfum.

Section 7

1. (a) I do not trust him who boasts (b) the enemy army is harrying in this land (c) they do honour to their friends and do harm to their enemies (d) the king is travelling with one person as a companion (e) those vikings who boast greatly will be afraid in battle (f) the Mercians are strengthening the fortress against the Danes

2. (a) se biscop losaþ ond forhtaþ swīðe (b) folga mec ond scēawa ðā āc sēo ðe is on mīnum æcere (c) ne forhta, sēo benn sārað ac ne dereþ þē (d) ic gehālsie mid mīnum frīend ðone ðe se cyning trūwað (e) settaþ rāp ymbe ðæt trēow ond cnyttað (f) þās menn sind Mierce, hīe ne eardiaþ on Seaxna lande.

Section 8

1. (a) When I call, my horse comes to me immediately. It is a good horse and a strong one, but it does not always obey. Sometimes it is hostile and does not do what I command. Then it angers me very much. (b) Wherever I go, you go there with me as a companion; you are a good and willing friend to me, and I trust what you say. (c) Learn something from this book – then you will be wise and well-taught.

2. (a) Swā hwæt swā ic dō lett mon mec. Menn ne lufiað mec ond ic forhtie ac mīne galdras weriaþ mec. (b) Þæs cyninges sunu rītt tō Burgredes tūne, his wines, on Mīercum. (c) Hē næfð gold on his lande ac hē is rīce nōðȳlǣs.

Section 9

1. (a) My hands are cold when I travel through open land in wintertime at my lord's behest. (b) In my homeland there is a great wood, in which elves live. (c) The floor of the house is covered with rushes. (d) Your son's bride loved him greatly and he protected her against the vikings. (e) The ploughmen were working in the fields, then travelled home in the early evening. (f) Danish vikings harried throughout England in those days, and people were very afraid until a certain English king saved them.

2. On þǣm dagum wæs micel Denisc here on þissum lande, se ðe hergode ond rēafode būton ende. Swā hwider swā hē fērde, hæfde hē sige ond þā Engle wǣron miclum ādrehte; ēac wæs unweder ond storm geond þæt land swā men ne eredon and hungor folgode hergunge

Section 10

1. ic hīerde blindne mann; hē wāt his cildru þā ðe ǣr miþon wīgendra ealu. Grime clipodon hīe and bismrodon hine and hē cweahte, ac hīe ne deredon him. Ðā cildru wrigon þæt ealu mid gōsa feþrum; hīe forhtodon swīþe. Heora fæder tāh hīe ond hīe bifodon; þonne sorgodon hīe.

2. At one time in this land (there) was a great and powerful magician, whose father was also a magician and had great power. His charms were effective and men trembled in front of his house.

Section 11

1. The warriors chose Berhtwulf as king and he ruled for twelve years in that land without peacebreaking. He was a very powerful war-leader and his enemies often fled from his army; their women mourned.

2. The sailors shoved their ship into the sea, but one slave dived from it and floated in the water, freezing, and the warriors shot with bows. Arrows flew, but did not harm him.

3. Se þēow gēat þæt ealu þā þā bodan lugon be heora heretogan naman. Gimmas scinon and līxton on ðǣm gyldenum bunum.

4. Twēgen smiþas worhton on smiþþan; hīe scierpton sweord, bugon īren ond scufon þæt on wæter þæt hit sēað.

Section 12

1. Torhta, the dark smith, began to toil, to sharpen his lord's sword; its edge he ground, the hilt he bound, carved his name on the ornamented sheath. While he toiled in the dark smithy, he sang and drank ale; the sparks flew around, fell and died. When the day grew dark, he became tired at his anvil; he had glorified the weapon with hard blows and with wise skill. When his lord fought with the great sword, he stabbed the enemy quickly. The sword did not fail him in battle.

3. Þā ic bealg, þā wearp ic mine gyldenan bunan on ðǣre flōra; mīn heorte swearc. Ic brēat æcsan wiþ trēow swā ic cearf hit ond tēah. Nāne bōte ne fand ic for þisse sace.

Section 13

1. The vikings fought against the English at the mouth of a stream; they had built a fortress there. Inside captives sat weaving and grinding, toiling with great sorrow. They were afraid because they were not free. The vikings' custom was that they did not protect their captives, but sent them out into the fighting, and there they died. A certain captive crept from the fortress and dived in the water, he swam to the horses of the English army and told the commander where the vikings' ships were. Then the English warleader sent some warriors out, and they crept among the rushes and sprang against the Danes, driving off the ship-keepers with great wounds. When the Danes perceived that their ships had been pierced, they began to be very afraid.

Section 14

1. Trumhere was a merchant. He had one large ship which he had loaded (ordered to be loaded) with English goods and then journeyed with seamen over the sea into foreign lands, sometimes eastwards, sometimes southwards. People there bought his cargo in exchange for golden coins which were very valuable in England. But Trumhere knew well that the coins were not as valuable as certain foreign commodities which he was looking for there. First he was seeking the foreign peoples' spice mixture; then gold, and garments, and weapons, and wine, and sundry foods.

2. Hwīlum drōg Trumhere ond his menn þæt scip on elðēodisc strand, ond þær sǣton ond ǣton oþþæt ðā ðēodiscan menn cōmon tō him. Hīe þrungon ymb þæt scip ond wundrodon þāra gōda þe hē gehladen hæfde; oftost guldon hīe mid silfrenum sceattum, oððe mid hiera agenum gōdum gif hīe nāne næfdon. Þās wǣron wearme brattas, ond tōla, ond wull; ond ealra betsta þā gimmas þā hīe worhton on þǣm lande.

Section 15

1. When Trumhere travelled from the foreign land and sailed over (the) sea towards England, there was bad weather and a stormy sea and the sailors did not know whether they would be able to cross over or be shipwrecked. One of them was afraid and began to chant an unfamiliar charm and the ship slid over the waves as if on ice. The sailor, who had previously been a captive of the Danish people, trembled greatly and called out, but his companions were glad at the ship's speed. They soon came into peaceful water, the men and the freight safe, and the ship floated up to an island.

On the island there was a small farm, but there was no person there; the big house's roof was burnt away, and sheep were living in there. Two seamen of Trumhere's rowed in a boat towards the island, and called out without reply. Then they all knew that the Danes had ravaged the island. Trumhere did not know where they were – they had become lost in the storm – but he knew that they must travel west. When they then began to travel away from the island, a sailor saw smoke rising from a headland; there was a little tent there.

2. Hīe hwurfon hīe tō ðǣm næsse, ond scēawodon þæt geteld – ān mann sæt binnan; þā hē þæt scip sēah, þā wolde hē hēlan, ac þā hē ongēat þæt þæt næs Denisc scip, þā clipode hē ond fægnode. Man hlōd hine on borde, ond rǣhte hīe þæt his nama wæs Torhta; se wæs smiþ. Dene nōmon ealle þā menn þā eardodon þǣr, ac hīe ne sǣwon his geteld on ðǣm hē wunode, wudu sēcende. His wīf ond cildriu wǣron nū wīcinga hæftlingas ond his fæder wæs dēad – Dene stang hine. Torhta wolde his cynren wrecan swā sōna swā hē mihte findan wīcing ungeweredne.

Section 16

1. Torhta ate gladly – he had gone hungry for three days after the vikings had come – and agreed that he would lead Trumhere up to the harbour which they had previously been seeking in the western part of England. Then they travelled for two days in rainy weather westwards, until they came into a large estuary and saw the market town in it. There in the river two Danish ships floated – one with a torn sail, the other without a mast and somewhat burnt – and no-one on board. Trumhere's ship soon came into the market town, and he looked for the town reeve to sell his goods which had been loaded in a foreign land. The town reeve, named Cuthred, took the king's portion of the cargo and himself bought a cloak, a golden container, a decorated sword and two vessels of wine. Then Trumhere asked what the ships were which had been seen in the river, and Cuthred answered him: "These are Danes' ships which were seized on the shore; the vikings fought against the king's force but we overcame them, killed some and brought the others here in fetters. They had English captives on their ships, who are now free. The king intends to send them back home, each with a part of the property which they took from us."

2. Þā clipode Torhta ond blissode, sēah his wīf on ðǣm geþrange, fundode tō hire, cysste ond ymbclypte, ond þā cildriu ēac. Ðās fēower blissodon swīðe ond ongunnon maþelian samod. On his pusan hæfde Torhta sume sylfrene sceattas, mid ðǣm wolde hē āgieldan Trumhere his fōre ond generednesse. And ēac for winescipe wolde hē edlēan sellan þām cēapmenn. Trumhere geþafode þā giefe tō ðicgenne, and sōna grētte Torhtan cynren. Hūrū Torhta hrēaw þæt hē ne mihte þone wīcing ācwellan, se þe his wīf ond cildriu nōm, ac hēo cwæð þæt se rēafere self wearþ ofslǣgen on þǣm gefeohte. Nōþȳleas sægde Cūþred þæt Torhtan wracu wæs cyninges þing, ond se cyning wæs bana þæs wīcinges, forþȳ scolde Torhta wesan glæd. Mid þissum wordum wearþ Torhta gefrēfred, ond se earma smið þancode him. Hē ongann sēcan strang hors mid þǣm hāme tō farenne.

Part Five

OE Glossary

Glossary of Words
Used in the Course

This glossary contains all the principal words appearing in the course; nouns and pronouns are marked for gender by abbreviation and appear in the nom.sing., adjectives in the nom.sing.masc. strong form and verbs in the infinitive (*wv.* marks a weak verb, *iv.* an irregular verb, *ppv.* a preterite-present verb and *sv.* a strong one).

OLD ENGLISH DICTIONARIES

It is worth mentioning a peculiarity of OE dictionaries which often serves to confuse the newcomer. This is in the matter of ordering the headword entries. There are two particular areas where problems can occur: the treatment of the prefix **ge-** and of the vowel **æ**.

There are large numbers of words in OE beginning with **ge-** and for the great majority there may be an alternative form which does not: **sēon** and **gesēon**, both meaning 'to see', for example. A common approach is to list the two verbs independently but ignore the prefix, so they both appear in the **s** section, with the *ge-* italicised or in parentheses to show that it is not always present. The noun **gebed** is thus listed under the **b** section. Another method, older and less common, lists all the words with **ge-** prefixes under the **g** section. The Clark-Hall Dictionary marks the presence of the **ge-** prefix with a 'plus' sign (+*weofu* = *geweofu*) and where it is optional or forms both with and without it are found, the 'plus or minus' sign is used (±*weorðan* = *weorðan* or *geweorðan*).

For the letter **æ** many books use a separate listing between **a** and **b**, while some treat the character as if it were **ae** and insert it between **ad** and **af**.

It is as well to be aware of these pitfalls when using dictionaries and glossaries in OE works.

ac	conj.	but, though	*āhwelc*	pron.	anyone, each one
āc	f.	oak	*ālīesan*	wv.	release, set free
ādreccan	wv.	afflict	*ān*	num.	one
āgan	ppv.	possess	*and*	conj.	and
āgen	adj.	own	*andcweðan*	sv.	contradict
āhēawan	sv.	cut off, lop	*andlang*	prep.	along
āhwā	pron.	anyone	*andsaca*	m.	opponent

andsacan	sv.	contend
andswarian	wv.	answer, reply
Angul	n.	Angeln, Schleswig
ārian	wv.	honour, endow
āscian	wv.	ask
æcer	m.	field, acre
æfen	n.	evening
æfentīd	f.	eventide
æftan	adv.	from the back
æfter	prep.	(1) after
	adv.	(2) behind, at the back
æftercweðan	sv.	repeat
æg	n.	egg
æghwā	pron.	anyone, each one
æghwelc	pron.	anyone, each one
ælmes	f.	alms, mercy
ælmesgiefu	f.	almsgiving, charity
ǣr	adv.	(1) previously, before
	prep.	(2) before
ǣror	adv.	first, beforehand
æt	prep.	at
ætlǣdan	wv.	lead away
ætwindan	sv.	escape from
ætwītan	sv.	blame
æðele	adj.	noble
æðeling	m.	prince
bannan	sv.	summon
bāt	m.	boat
bæcere	m.	baker
bǣr	f.	bier
bærnan	wv.	burn
be	prep.	by, about, beside
bearm	m.	lap, bosom
bearn	n.	child, son
bēatan	sv.	beat
bebūgan	sv.	bend round
bedǣlan	wv.	deprive
bedrēosan	sv.	deprive of
befæstan	wv	entrust
beforan	prep.	before
bēgen	num.	both
behēafdian	wv.	behead
behindan	prep.	behind
belgan	sv.	be angry
benn	f.	wound
bēodan	sv.	offer, command
bēon	iv.	be, will be
beorgan	sv.	protect
beorhtnes	f.	brightness
beran	sv.	bear, carry
besierwan	wv.	ensnare, deceive
betǣcan	wv.	entrust
betera	adj.	better
betst	adj.	best
betwēonan	prep.	between
betwēonum	prep.	between
betwux	prep.	betwixt
bī	prep.	by, about, beside
bīdan	sv.	wait
biddan	sv.	ask
bindan	sv.	bind, tie
bītan	sv.	bite
blāwan	sv.	blow
blēdan	wv.	bleed
blīcan	sv.	shine, glitter
blind	adj.	blind
blissian	wv.	be happy
blōd	n.	blood
blōwan	sv.	blossom, bloom
bōc	f.	book
boda	m.	messenger, herald
bodian	wv.	announce, preach
bora	m.	bearer
bōt	f.	(1) remedy (2) compensation
brād	adj.	broad, wide
brecan	sv.	break
brēdan	wv.	breed
bregdan	sv.	pull, draw, brandish
brengan	wv.	bring, fetch
brēost	m.	breast, heart
brēotan	sv.	break
brim	n.	sea
brōd	f.	foetus, brood
brōðor	m.	brother
brūcan	sv.	enjoy, use
brȳd	f.	bride
būgan	sv.	bend, bow, turn
burg	f.	fortress, stronghold, borough
būtan	prep.	without, except for
būtan ðǣm ðe	conj.	unless, but for

bycgan	wv.	buy
byrd	f.	(1) burden
		(2) birth
byrde	adj.	of noble birth
byre	m.	(1) opportunity
		(2) son
byrele	m.	cup-bearer
byrne	f.	mailcoat
ceald	adj.	cold
cearu	f.	care, worry, trouble
cempa	m.	warrior
ceorfan	sv.	carve, cut
cēosan	sv.	choose
cild	n.	child
cirice	f.	church
cnāwan	sv.	know
cniht	m.	boy
cnyssan	wv.	strike
cnyttan	wv.	tie a knot
crēopan	sv.	creep
cū	f.	cow
cuma	m.	guest
cuman	sv.	come
cunnan	ppv.	know (how to)
cweccan	wv.	quake, shake
cwelan	sv.	die
cwellan	wv.	kill
cweorn	f.	quern, handmill
cweðan	sv.	say
cwīðan	wv.	mourn
cynedōm	m.	kingdom
cynelic	adj.	kingly, royal
cyning	m.	king
cynn	n.	kin, family, ancestry
cȳssan	wv.	kiss
daroþ	m.	javelin, throwing spear
daru	f.	injury, harm
dæg	m.	day
dǣlan	wv.	share, divide
delfan	sv.	delve, dig
dēman	wv.	judge
dēmend	m.	judge
Dene	mpl.	Danes
dēop	adj.	deep
dēore	adj.	dear
derian	wv.	harm, hurt
dohtor	f.	daughter
dōm	m.	judgement
dōn	iv.	(1) do
		(2) carry on
		(3) put
dragan	sv.	draw, drag, pull
dreccan	wv.	afflict
drēogan	sv.	endure, undergo
drēosan	sv.	fall
drīfan	sv.	drive
drincan	sv.	drink
drūgian	wv.	dry up
drȳlic	adj.	magical
dūfan	sv.	dive
dugan	ppv.	be of use, avail, be worthy
durran	ppv.	dare
duru	f.	door
dwellan	wv.	be mistaken
dynnan	wv.	make a loud noise
ēac	conj.	also, in addition
ēage	n.	eye
eahta	num.	eight
eahtoða	adj.	eighth
eald	adj.	old
eall	adj.	all
ealles	adv.	completely, at all
eallunga	adv.	entirely
ealoð	n.	ale, beer
ealu	n.	ale, beer
eard	m.	homeland
eardian	wv.	dwell
eardung	f.	dwelling
ēare	n.	ear
earm	adj.	poor
ēast	adv.	east, eastwards
ēastan	adv.	from the east
ēaþe	adv.	easily
ecg	f.	edge, sword
egesful	adj.	fearsome, terrible
elles	adv.	else, otherwise
endleofon	num.	eleven
endleofoða	adj.	eleventh
Englaland	n.	England
Engle	mpl.	Angles, English
eoh	m.	horse

eorðe	f.	earth
eorþlic	adj.	worldly
eorðling	m.	farmer, ploughman
ēower	adj.	your
erian	wv.	plough
etan	sv.	eat
fāh	adj.	hostile
fandian	wv.	test, try out
faran	sv.	travel, go
faroþ	m.	shore, stream
faru	f.	course
fæder	m.	father
fæderen	adj.	paternal, fatherly
fægnian	wv.	rejoice
fær	n.	way, expedition
færeld	n.	way, passage
fæst	adj.	firm
fealdan	sv.	fold
feallan	sv.	fall
fealu	adj.	dark
fēdan	wv.	feed
fela	adj.	many
feld	m.	open country
feohtan	sv.	fight
fēond	m.	enemy
fēorr	adv.	afar, at a distance
fēorran	adv.	from afar
fēorða	adj.	fourth
fēower	num.	four
fēowertīene	num.	fourteen
fēowertig	num.	forty
fēran	wv.	travel
ferian	wv.	carry
fēðe	n.	walking, gait
fēþecempa	m.	infantryman, footsoldier
feðer	f.	(1) feather
		(2) wing
fīf	num.	five
fīfta	adj.	fifth
fīftig	num.	fifty
findan	sv.	find
fiscoð	m.	fishing
flāh	adj.	treacherous
flēogan	sv.	fly
flēotan	sv.	float
flīema	m.	exile, outlaw
flīeman	wv.	rout
flītan	sv.	contend
flōr	f	floor
flōwan	sv.	flow
fōda	m.	food
fōn	sv.	sieze, grab, get
for	prep.	for, on behalf of
fōr	f.	journey
foran	adv.	from the front
ford	m.	ford, river crossing
fordēman	wv.	condemn
fordrūgian	wv.	wither
fore	prep.	(1) before, in front of
	adv.	(2) in front
forhtful	adj.	fearful, afraid
forlīþan	sv.	be shipwrecked
forma	adj.	first
formonig	adj.	too many
foroft	adv.	too often
forþ	adv.	to the front, forwards
forðæm	conj.	therefore
forðæm ðe	conj.	because
forþcuman	sv.	proceed
forðȳ	conj.	thus, therefore
fōt	m.	foot
fram	prep.	from, by
frec	adj.	greedy, dangerous
freca	m.	warrior
fremman	wv.	carry out, perform
frēoh	adj.	free
frēond	m.	friend, lover
frēosan	sv.	freeze
frōfor	f.	comfort, solace
fugel	m.	bird, fowl
fulgān	iv.	accomplish
furþum	conj.	moreover, even
fylgan	wv.	follow
fylstan	wv.	assist, help
fȳr	n.	fire
fyrmest	adj.	foremost
galan	sv.	sing, chant, charm
gān	sv.	go
gārberend	m.	spear-carrier, warrior
ge ... ge	conj.	both ... and

gē	pron.	ye, you
gearu	adj.	ready
geāscian	wv.	find out, get to hear
gebǣran	wv.	behave, bear oneself
gebeorg	f.	defence
gebrōþor	n.	one of the brethren
gebrōðru	npl.	brethren
gebyrd	f.	fate
gebyrde	adj.	innate, inborn
gebyrdo	f.	parentage, family
gebyrga	m.	(1) protector (2) surety
gedafenian	wv.	befit, suit
gefara	m.	travelling companion
gefēon	sv.	rejoice
gefēra	m.	companion, fellow-traveller
gefēre	adj.	fit to travel
geferian	wv.	bring, carry, convey
gefērscipe	m.	fellowship
gefremman	wv.	benefit, serve
gehātan	sv.	(1) call (2) be called
gehwā	pron.	everyone
gehwǣr	pron.	everywhere
gehwilc	adj.	whichever
gelīc	adj.	alike, similar
gelīefan	wv.	believe
gelimp	n.	event
gelimpan	sv.	happen
gemunan	ppv.	remember
gemyndig	adj.	mindful
genēalǣcan	wv.	approach, near
genesan	sv.	survive, be saved, escape
geond	prep.	across, throughout
gēotan	wv.	pour out
gescȳ	n.	pair of shoes
gesīðcund	adj.	of the rank of retainer
gewendan	wv.	translate
gewinnan	sv.	win, gain
gewītan	sv.	go along
gicel	m.	icicle
giefa	m.	donor
giefan	sv.	give
giefu	f.	gift, act of giving
gieldan	sv.	pay, give up
giellan	sv.	shout
gielpan	sv.	boast, vow
gif	conj.	if
gingest	adj.	youngest
gingra	adj.	younger
git	pron.	you two
glæd	adj.	happy
glīdan	sv.	glide
gōd	adj.	good
godcund	adj.	godly, divine, sacred
gōs	f.	goose
gram	adj.	fierce, angry
grǣdig	adj.	greedy
grēne	adj.	green
grētan	wv.	greet
grindan	sv.	grind
grōwan	sv.	grow
guma	m.	man, warrior
habban	wv.	have
hāmweardes	adv.	homewards
hand	f.	hand
hātan	sv.	(1) call, call out (2) be named
hatian	wv.	hate
hǣlend	m.	saviour, healer
hæleð	m.	hero
hǣlo	f.	health
hǣlu	f.	health
hē	pron.	he, it
hēafod	n.	head
hēah	adj.	high
healdan	sv.	hold
healf	f.	half
heard	adj.	hard
hēawan	sv.	hew, chop, cut
hebban	sv.	raise, lift, heave
helan	sv.	hide
helpan	sv.	help
hengest	m.	stallion
hēo	pron.	she, it
heonan	adv.	hence, from this place
heorte	f.	heart
hēr	adv.	here

here	m.	army, military force
herian	wv.	praise
hider	adv.	hither, to this place
hīe	pron.	they
hīehst	adj.	highest
hīerra	adj.	higher
hiera	adj.	their
hīeran	wv.	hear, obey
hierde	m.	herdsman
hīersumian	wv.	obey
hild	f.	battle, fighting
hildegicel	m.	sword
hindan	adv.	(1) behind
		(2) from behind
hinder	adv.	to the back
hire	adj.	her, its
his	adj.	his, its
hit	pron.	it
hladan	sv.	load
hlāf	m.	loaf, bread
hlǣfdige	f.	lady
hlēapan	sv.	leap, dance
hlēapestre	f.	dancer
hnutu	f.	nut
hōn	sv.	hang
hōr	n.	adultery
hōring	m.	adulterer
hors	n.	horse
hrēoh	adj.	cruel, fierce
hrēohmōd	adj.	cruel at heart
hrēosan	sv.	fall
hrēowan	sv.	rue, be sorry
hrīnan	sv.	touch
hrōf	m.	roof, ceiling
hrōffæst	adj.	firmly-roofed
hū	pron.	how?
hund	n.	hundred
hundeahtatig	num.	eighty
hundend-leofontig	num.	one hundred and ten
hundnigontig	num.	ninety
hundred	num.	hundred
hundseofontig	num.	seventy
hundtēon-tigoða	adj.	hundredth
hundtigontig	num.	hundred

hundtwelftig	num.	one hundred and twenty
hunta	m.	hunter
huntian	wv.	hunt
huntoþ	m.	hunting
hūru	conj.	however
hūs	n.	house
hwā	pron.	(1) who?
		(2) anyone
hwanon	adv.	whence? from which place?
hwǣm		to whom?
hwǣr		where?
hwæs		whose?
hwæt	adj.	bold, daring
hwæt		what?
hwæthwugu	pron.	something
hwæðer		which (of two)?
hwelchwugu	pron.	someone
hweorfan	sv.	turn, go
hwider		whither? to which place?
hwīl	f.	period of time
hwilc	adj.	which one?
hwīlum	adv.	sometimes
hwon		by whom?
hwonan	adv.	whence?
hwone		whom?
hwonne		when?
hwȳ		why?
hyse	m.	youngster, youth
hysecild	n.	male child
ic	pron.	I
īeðe	adj.	easy
ieldest	adj.	eldest, oldest
ieldra	adj.	elder, older
ierre	adj.	angry
inn	adv.	to the inside
innan	adv.	from the inside
inne	adv.	on the inside
īsig	adj.	icy
lēan	sv.	blame
lamb	n.	lamb
land	n.	land
lār	f.	knowledge
lāðlic	adj.	hateful
lǣccan	wv.	catch, grab

lǣce	m.	doctor, healer
lǣdan	wv.	lead, direct
lǣran	wv.	teach
lǣssa	adj.	less
lǣst	adj.	least
lǣtan	sv.	let, allow
leccan	wv.	moisten
lengest	adj.	longest
lengra	adj.	longer
lengu	f.	length
lengðu	f.	length
lēode	mpl	people
lēof	adj.	dear, precious
lēogan	sv.	tell lies
lēon	sv.	lend
leorning	f.	learning
leorningcniht	m.	student, disciple
lēosan	sv.	lose
lettan	wv.	hinder
licgan	sv.	lie down
līcian	wv.	please
linnan	sv.	desist
līðan	sv.	travel by sea
līðmann	m.	sailor
lof	n	praise
līxan	wv.	gleam
lūcan	sv.	lock, close
lufian	wv.	love
luflic	adj.	lovely
lufsum	adj.	lovable
lūs	f.	louse
lystan	wv.	be pleasing
lȳt	adv.	little
mā	adv.	more, greater
magan	ppv.	be able to
man	pron.	one, someone, anyone
mann	m.	man, person
māra	adj.	more, greater
māwan	sv.	mow
mægen	n.	strength
mægþ	f.	maid, girl
mægþhād	f.	maidenhood, virginity
mǣre	adj.	famous, renowned
mǣst	adj.	most, greatest
mearh	m.	horse
meltan	sv.	melt
mennisc	adj.	human
meodu	m.	mead
mētan	wv.	meet
metan	sv.	measure
micle	adv.	much, greatly
mid	prep.	with
Mierce	mpl.	Mercians
miltsian	wv.	take pity on
mīn	adj.	my
mislimpan	sv.	go wrong
misðyncan	wv.	displease
mīðan	sv.	hide
mōd	m.	mind, soul
mōdor	f.	mother
mōna	m.	moon
monig	adj.	many
mōtan	ppv.	be allowed, have the opportunity
mund	f.	(1) hand (2) protection
munt	m.	hill, mound
mūs	f.	mouse
nā	adv.	not at all
nabban	wv.	have not
nāgan	ppv.	have not
nama	m.	name
nān	adj.	none, no
nāthwā	pron.	someone
nāthwelc	pron.	someone
nǣfre	adv.	never
nǣlles	adv.	by no means
nǣnig	pron.	none, no-one
ne	adv.	not
ne ... ne	conj.	neither ... nor
nēah	adj.	close, near
	adv.	near
nēan	adv.	from close by
nēar	adv.	to close by
nearu	adj.	narrow, close
nefne	conj.	unless, except, but for
nemnian	wv.	name, call
neopan	adv.	underneath, from beneath
nerian	wv.	save
nigon	num.	nine

231

nigoða	adj.	ninth
niþer	adv.	under, beneath
nīw	adj.	new
norð	adv.	north, northwards
norðan	adv.	from the north
Norðanhymbre	mpl.	Northumbrians
nōðȳlēas	conj.	nevertheless
nunne	f.	nun
nyllan	ppv.	want not to
nytan	ppv.	know not
of	prep.	off, from
ofer	prep.	over, beyond
ofercuman	sv.	overcome
oferfaran	sv.	cross, travel over
oferflītan	sv.	outdo, overcome
oferflōwan	sv.	overflow
ofost	f.	haste
ōleccan	wv.	flatter
on	prep.	on(to), in(to), against
ondrǣdan	sv.	dread
oneardian	wv.	inhabit
onfeohtan	sv.	assail, attack
onfōn	sv.	receive, acquire
ongēan	prep.	towards, against
ongietan	sv.	realize, perceive
onginnan	sv.	begin
oþ	prep.	as far as, until
ōþer	adj.	(1) other (2) second
oððe ... oððe	conj.	either ... or
rǣd	m.	advice
rǣdan	sv.	advise
reccan	wv.	care for
reccan	wv.	tell, reckon
rīce	adj.	powerful
rīce	n.	kingdom
rīdan	sv.	ride
riht	adj.	(1) right, correct (2) direct
rihtfæder-encynn	n.	direct paternal lineage
rīsan	sv.	rise
rōwan	sv.	row
sacan	sv.	contend
sārlic	adj.	painful
sāwan	sv.	sow
sǣ	m,f	sea
sǣlan	wv.	happen
scacan	sv.	shake
sceamian	wv.	be shameful
scēap	n.	sheep
scēotan	sv.	shoot
sceððan	wv.	injure
scīeran	sv.	shear, cut
scieppan	sv.	shape, create
scierpan	wv.	sharpen, whet
scīnan	sv.	shine
scip	n.	ship
scōh	m.	shoe
scrīðan	sv.	move
scūfan	sv.	shove
sculan	ppv.	must, be obliged to
se	m.	(1) (dem.) the, that (2) (rel.pron.) who, which
Seaxe	mpl.	Saxons
sēcan	wv.	seek, look for
secgan	wv.	say
sēfte	adj.	soft
sēlest	adj.	best
sellan	wv.	hand over
sēlra	adj.	better
sendan	wv.	send
sēo	f.	(1) (dem.) the, that (2) (rel.pron.) who, which
sēoc	adj.	sick
seofon	num.	seven
seofoða	adj.	seventh
sēon	sv.	see
sēoðan	sv.	boil, seethe
settan	wv.	set, put
sīde	f.	side
sidu	m.	custom, habit
sierwan	wv.	plot, devise
siex	num.	six
siexta	adj.	sixth
siextig	num.	sixty
sīn	adj.	one's/his/her/its own
singan	sv.	sing
sittan	sv.	sit
slǣpan	sv.	sleep

slēan	sv.	slay, strike	*sweorcan*	sv.	grow dark
slīdan	sv.	slide	*sweord*	n.	sword
slītan	sv.	tear	*sweostor*	f.	sister
smēðe	adj.	smooth	*swerian*	sv.	swear, promise
smōðe	adv.	smoothly	*swēte*	adj.	sweet
snīðan	sv.	cut	*swica*	m.	traitor
sōfte	adv.	softly	*swīcan*	sv.	fail
sōna	adv.	soon, straightaway	*swicol*	adj.	deceitful, treacherous
spanan	sv.	seduce, entice			
spannan	sv.	span, link	*swift*	adj.	swift, fast
specan	sv.	speak	*swimman*	sv.	swim
spōwan	sv.	succeed	*swincan*	sv.	labour, toil
sprecan	sv.	speak	*swingan*	sv.	flog
sprecul	adj.	talkative, loquacious	*swingere*	m.	scourge
			swōte	adv.	sweetly
springan	sv.	jump, spring up	*swylc*	adj.	such
spyrian	wv.	ask, inquire	*talu*	f.	tale, story
stān	m.	stone, rock	*tǣcan*	wv.	teach
standan	sv.	stand, be upright	*tela*	adv.	well
stede	m.	place, location	*tellan*	wv.	count
stelan	sv.	steal	*tēon*	sv.	(1) accuse
stellan	wv.	set down		sv.	(2) draw, pull
stēorbord	n.	starboard, steering paddle	*tēoða*	adj.	tenth
			teran	sv.	tear
steorra	m.	star	*tīen*	num.	ten
stīgan	sv.	climb, go up	*til*	adj.	gainful, good
stingan	sv.	stab	*tō*	prep.	to, as, upto
stōw	f.	place, site	*tō ðæs*	adv.	to that degree, so
strang	adj.	strong, powerful	*tō ðæs ðe*	conj.	so that
streccan	wv.	stretch	*tōbrecan*	sv.	break apart
strengest	adj.	strongest	*tōcuman*	sv.	arrive
strengo	f.	strength	*tōforan*	prep.	in front of
strengra	adj.	stronger	*tōð*	m.	tooth
strengðo	f.	strength	*tredan*	sv.	tread
strengu	f.	strength	*trēow*	n.	tree
sum	pron.	a certain one	*trum*	adj.	firm, stout
sumor	m.	summer	*trymman*	wv.	strengthen
sunne	f.	sun	*tū*	num.	two (n.)
sunu	m.	son	*tū hund*	num.	two hundred
sūð	adv.	south, southwards	*tūn*	m.	enclosure, estate
sūðan	adv.	from the south	*tunge*	f.	tongue
swā	adv.	(1) so	*twā*	num.	two (f.)
	adv.	(2) as, so much	*twēgen*	num.	two (m)
swā swā	adv.	just as	*twelf*	num.	twelve
swelgan	sv.	swallow	*twelfta*	adj.	twelfth
sweltan	sv.	die	*twentig*	num.	twenty
swencan	wv.	distress	*twēolic*	adj.	doubtful

twintigoða	adj.	twentieth		*ufan*	adv.	above, from above
ðā	all	(1) (dem.) the, those		*unearg*	adj.	not cowardly, bold
		(2) (rel.pron.) who, which		*ungemete*	adj.	large
				unnan	ppv.	grant, allow, bestow
		(3) when				
		(4) then		*unrǣd*	adj.	poor advice
ðās	all	(dem.) this, these		*unscyldig*	adj.	not guilty, innocent
ðǣr	adv.	(1) there, in that place		*untrumian*	wv.	become infirm, weaken
	conj.	(2) if, under those conditions		*untrumnes*	f.	infirmity
				unþēaw	m.	evil custom
ðæt	dem.	(1) the, that		*unwearnum*	adv.	irresistably
	pron.	(2) who, which		*unweder*	n.	bad weather, storm
	conj.	(3) that		*upp*	adv.	upwards
ðēah	conj.	though, although		*uppan*	adv.	from above
ðēaw	m.	custom, habit		*uppe*	adv.	above
ðeccan	wv.	cover over		*ūre*	adj.	our
þegn	m.	thane		*ūser*	adj.	our
ðegnian	wv.	serve		*ūt*	adv.	to the outside
ðencan	wv.	think		*ūtan*	adv.	from the outside
þēof	m.	thief		*ūte*	adv.	on the outside
ðēon	sv.	thrive		*wadan*	sv.	go, walk
ðēos	f.	(dem.) this		*waru*	f.	shelter, care
ðēowian	wv.	serve		*wē*	pron.	we
ðes	m.	(dem.) this		*weald*	m.	woodland
þicgan	sv.	partake, receive, taste		*wealdan*	wv.	wield, rule
				wealh	m.	foreigner, Briton
ðider	adv.	thither, to that place		*wealisc*	adj.	foreign, Welsh
ðīn	adj.	thy, your		*weallan*	sv.	surge, well
ðingian	wv.	talk, reconcile		*wearn*	f.	refusal
ðis	n.	(dem.) this		*weaxan*	sv.	grow
ðonan	adv.	thence, from that place		*weccan*	wv.	wake up
				wēdan	wv.	rage
ðrēotēoða	adj.	thirteenth		*weder*	n.	weather
ðrēotīene	num.	thirteen		*wefan*	sv.	weave
ðrēo	num.	three (f.)		*wel*	adv.	well
ðridda	adj.	third		*wēnan*	wv.	hope, expect
ðrīe	num.	three (m., n.)		*weorpan*	sv.	throw
þrīnes	f.	threeness, trinity		*weorðan*	sv.	become
ðringan	sv.	throng, crowd		*wer*	m.	adult male
ðrītigoða	adj.	thirtieth		*werian*	wv.	defend protect
ðū	pron.	thou, you		*wērig*	adj.	weary
ðurfan	ppv.	need		*werod*	n.	bodyguard, defensive troop
ðurh	prep.	through, by				
ðūsund	num.	thousand		*wesan*	iv.	be
ðweorh	adj.	awkward, perverse		*west*	adv.	west, westwards
ðyncan	wv.	seem		*westan*	adv.	from the west

wiersa	adj.	worse
wierst	adj.	worst
wīf	n.	adult female
wīgan	wv.	fight
wīgend	m.	warrior
willa	m.	wish, desire, intention
willan	wv.	wish, want, intend
wilsum	adj.	enjoyable
windan	sv.	wind
wine	m.	friend
winnan	sv.	fight
winter	n,m	(1) winter (2) year
wīsian	wv.	guide
wit	pron.	we two
wita	m.	(1) wise man (2) adviser
witan	ppv.	know
wītan	sv.	blame
wītelēas	adj.	without penalty
witlēas	adj.	witless, foolish
wið	prep.	against, towards, along
wōd	adj.	maddened, angry
word	n.	word, speech
wrāð	adj.	angry
wrecan	sv.	avenge
wrēon	sv.	cover
wrītan	sv.	write
wudu	m.	wood, forest
wundrian	wv.	wonder, be amazed
wyrcan	wv.	work, make, create
yfel	adj.	evil, bad
yfle	adv.	badly
ylfe	mpl.	elves
ylde	mpl.	men
ymbe	prep.	around, about
yrhðo	f.	(1) cowardice (2) worthlessness
yrmðo	f.	poverty

First Steps in Old English
A Correspondence Course in the Old English Language
by Stephen Pollington

A correspondence course based around the *First Steps in Old English* textbook book is available offering further advice and assistance for those wishing to read Old English but wanting to make use of the additional benefits of a tutored course – personal marking of the student's written work and answers to those difficult questions the grammars never touch upon.

The three-part course is keyed directly to the *First Steps in Old English* textbook so that the student can co-ordinate his reading from that book with his progress in the course, thus avoiding the temptation to move on quickly through the early stages before a full understanding has been achieved. Annotated marking helps the student identify areas of weakness and offers the opportunity, where necessary, of clarification.

For further details please write to Stephen Pollington, c/o Anglo-Saxon Books, Frithgarth, Thetford Forest Park, Hockwold-cum-Wilton, Norfolk IP26 4NQ

Ærgeweorc: Old English Verse and Prose
read by Stephen Pollington

This audiotape cassette can be used with *First Steps in Old English* or just listened to for the sheer pleasure of hearing Old English spoken well.

Tracks: 1. Deor. 2. Beowulf – The Funeral of Scyld Scefing. 3. Engla Tocyme (The Arrival of the English). 4. Ines Domas. Two Extracts from the Laws of King Ine. 5. Deniga Hergung (The Danes' Harrying) Anglo-Saxon Chronicle Entry AD997. 6. Durham 7. The Ordeal (Be ðon ðe ordales weddigaþ) 8. Wið Dweorh (Against a Dwarf) 9. Wið Wennum (Against Wens) 10. Wið Wæterælfadle (Against Waterelf Sickness) 11. The Nine Herbs Charm 12. Læcedomas (Leechdoms) 13. Beowulf's Greeting 14. The Battle of Brunanburh 15. Blacmon – by Adrian Pilgrim.

£7·50   ISBN 1–898281–20–3   C40 audiotape

Wordcraft: Concise English/Old English Dictionary and Thesaurus
Stephen Pollington

This book provides Old English equivalents to the commoner modern words in both dictionary and thesaurus formats. The Thesaurus presents vocabulary relevant to a wide range of individual topics in alphabetical lists, thus making it easily accessible to those with specific areas of interest. Each thematic listing is encoded for cross-reference from the Dictionary. The two sections will be of invaluable assistance to students of the language, as well as to those with either a general or a specific interest in the Anglo-Saxon period.

£11·95   A5   ISBN 1–898281–02–5   256 pages

Leechcraft
Early English Charms, Plantlore and Healing
Stephen Pollington

An unequalled examination of every aspect of early English healing, including the use of plants, amulets, charms, and prayer. Other topics covered include Anglo-Saxon witchcraft; tree-lore; gods, elves and dwarves.

The author has brought together a wide range of evidence for the English healing tradition, and presented it in a clear and readable manner. The extensive 2,000-entry index makes it possible for the reader to quickly find specific information.

The three key Old English texts are reproduced in full, accompanied by new translations.
Bald's Third Leechbook; *Lacnunga*; *Old English Herbarium*.

£35 ISBN 1–898281–23–8 254 x 170mm / 10 x 6¾ inches hardcover 28 illustrations   544 pages

The English Warrior from earliest times to 1066
Stephen Pollington

This important new work is not intended to be a bald listing of the battles and campaigns from the Anglo-Saxon Chronicle and other sources, but rather it is an attempt to get below the surface of Anglo-Saxon warriorhood and to investigate the rites, social attitudes, mentality and mythology of the warfare of those times.

The book is divided into three main sections which deal with warriorhood, weaponry and warfare respectively. The first covers the warrior's role in early English society, his rights and duties, the important rituals of feasting, gift giving and duelling, and the local and national military organizations. The second part discusses the various weapons and items of military equipment which are known to have been in use during the period, often with a concise summary of the generally accepted typology for the many kinds of military hardware. In the third part, the social and legal nature of warfare is presented, as well as details of strategy and tactics, military buildings and earthworks, and the use of supply trains. Valuable appendices offer original translations of the three principal Old English military poems, the battles of *Maldon*, *Finnsburh* and *Brunanburh*.

The author combines original translations from the Old English and Old Norse source documents with archaeological and linguistic evidence to present a comprehensive and wide-ranging treatment of the subject. Students of military history will find here a wealth of new insights into a neglected period of English history.

£14·95   ISBN 1–898281–10–6   272 pages   10" x 7" (250 x 175mm) with over 50 illustrations

An Introduction to the Old English Language and its Literature
Stephen Pollington

The purpose of this general introduction to Old English is not to deal with the teaching of Old English but to dispel some misconceptions about the language and to give an outline of its structure and its literature. Some basic knowledge of these is essential to an understanding of the early period of English history and the present form of the language.

£4·95   A5   ISBN 1–898281–06–8   48 pages

Dark Age Naval Power: A Reassessment of Frankish and Anglo-Saxon Seafaring Activity
John Haywood

In the first edition of this work, published in 1991, John Haywood argued that the capabilities of the pre-Viking Germanic seafarers had been greatly underestimated. Since that time, his reassessment of Frankish and Anglo-Saxon shipbuilding and seafaring has been widely praised and accepted.

In this second edition, some sections of the book have been revised and updated to include information gained from excavations and sea trials with sailing replicas of early ships. The new evidence supports the author's argument that early Germanic shipbuilding and seafaring skills were far more advanced than previously thought. It also supports the view that Viking ships and seaborne activities were not as revolutionary as is commonly believed.

'The book remains a historical study of the first order. It is required reading for our seminar on medieval seafaring at Texas A & M University and is essential reading for anyone interested in the subject.'

F. H. Van Doorninck, *The American Neptune* (1994)

£14·95   ISBN 1–898281–22–X   approx. 10 x 6½ inches - 245 x 170 mm   224 pages

English Heroic Legends
Kathleen Herbert

The author has taken the skeletons of ancient Germanic legends about great kings, queens and heroes, and put flesh on them. Kathleen Herbert's encyclopaedic knowledge of the period is reflected in the wealth of detail she brings to these tales of adventure, passion, bloodshed and magic.

The book is in two parts. First are the stories that originate deep in the past, yet because they have not been hackneyed, they are still strange and enchanting. After that there is a selection of the source material, with information about where it can be found and some discussion about how it can be used. The purpose of the work is to bring pleasure to those studying Old English literature and, more importantly, to bring to the attention of a wider public the wealth of material that has yet to be tapped by modern writers, composers and artists.   This title was previously published as *Spellcraft: Old English Heroic Legends*.

£11·95   A5   ISBN 1–898281–25–4   292 pages

An Introduction to Early English Law
Bill Griffiths
Much of Anglo-Saxon life followed a traditional pattern, of custom, and of dependence on kin-groups for land, support and security. The Viking incursions of the ninth century and the reconquest of the north that followed both disturbed this pattern and led to a new emphasis on centralized power and law, with royal and ecclesiastical officials prominent as arbitrators and settlers of disputes. The diversity and development of early English law is sampled here by selecting several law-codes to be read in translation - that of Æthelbert of Kent, being the first to be issued in England, Alfred the Great's, the most clearly thought-out of all, and short codes from the reigns of Edmund and Æthelred the Unready.

£6·95   A5   ISBN 1–898281–14–9   96 pages

The Battle of Maldon: Text and Translation
Translated and edited by Bill Griffiths
The Battle of Maldon was fought between the men of Essex and the Vikings in AD 991. The action was captured in an Anglo-Saxon poem whose vividness and heroic spirit has fascinated readers and scholars for generations. *The Battle of Maldon* includes the source text; edited text; parallel literal translation; verse translation; a review of 103 books and articles. This new edition has a helpful guide to Old English verse.

£6·95   A5   ISBN 0–9516209–0–8   96 pages

Beowulf: Text and Translation
Translated by John Porter
The verse in which the story unfolds is, by common consent, the finest writing surviving in Old English, a text that all students of the language and many general readers will want to tackle in the original form. To aid understanding of the Old English, a literal word-by-word translation is printed opposite the edited text and provides a practical key to this Anglo-Saxon masterpiece.

£8·95   A5   ISBN 0–9516209–2–4   192 pages

A Handbook of Anglo-Saxon Food: Processing and Consumption
Ann Hagen
For the first time information from various sources has been brought together in order to build up a picture of how food was grown, conserved, prepared and eaten during the period from the beginning of the 5th century to the 11th century. Many people will find it fascinating for the views it gives of an important aspect of Anglo-Saxon life and culture. In addition to Anglo-Saxon England the Celtic west of Britain is also covered. Now with an extensive index.

£9·95   A5   ISBN 0–9516209–8–3   192 pages

A Second Handbook of Anglo-Saxon Food & Drink: Production and Distribution
Ann Hagen
Food production for home consumption was the basis of economic activity throughout the Anglo-Saxon period. This second handbook complements the first and brings together a vast amount of information on livestock, cereal and vegetable crops, fish, honey and fermented drinks. Related subjects such as hospitality, charity and drunkenness are also dealt with. Extensive index.

£14·95   A5   ISBN 1–898281–12–2   432 pages

The Hallowing of England
A Guide to the Saints of Old England and their Places of Pilgrimage
Fr. Andrew Philips
In the Old English period we can count over 300 saints, yet today their names and exploits are largely unknown. They are part of a forgotten England which, though it lies deep in the past, is an important part of our national and spiritual history. This guide includes a list of saints, an alphabetical list of places with which they are associated, and a calendar of saint's feast days.

£5·95   A5   ISBN 1–898281–08–4   96 pages

Peace-Weavers and Shield-Maidens: Women in Early English Society
Kathleen Herbert

The recorded history of the English people did not start in 1066 as popularly believed but one-thousand years earlier. The Roman historian Cornelius Tacitus noted in *Germania*, published in the year 98, that the English (Latin *Anglii*), who lived in the southern part of the Jutland peninsula, were members of an alliance of Goddess-worshippers. The author has taken that as an appropriate opening to an account of the earliest Englishwomen, the part they played in the making of England, what they did in peace and war, the impressions they left in Britain and on the continent, how they were recorded in the chronicles, how they come alive in heroic verse and jokes.

£4·95　A5　ISBN 1–898281–11–4　64 pages

Looking for the Lost Gods of England
Kathleen Herbert

Kathleen Herbert sifts through the royal genealogies, charms, verse and other sources to find clues to the names and attributes of the Gods and Goddesses of the early English. The earliest account of English heathen practices reveals that they worshipped the Earth Mother and called her Nerthus. The tales, beliefs and traditions of that time are still with us and have played a part in giving us *A Midsummer Night's Dream* and *The Lord of the Rings*.

£4·95　A5　ISBN 1–898281–04–1　64 pages

Rudiments of Runelore
Stephen Pollington

This book provides both a comprehensive introduction for those coming to the subject for the first time, and a handy and inexpensive reference work for those with some knowledge of the subject. The *Abecedarium Nordmannicum* and the English, Norwegian and Icelandic rune poems are included in their original and translated form. Also included is work on the three Brandon runic inscriptions and the Norfolk 'Tiw' runes.

£5·95　A5　ISBN 1–898281–16–5　Illustrations　88 pages

English Martial Arts
Terry Brown

By the sixteenth century English martial artists had a governing body that controlled its members in much the same way as do modern-day martial arts organisations. The *Company of Maisters* taught and practised a fighting system that ranks as high in terms of effectiveness and pedigree as any in the world.

In the first part of the book the author investigates the weapons, history and development of the English fighting system and looks at some of the attitudes, beliefs and social pressures that helped mould it.

Part two deals with English fighting techniques drawn from sources that recorded the system at various stages in its history. In other words, all of the methods and techniques shown in this book are authentic and have not been created by the author. The theories that underlie the system are explained in a chapter on *The Principles of True Fighting*. All of the techniques covered are illustrated with photographs and accompanied by instructions. Techniques included are for bare-fist fighting, broadsword, quarterstaff, bill, sword and buckler, sword and dagger.

£25　ISBN 1–898281–18–1　250 x 195mm /10" x 7½"　220 photographs　240 pages

Anglo-Saxon Books
Frithgarth, Thetford Forest Park, Hockwold-cum-Wilton, Norfolk IP26 4NQ
Tel: +44 (0) 1842 828430　Fax: +44 (0) 1842 828332　email: sales@asbooks.co.uk

For a full list of titles and details of our North American distributor see our web site at
www.asbooks.co.uk or send us a s.a.e.

We accept payment by cheque, Visa and MasterCard. Please add 10% for UK delivery, up to a maximum charge of £2·50. For delivery charges outside the UK please contact us or see our website.

Regia Anglorum

Regia Anglorum is a society that was founded to accurately re-create the life of the British people as it was around the time of the Norman Conquest. Our work has a strong educational slant and we consider authenticity to be of prime importance. We prefer, where possible, to work from archaeological materials and are extremely cautious regarding such things as the interpretation of styles depicted in manuscripts. Approximately twenty-five per cent of our membership of over 500 people are archaeologists or historians.

The Society has a large working Living History Exhibit, teaching and exhibiting more than twenty crafts in an authentic environment. We own a forty foot wooden ship replica of a type that would have been a common sight in Northern European waters around the turn of the first millennium AD. Battle re-enactment is another aspect of our activities, often involving 200 or more warriors.

For further information see www.regia.org or e-mail kim_siddorn@compuserve.com
or write to K. J. Siddorn, 9 Durleigh Close, Headley Park, Bristol BS13 7NQ, England

Þa Engliscan Gesiðas - *The English Companions*

Þa Engliscan Gesiðas is a historical and cultural society exclusively devoted to Early English (Anglo-Saxon) history. Its aims are to bridge the gap between scholars and non-experts, and to bring together all those with an interest in the Anglo-Saxon period so as to promote a wider interest in, and knowledge of, its language, culture and traditions. The Fellowship publishes a journal, *Wiðowinde,* which helps members to keep in touch with current thinking on all relevant topics. The Fellowship enables like-minded people to keep in contact by publicising conferences, courses and meetings that might be of interest to its members.

For further details see www.kami.demon.co.uk/gesithas/ or write to:
The Membership Secretary, Þa Engliscan Gesiðas, BM Box 4336, London, WC1N 3XX England.

Sutton Hoo near Woodbridge, Suffolk

Sutton Hoo is a group of low burial mounds overlooking the River Deben in south-east Suffolk. Excavations in 1939 brought to light the richest burial ever discovered in Britain – an Anglo-Saxon ship containing a magnificent treasure that has become one of the principal attractions of the British Museum. The mound from which the treasure was dug is thought to be the grave of Rædwald, the English king who died in 624/5 AD.

For tour details contact:–

The Sutton Hoo Guiding and Visits Secretary, Tailor's House, Bawdsey, Woodbridge, Suffolk IP12 3AJ
e-mail: visits@suttonhoo.org   website: www.suttonhoo.org

The Sutton Hoo Society

Our aims and objectives focus on promoting research and education relating to the Anglo Saxon Royal cemetery at Sutton Hoo, Suffolk in the UK. The Society publishes a newsletter SAXON twice a year, which keeps members up to date with society activities, carries resumes of lectures and visits, and reports progress on research and publication associated with the site. If you would like to join the Society please write to:

Membership Secretary, Sutton Hoo Society, 28 Pembroke Road, Framlingham,
Woodbridge, Suffolk IP13 9HA, England   website: www.suttonhoo.org

West Stow Anglo-Saxon Village

An early Anglo-Saxon Settlement reconstructed on the site where it was excavated consisting of timber and thatch hall, houses and workshop. Open all year 10a.m.– 4.15p.m. (except Christmas). Free tape guides. Special provision for school parties. A teachers' resource pack is available. Costumed events are held at weekends, especially Easter Sunday and August Bank Holiday Monday. Craft courses are organised.

For further details see www.stedmunds.co.uk/west_stow.html or contact:
The Visitor Centre, West Stow Country Park, Icklingham Road, West Stow
Bury St Edmunds, Suffolk IP28 6HG   Tel: 01284 728718